Internet Research Companion

Geoffrey W. McKim

Indiana University

Internet Research Companion

Library of Congress Catalog No.: 95-74875

ISBN: 1-57576-050-9

98 97 96   4   3   2   1

Interpretation of the printing code: the rightmost double-digit number is the year of the book's printing; the rightmost single-digit number, the number of the book's printing. For example, a printing code of 96-1 shows that the first printing of the book occurred in 1996.

Screens reproduced in this book were created using Collage Plus from Inner Media, Inc., Hollis, NH.

Publisher: David P. Ewing

Associate Publisher: Chris Katsaropoulos

Product Marketing Manager: Susan J. Dollman

Managing Editor: Sheila Cunningham

Acquisitions Editor	Acquisitions Coordinator	
Satbir Bedi	Elizabeth D. Brown	
Production Editor	**Production Team**	
Virginia Noble	Mona Brown	Paula Lowell
Technical Editor	Chris Cleveland	Steph Mineart
Mary Beth Maddox	Mike Dietsch	Bobbi Satterfield
	Jason Hand	SA Springer
Cover Designer	Sonja Hart	Andy Stone
Anne Jones	Ayanna Lacey	Mark Walche
	Clint Lahnen	

Trademark Acknowledgments

About the Author

Geoffrey McKim has developed, managed, and taught Internet-based information resources for over five years. He holds a degree in Library and Information Science from the Indiana University School of Library and Information Science. He continues to teach courses and workshops on UNIX, computer skills, Internet skills, digital libraries, and World Wide Web disign and programming. Mr. McKim is currently the Director of Information Technology at the Indiana University School of Library and Information Science, and his research interests include Computer Supported Cooperative Work.

Acknowledgments

I would first and foremost like to thank Amy Cornell for all of her advice, patience, and constant support. Without her editing skill, incisive questioning, and love, this book would not have been possible.

I would also like to thank Julie Fore, also without whom this project would not have happened. Her Internet expertise, her trenchant and perceptive understanding of user behavior, and her friendship have all been invaluable throughout the process.

A generous measure of thanks also goes to the editing team at Que Education and Training. Thanks to Satbir Bedi for managing the whole project, for keeping me on task, and for giving me the opportunity to write this book. Thanks also to Ginny Noble for making sure that what I write makes sense to anyone else, and for her always enjoyable editor's comments. Finally, thanks to Mary Beth Maddox, both for her technical editing and for introducing me to Que Education and Training.

I would like to thank my colleagues at the Indiana University School of Library and Information Science, in particular Blaise Cronin and Howard Rosenbaum, for providing a dynamic and exciting environment, in which the information and communications provided by the Internet play an integral role.

Finally, I would like to thank my parents, William and Karen McKim, for always having challenged me and for having provided a wonderful home environment, in which learning was promoted and supported. Not a day goes by in which I don't recognize their influence in what I do.

Composed in *Sabon* and *MCPdigital* by Que Corporation

Table of Contents

Introduction

Electronic information on the Internet has recently become useful for college students who do research and write term papers. These Internet-based resources may serve as primary material, providing new and original research, or as reference material, bringing together existing materials in the form of annotated bibliographies, directories, atlases, and resource lists. Some instructors are even recommending that students consult certain Internet sites for information.

For college students, Internet-based information has many advantages over traditional paper-based materials. First, electronic resources have the potential of being up-to-date in a way that was impossible in the print world, even with periodicals. Students now have the opportunity to do original and innovative research, beyond what was traditionally expected of them. Second, electronic resources are searchable, enabling students to access and retrieve easily the exact information they need. Third, as the Internet becomes more accessible in both the home and the residence hall, students have more flexibility in where and when they do research. Finally, the Internet enables students to determine the scope and breadth of a particular subject or discipline with ease, giving them a snapshot of the relevant issues, documents, and centers of activity.

Along with the advantages, however, come some disadvantages. First, although Internet resources have the potential to be current, they frequently are not. Quite often, the managers of Internet-based resources maintain them for fun or out of professional interest, so the managers have little incentive to keep the resources up-to-date. This problem is magnified because you can't always tell when an electronic resource is up-to-date. You can't simply check the date of publication, as you can with a published work.

The most serious problem is the lack of quality control in resources found on the Internet. Although inaccuracy is not a stranger to the print world, the publisher of print materials at least puts an *imprimatur*, or seal of quality, on the work; in fact, the publisher's reputation depends on the quality of the material published. But on the Internet anyone can be a publisher, from a large media company to a high school student. Because this publisher seal of quality no longer exists, the student researcher must play the unfamiliar role of evaluator. The student must be responsible for assessing the quality of the resources.

Certain academic disciplines and areas of study present students with a rich and useful set of information resources on the Internet. The fields of government, computing and computer technology, and popular culture are especially notable. However, students in all areas of study—from postmodern literary studies to medieval history to genetics to political science—can benefit academically from the vast number of resources on the Internet.

Of course, the challenge to the student who wants to make use of these new sources of information is to *find* them. Greg Rawlins, in an influential paper (published on the Internet), referred to three emerging roles—what he called "mapmakers, filters, and ferrets"—that people and programs will have to assume in order to make use of information in the new networked, electronic world. This book is about the third role, that of ferret. Students now have both a great opportunity and a great incentive to become "information ferrets" on the Internet, to be able to search for and retrieve information that they can read, synthesize, and incorporate in their research and term papers.

Becoming such seekers of information will require that students pick up a new set of skills. First, they must learn to use new computer tools, ones that enable them to access electronic resources. Second, students must learn how to search for information, particularly when the potential number of sources is open-ended. Many students leave high school never knowing how to use information sources beyond the encyclopedia and *Readers' Guide to Periodical Literature*. Finally, students must learn to evaluate the quality of the resources they find on the Internet. If the quality is poor, students will not want to rely on such resources for papers.

Students do not need to learn these skills by themselves. Many sources can help. Books are available on the search and access tools. The first two chapters of this book, in fact, discuss some of these tools. College and university librarians can be an invaluable resource for students wanting to learn to use Internet-based tools and materials. Although librarians can help students use the tools, these professionals can be of most help in knowing where to find information, in guiding students to the best resources and avoiding those of poor quality. Many libraries have even hired librarians whose sole job is to work with Internet-based resources. Every student should think of the librarian as one of the primary sources of assistance in finding, retrieving, evaluating, and using information on the Internet.

How This Book Is Organized

This book is divided into four parts. Part I, "Tools of the Trade: The Technologies of the Internet," describes the programs that enable you, the student researcher, to access information on the Internet. These tools include Telnet, FTP, Gopher, and the World Wide Web. Because the World Wide Web is clearly the most useful tool, much of the discussion focuses on the Web.

Part II, "Retrieving and Working with Information on the Internet," shows you how to find and retrieve documents that may be of use in researching and writing papers.

Part III, "People as Resources," focuses also on finding information on the Internet, but the focus is not on documents. It is on getting information from people—an equally (if not more) important information resource. Tools such as e-mail, LISTSERVs, electronic discussion groups, and Usenet newsgroups (electronic bulletin boards) are discussed in Part III.

Part IV, "Evaluation and Citation," deals with what you do after you have the information. You learn how to evaluate Internet information and how to incorporate citations to such Internet information in your bibliographies and footnotes.

An appendix is also included, which lists the Internet addresses of the research tools discussed in the book.

Who This Book Is For

This book is not a comprehensive guide to using the Internet, or even to using a particular part of it. Instead, this book is aimed at students who want to make use of the Internet as a research tool in their studies. Students who want to become technologists or Internet "gurus" will probably not benefit from this book; in fact, they may know most of the information in it. This book is for the rest of us, those who want to use the Internet for research but may be a little bewildered by the scope and breadth of information available, as well as the difficulty in learning the necessary tools.

In writing this book, I followed two guidelines:

- Don't "dumb down" explanations, but don't include unnecessary technical detail.

- Present the most valuable techniques and resources, and don't include those of limited value or those whose difficulty of use outweighs any potential value.

If your favorite search tool is not covered in this book, keep in mind that I included only those resources and tools that I believe are of the most value for the effort expended in learning them.

I also maintained a scholastic focus throughout the book. There are already plenty of books available on recreational materials on the Internet, and most students will find these on their own. The techniques and tools presented in this book will increase your academic productivity and give you access to a variety of materials and resources for use in researching and writing papers.

Conventions Used in This Book

Certain conventions are followed in this book to help you easily understand the information presented.

Words or phrases defined for the first time appear in *italic*. Words or phrases that you are asked to type are in **boldface**. Screen displays and on-screen messages appear in a special monospace typeface. Internet addresses appear in **monospace and boldface.**

Keys are represented as they appear on your keyboard. Key combinations, such as Ctrl+B and Alt+Enter, are connected by a plus sign (+). In menu commands and dialog box options, access keys are in boldface and underlined. An example is the Open **L**ocation command on the **F**ile menu.

The Enter key is often mentioned in this book. Note that this key may be labeled differently on your keyboard. On Macintosh keyboards and on many older PC keyboards, this key is labeled Return. If you are using such a keyboard, simply press the Return key whenever you are instructed to press the Enter key.

Although the Macintosh keyboard has a key labeled Control, this key isn't used as frequently as it is on the PC. Most often, Macintosh commands require that you use the Command key instead of the Control key. Please note that the Command key is often called the "apple" key or the "cloverleaf" (⌘) key.

Internet Access Tools

Objectives

After reading this chapter, you will be able to

- Understand the differences between host-based and direct Internet connections

- Recognize the basic Internet tools: Telnet, FTP, Gopher, and the World Wide Web

- Understand how Uniform Resource Locators (URLs) are used to refer to Internet resources

This book is not solely about the technologies of the Internet, as there are many excellent books already on the market about that topic. However, an understanding of a few key technological issues is critical to making full use of this book. This chapter presents several technological issues and introduces four key technologies: FTP (File Transfer Program), Telnet, Gopher, and the World Wide Web. Although some of these technologies are newer than others (in particular, the World Wide Web has become dominant), all of them can be useful at different times for student research.

Issues to Consider

To make use of the Internet and its technologies, you first need to consider three important issues. These issues affect how the Internet tools *look* to you and thus how you *read* some of the text. This discussion covers the following key issues: the type of Internet connection you use, the Internet software available to you, and the type of computer you have.

Direct Internet Access versus Host-Based Internet Access

You can access the Internet in one of two modes: host-based mode and direct-access mode. In host-based mode, all interaction with the Internet is done in the form of lines of text. Generally, this mode is associated with accessing the Internet through other online systems, such as local bulletin boards, campus computers running UNIX, and some commercial online services. Direct-access mode, which is becoming more common, has the distinct advantage of enabling you to view multimedia information, such as sound and movies, as well as text. Interaction with the Internet in direct-access mode is often in the form of mouse clicks instead of typed text. In addition, you usually use graphical user interfaces such as Microsoft Windows, Microsoft Windows 95, and the Macintosh.

Internet information access programs such as Mosaic, Netscape, TurboGopher, WinGopher, and HGopher require that you have access to a direct Internet connection of some sort. Because much of the information available on the Internet is composed of multiple media, having graphical access is an advantage. Although the information available is generally the same with host-based access, you won't be able to view any graphics or movies in host-based mode (at least not with ease); nor will you be able to listen to sounds.

To make use of direct-access Internet tools, you need a couple of things. First, you need to be using an operating system that provides a graphical environment, such as Windows 95 or the Macintosh. (The X Window environment on UNIX machines will also work, but if you are using that, you probably already know how to use the Internet!) Second, you need some sort of network connection to the Internet.

If you are accessing the Internet from an on-campus lab or classroom, or if you are in a residence hall that provides a network connection, you probably have a direct network connection. Otherwise, you can still have a network connection even if you are dialing in to a network with a modem over the telephone lines from home. In that case, you need to be using either PPP (point-to-point protocol) or SLIP (serial-line Internet protocol). Both of these systems enable your computer to pretend that it actually has a network connection to the Internet. Your campus computing staff should be able to tell you whether SLIP or PPP access is available at your site.

If you don't have access to a network connection to the Internet, you are probably dialing in through some sort of terminal software (like ProComm, Terminal, Smartcom, or Zterm). In addition, you are most likely using the Internet tools on a computer running a computer operating system called UNIX. (This doesn't mean that you have a computer running UNIX sitting on your desk; it just means that the computer you are dialing into is running UNIX.) In this case, you are limited to text-only tools, although you still should have access to all the resources.

> **NOTE** *This book is directed to both direct-access and host-based Internet users. Although direct-access and host-based modes may look quite different (primarily because direct-access mode is graphics-based), all the examples in this book illustrate basic principles that are valid no matter which mode you are using. Don't panic if things don't look exactly the same for you—you should still benefit from the basic tasks presented in these chapters.*

The Internet Tools Available to You

Not all Internet tools are available on all systems. If you have a direct connection to the Internet, you are capable of running all the available tools. In that case, there is no reason why you shouldn't have one of each type of tool discussed in this book. (The appendix describes where to obtain various types of Internet software.)

If, however, you have a host-based connection to the Internet, usually through a UNIX computer, you will have available only what the system administrator put on the system. If you are lucky enough to have a World Wide Web browser (usually Lynx—if you have access through a UNIX computer), you can access almost any Internet resource. Much of this book deals with World Wide Web–based resources. Yet even if you cannot access the World Wide Web but have access to all the other tools (Telnet, FTP, and Gopher), there is still much that you can do, using this book for assistance.

The Type of Computer You Use

Although it would make life easier if we all had the same kind of computer, that is not the nature of the marketplace, and ultimately, we are probably the better for it. However, writing computer books is certainly more challenging. The fact is that some people use Windows-based computers to access the Internet, others use Macintoshes, and still others use nongraphical UNIX accounts.

Fortunately, many of the tools for the Macintosh and for Windows (particularly the World Wide Web browsers) look very much the same. The tools used with host-based Internet access, of course, look quite different. Throughout this book, Windows examples are used, and the screen displays are taken from a Windows-based computer. Macintosh users should be able to get the same information from these examples, even though their screens might look slightly different. This book also includes many text-only examples, particularly when the text-only tools are different in substance as well as in look.

The following sections discuss four tools used in the Internet. These core tools are Telnet, FTP, Gopher, and the World Wide Web. Later in the book, you learn about a couple of other tools: electronic mail and Usenet news.

Telnet—Terminal Access to the Internet

Telnet was one of the earliest technologies used to access the Internet. This technology reflects the way computers were used in the days before personal computers, when people used terminals to access central shared computers. A terminal generally looks like a computer: It has a screen and a keyboard but has no processor, which is the "brain" of a computer. All that a terminal can do is display data sent to it from another computer, allow the user to type data at the keyboard, and then send the data back to that computer. Terminals tend to be limited to text only (with some exceptions). The key distinguishing feature of a terminal, though, is that it doesn't actually do any processing—it just connects to a central shared computer that does the processing.

Nowadays, few people use terminals; they instead use personal computers of various kinds. However, many electronic resources on the Internet were developed for terminal access, and often you will need to access these resources as though you were using a terminal. To access these resources, you need a program called Telnet, which makes your personal computer look like a terminal and connects it to a remote shared computer.

Using Telnet to Connect to Internet Resources

Many different versions and brands of Telnet software are available, enabling you to connect to remote shared computers to access terminal-based Internet resources. Some names that you might encounter are NCSA Telnet, PCTCP, CUTCP, WinQVT for IBM PC compatibles, and NCSA Telnet for the Macintosh. In addition, every UNIX system comes with a Telnet program simply called telnet. Almost everyone who has access to the Internet has access to a UNIX account, so the UNIX telnet program is used in the following example. Keep in mind that the basic principles are the same, no matter which Telnet program you use or what your Telnet program looks like.

Before you can connect to a remote computer using Telnet, you need to know the Internet address of that computer. Internet addresses can be in one of two forms: a series of letters or words connected by periods (such as **ezinfo.ucs.indiana.edu** or **velcome.iupui.edu**), or a series of four numbers connected by periods (such as **129.79.33.75**). Ultimately, all computers on the Internet can be addressed through a series of four numbers connected by periods, called an *IP number*. However, because people don't tend to work well with such numbers, computers on the Internet can be addressed with addresses of the first form as well. A system on the Internet known as Domain Name Service (DNS) translates between the names and numbers that computers go by. DNS can be thought of as a telephone directory for computers. These are all technical details, however. Simply put, to connect to a remote computer using Telnet, you need to know the address of the remote computer.

In the following example, you use the UNIX version of Telnet to connect to a remote computer at the address **infogate.ucs.indiana.edu**. This is the address of the library catalog at Indiana University. Before you begin, take a quick look at this Internet address. The last two elements, **indiana** and **edu**, tell you something about where the resource is located. **indiana** means that the resource is at Indiana University. (If **purdue** were in that location, the resource would be located at Purdue University.) Each institution, organization, and business with Internet resources has its own identifying suffix on the Internet. The **edu** part of the address identifies the computer as being located at an educational institution. Other types of institutions have identifying suffixes in their Internet addresses: **com** for commercial organizations, **org** for not-for-profit organizations, and **gov** for government agencies.

To connect to a remote computer using the UNIX telnet program, follow these steps:

1. Make sure that you are at the UNIX prompt. How this prompt looks will vary, depending on what kind of UNIX computer you are using and how your local system is set up. My UNIX prompt, for instance, is just %.

2. Type **telnet infogate.ucs.indiana.edu** at the UNIX prompt.

   With this command, you are telling your UNIX telnet program to open a connection to the remote computer (often called a host computer), located at address `infogate.ucs.indiana.edu`. If you are using a different Telnet program, you will use different commands. For example, if you are using a Windows- or Macintosh-based client, you will probably choose an option from a menu (such as Open Connection to Host) to tell your Telnet program to connect to a remote computer. However, the basic principle is the same.

   Your screen should look something like figure 1.1.

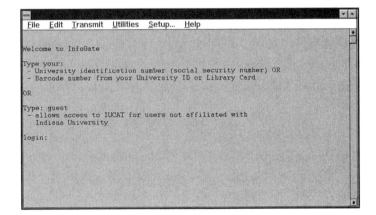

Figure 1.1

Using Telnet to connect to InfoGate.

This text is actually coming to you from the remote host, InfoGate at Indiana University. Each host that you connect to will probably look completely different. However, *logging in*—that is, identifying yourself to the computer—is a common requirement of most remote computers. In this case, if you were at Indiana University, you would log in using your own student ID number. Other computers will make you identify yourself through a *user name* or *login name*, which is a name given to you by your campus computing center.

In addition, you may need to enter a *password*, a secret word that allows the computer to verify that you are who you say you are. However, many hosts that are intended for public use often provide a way to log on to them even if you don't have a user name and password on the computer. You may be able to log in with a generic user name—usually guest, visitor, or anonymous.

In the case of InfoGate, the generic user name is guest. Generally, systems that allow a guest login don't give people who log in as guest as many features as those who have their own user names and passwords. With InfoGate, people who log in with their own user names and passwords on the system are presented with an entire menu of information resources; users who log in with guest are permitted to access only the library catalog.

3. Type **guest** and press Enter to log into InfoGate.

After you have logged in as guest, you will be connected to the Indiana University library catalog, as shown in figure 1.2.

Figure 1.2

Using Telnet to connect to the Indiana University library catalog.

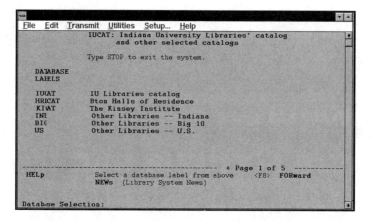

TIP | *Don't take too long between connecting to a computer with Telnet and logging in to the computer. If you do, the remote computer may "time you out"—that is, disconnect you because you took too long. If this happens, you need to connect again, before logging in.*

FTP—Transferring Files over the Internet

Although Telnet enables you to access resources located on remote computers, FTP, or File Transfer Program, has a different mission. It allows you to transfer files of information from one computer on the Internet to another computer on the Internet. Usually, you use FTP to *download* files—to transfer files of information from a remote computer to your own computer for use and viewing.

With the development of the World Wide Web, the need for FTP has diminished greatly. However, there are still some files and resources that can be accessed only through FTP. Just as with Telnet, many different programs enable you to use FTP to transfer files, and these programs go by many different names. For example, the most popular FTP programs for the Macintosh are called Fetch and X-Ferit. The most popular programs for the PC include NCSA FTP, RapidFiler, and WinQVT. In UNIX, the most common program is simply called ftp.

The basic concept behind FTP is simple. The computer from which you want to transfer files is called the *server*. The computer to which you want to transfer files (either your own desktop computer or, if you are logged into a nongraphical UNIX account, the computer running UNIX) is called the *client*. The goal of FTP is to transfer files from the client to the server (or from the server to the client). A way to remember this is to think of the client as the computer that initiates the FTP connection.

JARGON ALERT!

*When you **log in**, you identify yourself to a computer. Logging in usually involves using both a user name (which lets the computer know who you are) and a password (which makes sure that no one else can claim to be you).*

*A **host** computer is one that provides information of some sort. In other words, the computer "hosts" information that you can access.*

***Downloading** files means transferring them from a remote computer to your own computer. The opposite is **uploading**— transferring files from your own computer to a remote computer.*

*Similar to a host computer, a **server** computer provides and stores information that is accessed by a client.*

*A **client** is a piece of software that allows one computer to access information stored on another computer (a server). A Web browser is a client that can access information stored on a Web server.*

The need for FTP has diminished partly because many resources originally made available through FTP are now available through other types of servers, such as Gophers and World Wide Web servers. Another reason is that Gopher and World Wide Web clients (that is, the software you use to access Gopher and World Wide Web resources) can also access information on FTP servers. Thus, there is little need for you to use FTP client software anymore.

> **TIP** *You can generally use a World Wide Web or Gopher client to access FTP-based information. The only time that you need to use an actual FTP client is when you must put information onto an FTP server for someone else to access.*

Gopher—Accessing Networked Information through Menus

When Gopher was originally developed at the University of Minnesota, it was a revolutionary advance in Internet information retrieval. Before then, information could be accessed only through Telnet or FTP—technologies that required you to know exactly where on the Internet something was located, and forced you to learn ugly and clumsy interfaces. Gopher, however, was a technology that allowed you to access information by picking options from menus.

The creator of a Gopher server can set up systems of menus that point to useful Internet resources. The person wanting to use the information can obtain the Gopher client, a piece of software that accesses Gopher-based information, and connect to the Gopher server. The person can then see the menus that have been set up and can retrieve the information based on the menus. The best part about this architecture, though, is that the information to which the menus point do not have to be on the server itself. The information can be located on another server, at another place in the Internet. The user doesn't even need to know this—the server takes care of all of the technical details.

Essentially, Gopher is a system that allows Internet-based information to appear as though it is all in one place and arranged in a uniform order, when in reality, the information may be scattered all over the Internet. Moreover, Gopher adds the capability to retrieve documents that aren't limited to text. Gopher is generally able to retrieve documents of different media types (graphics, sounds, and movies). The Gopher clients themselves don't deal with these different media formats; instead, a Gopher client merely retrieves the data and passes it on to other programs that display the graphics. Furthermore,

Gopher provides access to two earlier types of Internet resources: Telnet-based resources and FTP-based resources. Actually, Gopher uses a Telnet program to provide Telnet-based resources, but at least Gopher makes Telnet-based data easier to locate and access.

Gopher is still in use, but its use is fading. The World Wide Web incorporates all the features of Gopher, and much more: The Web not only retrieves other types of media but also integrates them in a format resembling the printed page. Furthermore, the Web is not restricted to a hierarchical menu organization. (Whether this is a good thing, though, is open to debate, because sometimes a menu is easier to navigate.) Finally, just as Gopher has incorporated the technologies of FTP and Telnet, the Web has incorporated FTP, Telnet, *and* Gopher.

Before learning how to use the World Wide Web, you should pause to consider an important issue: how to refer to Internet information in a consistent and uniform way. Because of the increased use of Gopher, FTP, and the Web, this urgent need required serious attention. The solution—the URL—is discussed in the next section.

Referring to Internet Resources through Uniform Resource Locators (URLs)

With all the Internet technologies and locations where information could be found, users needed a way of identifying a resource regardless of the technology used to get the resource. A simple code could refer to a resource on the Internet, giving you all the information required to find that resource. The code that was developed to fill this need is known as a *Uniform Resource Locator*, or *URL*. A URL is similar to the library catalog call number of a book. If I give you the call number of a book, you can go to the library and find the book. Similarly, if I give you the URL for a resource on the Internet, you have all the information you need to find that resource.

Here are some examples of URLs for actual resources on the Internet:

```
ftp://ftp.indiana.edu/goober/simple.hqx

gopher://boombox.micro.umn.edu

http://www-slis.lib.indiana.edu

http://www.mcp.com/home.html

news:comp.infosystems.www.browsers.ms-windows
```

```
telnet://iuis.ucs.indiana.edu

http://www-slis/mambo.html
```

A URL contains three pieces of information:

- *The tool used to access the resource.* Such tools include telnet (for Telnet-based resources), ftp (for FTP-based resources), news (for Usenet newsgroups), gopher, and http (for Web-based resources). For example, if a URL begins with **gopher**, you know that the resource is a Gopher resource and that you need to use a Gopher browser to access the resource. The tool identifier is usually followed by two slashes (*//*).

  Why http? You might wonder why http is the code given for Web-based resources. In fact, http (which stands for hypertext transfer protocol) is the underlying network protocol the World Wide Web uses. Just think of an http resource as synonymous with a Web-based resource.

- *The address of the computer on which the resource is located.* This address uniquely identifies the computer on which the resource is located, anywhere on the Internet. In the first example in the preceding list, the name of the computer is **ftp.indiana.edu.**

- *The path name of the resource itself.* The path name tells you the resource's location (that is, the names of the directories and subdirectories) on the computer where the resource can be found. This piece of information is not always present. In the first example in the preceding list, the file referred to is called **simple.hqx**, which is in a directory called **goober**. However, in the second example, the path of the resource is not present. In the case of a URL of a Gopher resource, if the path is not present, the resource referred to is, by default, the top level of the Gopher menu. In the third example in the list, it doesn't make any sense to refer to a path name on a Telnet-accessible resource—the URL simply refers to an interactive login to the host.

> **NOTE** *If you are already familiar with the UNIX system, these naming conventions, particularly for the path of the resource, will make sense. Just think of the path as the series of directories and subdirectories at which a file is located on a computer.*

Note some additional examples:

```
http://www-slis.lib.indiana.edu/FallCourses.html

telnet://archie.sura.net

ftp://ftp.indiana.edu/pub/departments/socpsy
/ReadMe.TXT

gopher://lib-gopher.lib.indiana.edu:7040/11/lilly
/finding-aid/guide-inventory/welles
```

Although the concept of the URL was originally developed for the Web (where it gained popularity), URLs are now used by many Internet tools to refer to resources. Most Gopher clients also accept requests for resources in the form of URLs. If you cite an Internet resource in a paper, you will almost certainly have to provide the URL, which tells the reader exactly how to obtain the resource you used. Citing (footnoting) Internet resources is covered in Chapter 17.

> **NOTE** *Pay attention to URLs because they give you a lot of information. They tell you what kind of tool you can use to access the resource, and where the resource is located. Essentially, they give you all the information you need to retrieve the file. In addition, the URL is often the form in which you will be told about a resource. A colleague or professor may send you an e-mail message referring to a resource with a URL, or you may be reading a magazine and come across a URL. Finally, this book uses URLs to refer to resources throughout the examples.*

World Wide Web—Networked Hypermedia

The World Wide Web began in 1989 as a project by high-energy physics researchers in Switzerland to distribute research results over the Internet to fellow physicists. Since then, the Web has rapidly moved into the forefront of Internet technologies. More people now use the Web on the Internet than all other technologies combined. To most of the general public, the Web is synonymous with the Internet itself and is, in fact, thought by many to have played the dominant role in moving the Internet from an academic research tool to a household word.

Why has the Web become dominant? There are two primary reasons. First, the Web is, by almost any measure, easier to use than any of its technological predecessors. Second, the Web is inherently multimedia based, therefore moving the Internet closer to the familiar domains of the printed page and the television screen.

However, the Web goes beyond multimedia to encompass what is often called *hypermedia* or *hypertext*. Traditional text, usually represented in a paper document, is linear in nature. You begin at the beginning and finish at the end, and there is only one order in which to read the document—the order determined by the author. Hypertext, a term coined by computer visionary Ted Nelson in 1965, refers to writing technologies that supposedly free the reader from the linear nature of text.

Hypertext uses *links*, known also as *hyperlinks*. You can be reading a hypertext document and come across a link. It is then your choice to continue in the document or follow the link. This link could go to another part of the document, or even another document entirely. If you have many documents, all linked to many other documents, you have a network (or web!) of text, with no fixed beginning, no fixed ending, and no fixed way to browse through the text.

Hypertext has attracted a strong group of supporters. They believe that hypertext is a new medium or new form of writing that frees the reader from the constraints of a conventional document and enables the reader to explore the information space at will. Some even say that hypertext mimics more closely the way in which the human mind works—jumping from topic to topic and following mental links to other ideas. However, hypertext also has an (almost) equal number of detractors. They say that hypertext can be confusing and that a person can easily get lost in a network of linked documents, just as a person can get lost in a maze or forest. Detractors say also that the choices available to the reader are still restricted by the individuals who create the links—that hypertext really isn't any more liberating for the reader. It is up to you to explore the hypermedia universe and examine how it is implemented in the form of the World Wide Web.

How the Web Works: WWW Architecture

Although you don't need to know much detail about the technical architecture of the Web, you do need to know generally how the Web works so that you can use it more effectively. The overall structure of Web technology is what is known in the computer business as "client-server architecture." Essentially, this means that the technology of the Web is composed of two parts: a client and a server. The *server* is where the information that the user accesses is actually stored. If you want to make information available to others over the Web, you put the information on a server. If you want to access the information, you get the information from a server. The *client* is the piece of software that allows you to access the information. Generally (but not always), you run the client on your own computer, and the server exists somewhere out on the Internet.

Once you have the client and the server in place, the client gets information from the server by means of a transaction. Here's how a transaction works: The client makes a connection to the appropriate server over the Internet, the client sends a request for a resource from the server, the server sends the requested resource back to the client, and the client breaks the connection with the server. All this activity generally happens in the space of a few seconds.

Now consider some of the details. The World Wide Web clients—that is, the software that enables you to access resources on the Web—are called *browsers*. Several popular Web browsers (such as Netscape, Mosaic, and Lynx) are discussed in the following section. Other browsers include InternetWorks, MacWeb, Cello, Samba, and Internet Explorer (the new browser developed by Microsoft for Windows 95). The resource requests sent by the client to the server are in the form of Uniform Resource Locators, or URLs. URLs are strings of characters that determine which server to connect to (there are thousands of Web servers on the Internet now) and which resource on that server to find. Because URLs are so important in doing research on the Internet, you should go back and reread the section on URLs if you have any questions about them. After the server locates the resource specified by the URL, the server sends the resource (the document) to the client, which displays it for you to work with, print, or save.

The documents sent by the server to the client are written in a language called HTML, or HyperText Markup Language. HTML is a language designed to transmit documents that potentially contain different media formats in the same document: text, graphics, movies, sounds, and, most interestingly, hypertext links to other documents and other resources. Your Web browser receives the HTML, allowing you to move around in the document and, if you want, follow the hypertext links to the linked-to documents.

How to Access the Web: Web Browsers

This section covers Web browsers in more detail. One interesting aspect of the HTML that is used to mark up Web documents is that it gives the Web browsers some freedom in interpreting the information in the document. If a

Web browser does not support a certain media type, the browser can simply ignore that part of the document, but display the rest of it. For example, even though the World Wide Web is intended to support graphics in documents, if you have a computer that doesn't support graphics (or you don't have graphical access to the Internet), you will still be able to read the text in a particular document. This feature makes the Web a flexible means of information distribution: If users can view graphics, they will see the graphics in documents; if users cannot view graphics, they can still read the text.

Basic Features of a Web Browser

Although the World Wide Web has become popular only recently, over a dozen different high-quality Web browsers are available and for almost every computer type and operating system, including DOS, Windows, Macintosh, UNIX, and OS/2. Although these Web browsers vary greatly in the features they provide, some capabilities are central to all Web browsers:

- Retrieving HTML documents from a Web server and displaying them to you in some form

- Saving and printing the document you retrieved

- Jumping to links specified in the document

The graphical browsers (such as Netscape, Mosaic, and MacWeb) display graphics along with the text. Other media types (such as sounds, movies, WordPerfect documents, and spreadsheets) are handled and displayed through what is known as *helper applications*—applications that help Web browsers display additional media formats. The next chapter discusses many of the media formats you may encounter on the Internet, as well as many helper applications that work with these formats.

Mosaic and Netscape—Graphical Browsers

Because much of the Web is multimedia based, you will probably want to have a graphical Web browser. Mosaic is one of the most popular graphical browsers and the first to achieve widespread use. Mosaic was developed (and is still being developed) at the National Center for Supercomputing Applications (NCSA) at the University of Illinois. One of the reasons that Mosaic is highly popular is that it is available to anyone without charge. Mosaic is also available for the Macintosh, for Windows, and for UNIX X Window–based systems. Figure 1.3 shows a sample screen from Mosaic for Windows.

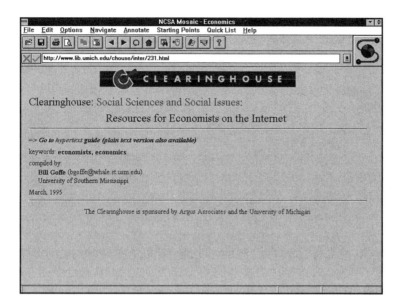

Figure 1.3
A Mosaic for
Windows sample
screen.

21

Mosaic looks similar for the Macintosh and for UNIX, so UNIX and Macintosh users can benefit equally from this discussion. The URL box contains the Uniform Resource Locator of the resource displayed in this example—the home page for Economic Resources on the Internet from the Clearinghouse for Subject-Oriented Internet Resource Guides. This is generally an excellent source for these subject-oriented guides to Internet-based resources. You can see why the Web has become more popular than any of its technological predecessors: The interface is simple, and its integrated text and resources resemble a printed page. Note that some of the words, such as `hypertext` and `plain text`, are colored or underlined. Mosaic (as well as Netscape) uses this convention to indicate a hypertext link. If you click an underlined word with the mouse, you will be taken to the resource to which the underlined word is linked, quite possibly on an entirely different server on the Internet.

The buttons at the top of the Mosaic screen are for navigation on the Web. For example, the house icon automatically takes you to the home page that has been predefined for the browser. (The user can set this home page. If you always come back to a particular home page, you can make it your default home page; when you want to go back to it, you just click the house icon.) The left-arrow icon takes you back to the page you just looked at, and the right-arrow icon takes you to the next page (assuming you have already used the left arrow). The left arrow is especially useful in navigating through hypertext: If you click a link that is uninteresting and you want to go back to what you were looking at before you followed the link, just click the left-arrow icon, and you will be right back where you were.

The Netscape browser, developed by Netscape Communications, has eclipsed Mosaic in popularity. The people who started Netscape Communications were some of the original developers of Mosaic. They decided that they could make more money if they turned out a commercial product (and they were right!). Netscape, unlike Mosaic, is therefore a commercial product, priced at around $40 per copy. However, people using Netscape within an educational institution (a school or university) do not have to pay anything for it. So Netscape is free to you as an educational user. (The latest version of Netscape is 1.22; however, new versions come out fairly frequently.)

You can tell from looking at Netscape that it was originally derived from Mosaic. Many of the menus are similar, and the program has a similar "look and feel." Generally, though, Netscape is considered a bit more stable, and it has many more features than Mosaic. For these reasons, Netscape is more commonly used. Figure 1.4 shows a screen from the Netscape browser for Windows (the Macintosh and UNIX versions are almost identical). This screen shows the same Internet resource, the Economic Resources page from the Clearinghouse for Subject-Oriented Internet Resource Guides.

Figure 1.4

A Netscape for Windows sample screen.

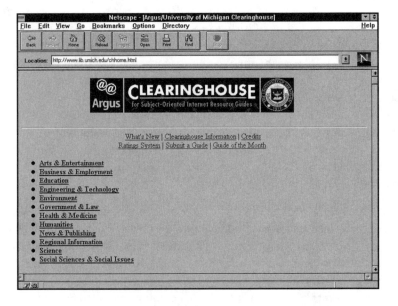

Notice the similarity of the screens. These browsers work almost the same. For example, you click the underlined words to follow hypertext links. The examples in this book use Netscape rather than Mosaic. However, Mosaic is so similar that the illustrations will still be useful if you are a Mosaic user.

Lynx—Text-Only Web Browser

Even though the Web was designed with multimedia in mind, and computers with graphical interfaces are able to make more effective use of the Web, all is not lost for those with text-only connections to the Internet. A text-only Web browser, known as Lynx, is available. Although Lynx is available for DOS and other operating systems, this browser is used mostly by those who have access to the Internet through a UNIX machine. Lynx enables you to access the same Web information from the same servers as other Web browsers, but you see only text; you don't get graphics, sounds, or other formats. Figure 1.5 shows a Lynx screen, accessing the same Economics Resources home page that you looked at with Netscape and Mosaic.

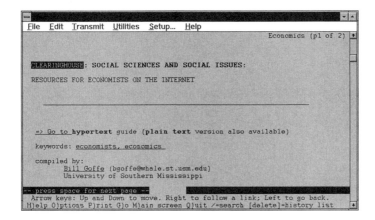

Figure 1.5

A Lynx sample screen.

Unfortunately, you can get lost more easily in Lynx than in one of the graphical browsers. With Lynx, you don't have many visual cues like graphics, different fonts, or different colors to break up the page. All you get is text. Note that hypertext links are in boldface or in some color other than the one used for normal text, depending on how your terminal emulator is set. In addition, a cursor will be on one of the links. Usually, the link where the cursor is located is highlighted or in reverse video. The up- and down-arrow keys move the cursor from link to link (but don't actually follow the link). The spacebar moves you down a screen of text, if the text of the Web page is more than a screenful. To follow a link, you move the cursor to the link (using the up- and down-arrow keys) and press either the Enter key or the right-arrow key.

> **NOTE** *The locations of the tools mentioned in this book are listed in the appendix rather than in the chapters. The reason is that if you have an Internet connection, you may already have the appropriate tools installed, and describing where to get every tool would clutter the text of each chapter. For the locations of tools you don't have, refer to the appendix.*

You now have an overview of the basic tools used on the Internet: Telnet, FTP, Gopher, and the World Wide Web. The next chapter describes some of the media formats you may encounter on the Internet.

Data Formats and Media

Objectives

After reading this chapter, you will be able to

- Understand the range of media types that can appear on the Internet (including text, hypertext, graphics, sound, and motion pictures)

- Understand Page Description Language formats and how they are used on the Internet

- Understand how helper applications enable you to view different media formats

- Understand compression and uncompression of files on the Internet

Beyond Text—Media on the Internet

Although most of the research that you do on the Internet will probably involve text resources, the Internet, particularly the World Wide Web and Gopher, offers much more. Many Internet tools provide opportunities for integrating different media types. Sounds, graphics, and even motion pictures can now be integrated along with text and hypertext. This chapter discusses the media types you may encounter on the Internet in your quest for useful resources. The chapter also explains what you need for viewing these media types.

Graphics on the Internet

Other than text, the most common media type that you will encounter on the Internet is graphics. Almost every Web-based resource includes graphics, and many Gopher resources include them as well. With Gopher, you must access the graphics as a separate document or menu item. With the World Wide Web, however, graphics can be integrated with the text just as they would be on a printed page. Most Web page designers have started to include graphics on every page, chiefly to add flash as well as content.

Graphics on the Internet usually come in one of two formats: GIF or JPEG. These formats describe standards that specify the internal structures used to store the graphics. Each format has its advantages and disadvantages, and if you were putting images out on the Internet for other users to access, you would probably want to know the details of these two formats. However, as things stand, you just need to know that these formats are different types of graphics.

Generally, you don't care which format the graphics are stored in; all you want to do is view the graphics on your screen. If you have access to a graphical Web browser, you are in luck. All graphical Web browsers can view graphics stored in GIF format without any difficulty or modification. In fact, these browsers display the graphic on the same page as the rest of the information, as though it were on a printed page (which is exactly the way it is supposed to be).

Most Web browsers, such as Netscape and Mosaic, display JPEG graphics the same way. Even if you use only a graphical Gopher client, or one of the few

Web browsers that don't directly support JPEG graphics, you can still view the images. However, you need to use a separate program, called a *helper application*, to view them. In this case, when you tell your Gopher or Web client to retrieve an image, the client retrieves the image but automatically invokes this separate helper application. It then displays the graphic in a separate window on-screen. The most common helper applications for displaying graphics are JPEGView for the Macintosh and LView for Windows. Both are available free of charge (their locations are given in the appendix), and both display JPEG and GIF graphics.

JARGON ALERT!

GIF *and* JPEG *are formats used to store graphics on the Internet. Most Web browsers will display these graphics formats by themselves, but Gopher requires a type of utility called a helper application to view them.*

Helper applications *are software programs that allow Internet tools like Web browsers to view different media types, including sounds, graphics, and motion pictures.*

You will need to configure your Web browser to use these helper applications. You do this by editing the configuration information for the Web browser (usually by choosing a menu item labeled Preferences). Incidentally, this concept of using helper applications to handle media types not handled by the clients and browsers themselves can be applied to other media types provided on the Internet.

Many resources on the Internet use graphics extensively to improve content (or even to be an integral part of it) and not just to make things look nicer. An example of a Web site that uses both GIF and JPEG graphics is the WebMuseum, located at **http://mistral.enst.fr**. The WebMuseum is a collection of art, art exhibits, and information about art, presented in a very informative way.

Figure 2.1 illustrates a page from the WebMuseum, about George Seurat's painting "Sunday Afternoon on the Isle of the Grand Jatte," complete with a graphic image of the painting. (The painting is actually a link to a much larger image of the same painting.)

Figure 2.1

A Web page from
the WebMuseum.

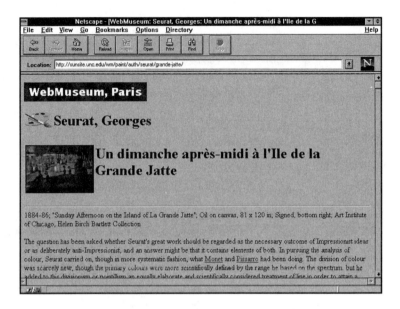

Sound on the Internet

Sounds on the Internet are generally not as useful to a student as graphics are. The reason is that not as many sites provide sounds for use in research. However, more sound resources will be available soon because libraries, schools, and businesses (particularly those connected with music) are currently building ambitious projects to deliver sound through the Internet.

Consider the basic requirements of accessing sounds. First, you need computer hardware that will support the playing of sounds. If you have an IBM PC-compatible computer, you must have a sound card installed in the computer in order to play sounds. (The sound card may go by many names; the most common is Sound Blaster.) If you have a Macintosh, you already have the hardware to play the sounds. Second, you need software programs that work with your Internet software and allow it to play sounds. The most common programs are probably SoundApp and SoundMachine for the Macintosh, and Mplayer for Windows. If you are using text-only UNIX, you really don't have an easy way of listening to sounds.

Page Description Languages

Although the World Wide Web comes close to presenting Internet information in a way that mimics the printed page, many Internet resource creators and publishers don't think the Web comes close enough. The Web doesn't give the author or publisher as much control over the exact look of the finished product in the way a printed page does (or even in the way a word processing file does). For example, each type of Web browser uses a different font in which to display text; and Gopher, FTP, and Telnet present information in even a less printlike format.

There are formats for information, however, that allow it to be stored and transmitted over the Internet in ways that mimic the look of the printed page. These formats are often called *page description language* formats—computer languages or data formats used to transmit data so that it looks like a printed page. In fact, files in a page description language format are used primarily so that the recipient of the document can then print it.

The oldest and most venerable page description language is called PostScript, owned by a company called Adobe. PostScript is still used for distribution of documents on the Internet that are intended to be printed. Although helper applications (such as GhostScript, the best known) will allow you to view PostScript-formatted documents on-screen, these applications really aren't very good. If you encounter a document in PostScript format on the Internet, your best bet is to retrieve that file (using any of the Internet tools) and send it to your printer. The way that you send a PostScript file to a printer varies from computer to computer, and from configuration to configuration. If you need help, ask a computer lab attendant.

A newer and more flexible page description language, also available from Adobe, has become fairly common on the Internet, particularly on the Web. This page description language, called Acrobat, can be viewed on-screen and printed with the aid of a helper application called the Acrobat Reader. Fortunately, Adobe has made the Acrobat Reader program available to the public free of charge. The program itself, for both Windows and the Macintosh, along with instructions on how to install the program and set it up with your Web browser, is available from the Adobe Web server, at location `http://www.adobe.com`. Netscape has also announced that it will provide the capability to read Acrobat documents directly in its next major version of Netscape.

> **TIP** *If you encounter a file name ending in .ps on the Internet, it is probably a PostScript file, which you can then print. If you see a file name ending in .pdf, it is probably an Adobe Acrobat file, and you will need to use the Adobe Acrobat Reader to view and print it.*

Compression and Data Files

Data on the Internet—especially software programs, sounds, graphics, and motion pictures—can grow extremely large. Even a minute or so of motion picture can be many megabytes of data. As a result, such information takes up a lot of space on servers, which have limited space available. Furthermore, such large files require a long time to transmit over a network when they are retrieved. For example, a two-minute sound clip may require over ten minutes to transmit over phone lines, and even a minute or so over a higher-speed network connection.

The solution implemented by most providers of information over the Internet is compression. *Compression* is the use of computer software to squeeze the same data into a smaller space *before* the data is stored on the Internet server. Compressed data takes up less space on the server itself, and because there is less data to transmit, retrieving a compressed file takes less time than retrieving the same file that is uncompressed. The capability to compress data is not limitless, however; there are mathematical limits on the degree to which data can be squeezed and still have none of the data lost. In addition, after you download the file, you must then uncompress it before you can use it.

Two types of compression are possible: compression that squeezes a single file into a smaller space, and compression that squeezes a number of files into a single file (often called archiving). Generally, you use these two types together. For example, if I have a set of files—such as a whole database of information, or a software program consisting of hundreds of files—I would want you to be able to download these files in one large chunk, instead of having to download and retrieve hundreds of individual files. In that case, I would archive all the files into one file and compress that archived file. You could then retrieve the file from the Internet and expand it into the original files on your own computer.

Unfortunately, the programs used for compression are quite different for UNIX, Windows, and the Macintosh. The following sections show how to uncompress a compressed file that you have retrieved from the Internet, using first UNIX, then Windows, and finally the Macintosh.

Uncompression with UNIX

Suppose that you have a UNIX file called readme.tar.gz. The .tar.gz extension to the file name tells you that you need to use two different programs to decompress this file. First, you need to use the gunzip program (which uncompresses), and then you need to use the tar program (which unarchives).

All UNIX systems have the tar program available, and almost all systems have gunzip. Follow these steps to decompress this file:

1. Type **gunzip readme.tar.gz** and press Enter.

   The gunzip program does the first level of uncompression, leaving the file readme.tar behind.

2. Type **tar pfxv readme.tar** and press Enter.

   The pfxv part is simply a series of options telling the UNIX tar program what you want it to do. This command unarchives the readme.tar file into one or more component files. The names of these files are listed on-screen as they are unarchived by tar.

Sometimes you will see files that end in .Z instead of .gz. The .Z means that they were compressed with the UNIX compression program, and they should be uncompressed with the UNIX uncompression program instead of gunzip.

> **TIP** *If you run across a file name ending in .tar on the Internet, you need to use the tar program to unarchive the file. If you see a file name ending in .tar.Z, you first use the UNIX uncompress command and then use the tar command to unarchive the file. If you encounter a file name ending in .gz, you use gunzip to uncompress it. Finally, if you see a file name ending in .tar.gz, you use gunzip first and then tar to unarchive it.*

Uncompression on the PC

Suppose that you have a file called MYFILE.ZIP on the PC. The ZIP extension tells you that this file should be uncompressed with the PKUNZIP uncompression program. Follow these steps:

1. At the DOS prompt, go into the directory where MYFILE.ZIP is located.

2. Type **pkunzip myfile.zip**.

   The PKUNZIP program decompresses this file and displays on-screen the file names of the expanded files. You can then work with the resulting files as you would with any other files. Of course, you must have the PKUNZIP program available on your computer so that you can use it to uncompress files.

Uncompression on the Macintosh

The Macintosh, like UNIX, uses several different types of compression. Files compressed on the Macintosh end in extensions like .sit and .hqx, or even .sit.hqx. Fortunately, all these types of files can be handled by a single decompression program called StuffItExpander.

If you have StuffItExpander on your computer, you just double-click the file icon ending in .sit.hqx, and the file will automatically be uncompressed.

Now that you have been introduced to various tools used to access the Internet, these tools are discussed in more detail in Part II. In the next several chapters, you practice retrieving information with the aid of different Internet tools.

3

Using the Web to Retrieve Information from the Internet

Objectives

After reading this chapter, you will be able to

- Retrieve a Web document with a known URL, using both Lynx and a graphical browser like Netscape or Mosaic

- Navigate the hypertext of a Web document, using both Lynx and a graphical browser

- Search the text of a particular Web document, using both Lynx and a graphical browser

- Save a Web page to disk, using both Lynx and a graphical browser

- Print a Web page, using both Lynx and a graphical browser

This chapter covers the basics of retrieving information from the World Wide Web, after you know the location of what it is you want. You learn how to move around in a Web document, follow links, and go back to where you started after you follow a link. You learn also how to search within a Web document, as well as how to save and print the information you have just located on the Web. Chapters 6, 7, and 8 cover searching in more detail.

In this chapter are examples of activities you might perform while using a Web browser: retrieving a resource, moving around and searching for text in the resource, printing and saving the resource, and following hypertext links in the resource. For many of these tasks, graphical Web browsers—such as Mosaic, Netscape, MacWeb, and Cello—look very different from nongraphical browsers like Lynx. For this reason, you see how each task is accomplished with a sample graphical browser (Netscape) and with a sample nongraphical browser (Lynx—really the only one still in use today).

Using a URL to Retrieve Information on the Web

This section uses, as an example, the Complete Works of William Shakespeare Web site, created and maintained by The Tech, an online news magazine from MIT. There are several reasons for using the Shakespeare Web site as an example here. First, the Shakespeare site is extremely well maintained. Second, it contains a body of work that most college and university students must work with at some time in their academic careers (so the content itself might be useful). Finally, the Shakespeare site exemplifies an excellent use of hypertext and electronic resources.

First, you retrieve the Complete Works of William Shakespeare home page by using the Web browsers Lynx and Netscape.

Retrieving the Shakespeare Home Page with Lynx

To retrieve the Shakespeare home page with Lynx, follow these steps:

1. Make sure that you are in Lynx. If you are at the command prompt and know that you have Lynx available, go into Lynx by typing **lynx**.

   You should now see the default home page for which your Lynx setup is configured. The default home page will be different for every site and will most likely be the home page for your particular school or department.

2. Type **g** from Lynx to tell it that you want to *go to* a particular URL.

   Lynx prompts you for the URL at the bottom of the screen:

   ```
   URL to open:
   ```

3. At this prompt, type the URL of the Shakespeare home page:

   http://the-tech.mit.edu/Shakespeare

   Then press Enter. You should now be at the Shakespeare home page, which is shown in figure 3.1.

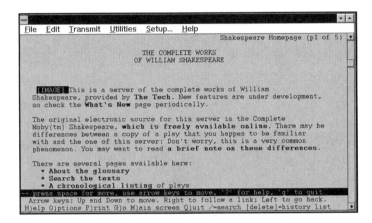

Figure 3.1

The Shakespeare home page in Lynx.

Note a couple of important things here. First, the line at the top, `Shakespeare Homepage (p1 of 5)`, refers to the number of screens of text that this home page contains. Right now, you are looking at the first of five screens of text. The entire five screens are referred to as the Web "page." (Thus, Web pages can be larger than a single screen, just as word processing document pages can.)

Second, the bottom two lines tell you what commands are available. The line

`Arrow keys: Up and Down to move. Right to follow a link; Left to go back.`

tells you how to move through the hypertext. The line

`H)elp O)ptions P)rint G)o M)ain screen Q)uit /=search [delete]=history list`

describes additional commands available to you.

Finally, and perhaps most important, the hypertext links to other documents are displayed in bold. Fortunately (or unfortunately), local programs like Procomm, Telnet, and Terminal—which enable you to access Lynx—can usually be customized, so you may not always see the hypertext links in bold.

However, the links will always be distinguished from normal text in some way. They may appear, for example, in inverse text or in some color other than the one used for normal text.

Notice the word [IMAGE] close to the upper left of the screen. This word means that a graphic is there and that you, with a nongraphical browser like Lynx, cannot look at the graphic. Let that be an incentive to get access to a graphical browser!

Retrieving the Shakespeare Home Page with Netscape

To retrieve the Shakespeare home page with Netscape or Mosaic, follow these steps:

1. Make sure that you are in Netscape. If you are not in this Web browser, double-click the Netscape icon to launch Netscape.

   You should now see the default home page for which your Netscape setup is configured. Again, this will be different for every site. In some cases, you may not even have a default home page configured, which is also OK.

2. Go to the File menu and choose Open Location.

   Netscape prompts you to enter a location for it to retrieve. What it actually wants is the URL for the resource to be retrieved.

3. In the box provided, type the URL of the Shakespeare home page:

   `http://the-tech.mit.edu/Shakespeare`

   Then click the Open button. You should now be at the Shakespeare home page, as shown in figure 3.2.

You have just done what is called opening a resource, going to a resource, or pointing your Web browser at a resource. Each of these expressions means using your Web browser to retrieve a particular resource and display it on-screen for browsing. The Shakespeare home page, as viewed with Netscape, is admittedly a bit more spectacular looking than the same document viewed with the Lynx browser. However, the same information is presented (with the exception of the graphics). The information, of course, looks quite different.

The title of the home page—in this case, Shakespeare Homepage—is in the title bar at the top of the Netscape screen. Netscape doesn't give you any idea of how many screens of data the page makes up—you pretty much have to move the scroll bar box up and down to find out. This time, the hypertext links to other documents are both underlined and in a different color. (The color can vary depending on how your copy of Netscape is set up, but the default is blue.)

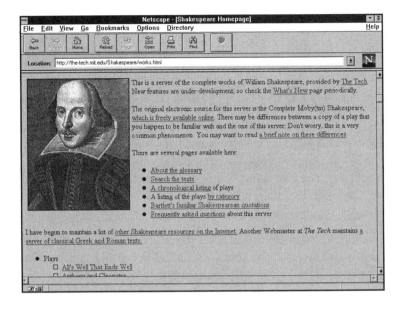

Figure 3.2
The Shakespeare home page in Netscape.

37

With the top row of buttons (labeled Back, Forward, Home, Reload, Images, Open, Print, Find, and Stop), you can perform different functions with the page, including the important task of moving between the pages and printing them. Note that the current location—the URL of the resource you are viewing—is displayed in a box labeled Location:. You can toggle (switch) on and off the display of the top row of buttons and the current location by selecting the Show Toolbar and Show Location options, respectively, from the Options menu.

After you have a Web document retrieved and displayed, you might want to do a number of things with the document, such as search for text within it, print the document, and navigate its hypertext links. To get familiar with the hypertext links, first try moving around a bit in the Shakespeare home page.

Moving Around in a Web Document

Now that you have the Shakespeare home page up, explore the hypertext a bit. Don't worry if you get lost. Hypertext should aid in navigation because it supposedly mimics human thought processes, jumping from place to place rather than following a single train of thought in a straight line. However, the hypertext you find on the Web most likely mimics the thought processes of the document's author rather than your own. For this reason, where you are and where you should go may not always seem as clear as they should be. Quite often, you will forget where you came from as well! Just keep at it, and you will eventually gain a feel for how to navigate hypertext without getting entirely lost.

Moving Around in a Web Document with Lynx

In this section, you use Lynx to move around in a Web document. In Lynx, the cursor, represented by inverse text, is always on top of one link. If you want to follow that link (that is, if you want to jump to the hypertext document pointed to by the link), all you do is press Enter while the cursor is on the link. If you want to follow a different link, you first need to use the up- and down-arrow keys to move the cursor to that link, and then press Enter to follow the link.

For this example, assume that you want to retrieve the first scene of the third act of *Hamlet*, a play that, for some reason, resonates particularly well with computer professionals! If you are not currently on the Shakespeare home page, follow the instructions in the preceding section to bring back the Shakespeare home page (the URL is `http://the-tech.mit.edu/Shakespeare`). Then follow these steps:

1. Using the down-arrow key, move the cursor down from link to link, until the cursor is on top of the link labeled `Hamlet`. If you go too far, you can always use the up-arrow key to move back up from link to link, until the cursor is on top of the `Hamlet` link.

> **NOTE** *On some computers, you won't be able to use the arrow keys. You can use the Tab key to move forward from link to link, and Shift+Tab to move backward from link to link.*

2. Press Enter to follow the link.

   The Hamlet page, shown in figure 3.3, is also larger than a single screen; in fact, it takes up five screens. Although you can move from link to link with the up- and down-arrow keys, you can also move from screen to screen of text (regardless of whether there is a link on the text) by using the spacebar and the hyphen key (-). The spacebar moves you down a screenful of text, and the hyphen moves you up a screenful.

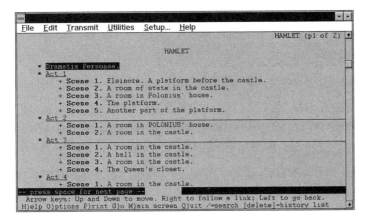

Figure 3.3

The Hamlet home
page in Lynx.

39

3. Using the up- and down-arrow keys, along with the spacebar and
   hyphen key, move the cursor so that it is on top of the link Act 3
   Scene 1. A room in the castle. This is the link you are looking for.

4. Press Enter to select the link.

   You are now viewing The Tech's "hypertextualized" version of the
   first scene of the third act of *Hamlet*. (*The Tech* is a student journal at
   the Massachusetts Institute of Technology.)

   Now you want to go back to where you were before, to the
   Shakespeare home page. You know you followed two different links,
   so you need to go back two links. However, if you forget where you
   are, Lynx provides a summary of all the links you've followed since
   you started Lynx. This summary is called the History page.

5. To view the History page, press the Backspace key (labeled Delete on
   Macintosh keyboards). Figure 3.4 shows the History page, which
   displays every link, in order, that you have traversed since beginning
   Lynx.

   The Indiana University WWW home page is my default home page
   for Lynx. Yours will most likely be different. What you see in this
   example is that you've retrieved four different Web documents since
   you began using Lynx earlier. The first document you retrieved was
   the default home page (in this example, the Indiana University WWW
   home page), automatically retrieved when you brought up Lynx. The
   second document was the Shakespeare home page, the third was
   Hamlet, and the fourth—which you are currently viewing—is the
   Hamlet, Act 3, Scene 1 document.

Figure 3.4

The History page
in Lynx.

40

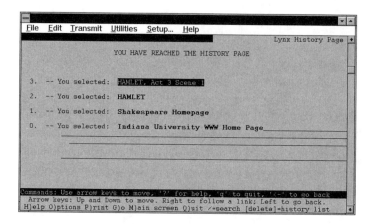

If you wanted, you could use the arrow keys directly from the History page to go back to any page previously visited. For example, to go back to the Hamlet page, you move the cursor to Hamlet and press Enter. You are then taken back to the Hamlet page. Note that the History page works just like any other hypertext document in Lynx. Links to other documents (such as those already visited) are shown in bold, inverse text, or a different color. You can also move from link to link with the same keys you've been using: the up- and down-arrow keys to move from link to link, and the spacebar and hyphen key to move up and down screens of text. However, for this example, you will not use the History page to go back to a previous page. Instead, you will go back directly.

6. Press the left-arrow key to go back to the Hamlet, Act 3, Scene 1 page—the page you were looking at before you went to the History page.

Already, you can see that the left-arrow key takes you back from the History page to where you were before. Indeed, the left-arrow key always takes you back to the previous page you had retrieved, before you followed a particular link.

> **TIP** *If you are using Lynx and you follow a link that doesn't lead you to where you want to be, just press the left-arrow key, and you will go back to where you started before you followed the link.*

Now you want to go back to the Hamlet document, your location before you followed the link to the current document (Hamlet, Act 3, Scene 1).

7. Press the left-arrow key to go back to the Hamlet home page.

   Now you get the picture. To move back even further, you can just press the left-arrow key again.

8. Press the left-arrow key again to go back to the Shakespeare home page.

   You've just reached your goal. You have successfully navigated the Shakespeare home page with the Lynx browser. Although this example featured the Shakespeare home page, everything discussed is generally applicable to other Web documents. These basic navigation skills (and much practice with them) will serve you well while searching for information on the Internet.

Table 3.1 summarizes the most important Lynx commands and actions.

Table 3.1	Summary of Lynx Navigation Keys
Key	**Function**
Up arrow	Moves to the previous link on a page
Down arrow	Moves to the next link on a page
Spacebar (or +)	Moves to the next screenful of text on a page
b or hyphen (-)	Moves to the previous screenful of text on a page
g	Enables you to go directly to a particular URL
/	Enables you to search within a single document for a particular word or phrase
h	Provides help for Lynx
d	Downloads the file to your account
a	Adds the current link to your bookmark file
m	Goes to your default home page (the main screen)
p	Prints or mails the current document
q	Quits
/	Searches the current document for a string
Backspace	Views the history of pages visited
=	Shows file and link information (such as the URL of the current page and link)

Moving Around in a Web Document with Netscape

Now you move around in "hyperspace" by using Netscape instead of Lynx. Navigating with a graphical browser is a bit easier than with Lynx because the graphics and different fonts on the screen can provide some cues. They certainly make it easier to recognize where you are. However, you can still get lost, even quite easily.

In Lynx, a cursor is always positioned on a particular link. Because you use a mouse to move around in Netscape (or Mosaic), the cursor is no longer needed. If you want to follow a link, you instead use the mouse to move the on-screen arrow pointer to the link, and then click once on the link.

> **TIP** *Even though you usually double-click to open a file or application in Windows and on the Macintosh, with Netscape and Mosaic (in Windows and on the Macintosh) you single-click to follow a link. Double-clicking can occasionally get you into trouble, if the second click accidentally takes you to another link.*

For this example, you want to retrieve the first scene of the first act of *Titus Andronicus*, Shakespeare's most unfortunate play. If you are not currently on the Shakespeare home page, follow the instructions given previously to bring back the Shakespeare home page (the URL is `http://the-tech.mit.edu /Shakespeare`). Then follow these steps:

1. Using your mouse, move the pointer until it is on top of the link `Titus Andronicus`. Depending on how large you have set your window and the size of your monitor, you may need to use the scroll bars to scroll to a different part of the document to find the `Titus Andronicus` link.

2. Click the mouse once to follow this link.

   You are now on the Titus Andronicus page, as shown in figure 3.5. Look at the document you have just retrieved, scrolling up and down, to get a feel for how long it is. Notice how scrolling works with the document. Notice also how the links are marked, usually with underlining and different colors.

3. Using your mouse, move the pointer so that it is on top of the `Act 1 Scene 1` link, which is the link you are looking for.

4. Click the link once to follow it.

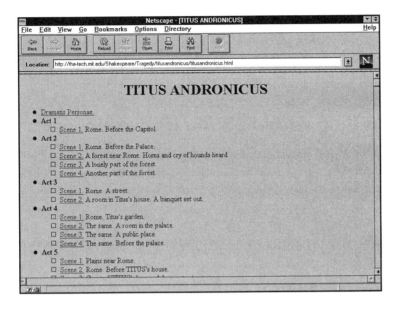

Figure 3.5

The Titus
Andronicus home
page in Netscape.

43

The computer retrieves the hypertext version of the first scene of the
first act of *Titus Andronicus*. Now, of course, you have probably
made a mistake—because no one wants to retrieve *Titus Andronicus*.
Thus, the next thing you need to do is go back to the previous link.
Fortunately, this task is simple: You just click the Back button (the
left-arrow icon) at the top of the Netscape screen.

5. Click the Back button at the top of the Netscape screen.

    You should now be back at the Titus Andronicus page.

6. Click the Back button again to go back to the Shakespeare page. You
    are now back where you started.

> **TIP** *If you are using Netscape or Mosaic and you follow a link
> that doesn't lead you where you want to be, just click the
> Back button at the top of the screen. You go back to
> where you started before you followed the link.*

Take a look at the hypertext links on the page again, particularly the link
pointing to the Titus Andronicus document. This link is a different color from
that of the rest of the links! This change of color means that you have already
followed the link once. Both Netscape and Mosaic change the color of a link

to let you know that you've already followed that link. This feature can be an enormous navigation aid when you are exploring a large set of hypertext documents, because you can easily tell what you haven't looked at yet by looking at the color of the links.

Searching within a Web Document

Although you can usually read very short Web documents easily (especially ones that don't contain more than a screenful of information), Web documents often can be quite long. (I've encountered Web documents with 75 pages or more.) With long documents, you may want to search for a particular word or phrase. For the following examples, imagine that you are writing a paper on nobility in *Hamlet*, and you want to search for the word *noble* in that first scene of the third act of *Hamlet*.

Searching within a Web Document with Lynx

To search within a Web document with Lynx, follow these steps:

1. Bring up the Lynx browser by typing **lynx** from the command prompt (if Lynx isn't already running).

2. Type **g** to go to a URL of your choice.

3. Type **http://the-tech.mit.edu/Shakespeare** and press Enter to go to the Shakespeare home page.

4. Follow the Hamlet link to the Hamlet page.

5. Follow the link Act 3 Scene 1. A room in the castle.

   Now you want to search for the word *noble*. The Lynx command that searches the text of a particular document is / (also known as the forward slash). Note that the / command does *not* search other documents on the Internet; / searches only the document you are viewing.

6. Press /. Lynx displays the prompt Enter a Search String:.

   At this prompt, you type the word or phrase you want to find.

7. Type **noble** and press Enter.

   The first line in which the word *noble* appears is now positioned at the top of the screen, as shown in figure 3.6. Note that, in this case, the word occurs as a substring of another word, *nobler*. Thus, Lynx searches only for the characters you type. Those characters can occur

anywhere in a word, or as part of a word. Now you want to find the
next instance of the word *noble*.

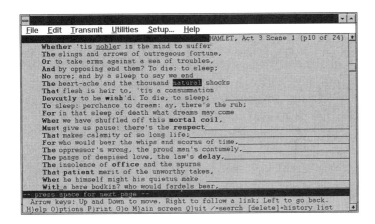

Figure 3.6
Finding the word
noble in *Hamlet*,
Act 3, Scene 1.

8. Press / and type **noble** again. Then press Enter.

The next line in which the word *noble* appears is now positioned at
the top of the screen. You can repeat these steps as many times as you
like. When the word you are searching for no longer appears, the
search goes back to the beginning of the document and starts over,
finding the same instances of the word again. However, if the document doesn't contain the word at all, Lynx tells you this through an
error message. For example, a search for the word *pipsqueak* in the
Hamlet document gives "pipsqueak" could not be found in this
document as an error message.

Searching within a Web Document with Netscape

To search within a Web document with Netscape (or Mosaic), follow these
steps:

1. Bring up the Netscape (or Mosaic) browser by double-clicking the
   appropriate icon, if the browser isn't already running.

2. Select Open Location from the File menu to go to a URL of your
   choice.

3. Type **http://the-tech.mit.edu/Shakespeare** and press Enter to go to
   the Shakespeare home page.

4. Follow the Hamlet link to the Hamlet page.

5. Follow the link Act 3 Scene 1. A room in the castle.

You want to search for the word *noble*, because you are studying nobility in *Hamlet*. To search for a word in a document with Netscape (or Mosaic), you choose the Find option from the Edit menu, and in the box that appears, type the word or phrase you want to search for. As a shortcut, instead of choosing Find from the menu, you can simply press ⌘+F on the Macintosh or press Ctrl+F in Windows.

6. Choose Find from the Edit menu. Netscape then prompts you to enter a word or phrase to search for.

7. Type **noble** and press Enter.

The first line in which the word *noble* appears is now positioned at the top of the screen (see figure 3.7). Note that the word occurs as part of a substring of another word, *nobler*. The reason is that Netscape (or Mosaic) searches for only the characters you type, which can occur anywhere in a word, or as part of a word. Now you want to find the next instance of *noble*. You don't need to type the word or phrase again; you simply choose the Find Again option from the Edit menu. As a shortcut for Find Again, you can press ⌘+G on the Macintosh or press Ctrl+G in Windows.

Figure 3.7

Using the Find command in Netscape.

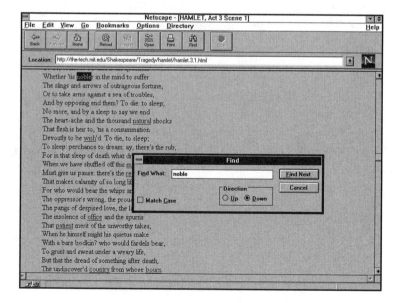

8. To move to the next instance of the word, press ⌘+G on the Macintosh or press Ctrl+G in Windows.

The next line in which the word *noble* appears is now positioned at the top of the screen. As with Lynx, you can repeat this process as many times as you like. When the word you are searching for is no longer found, the search starts again at the beginning of the document, finding the same instances of *noble* again. However, if the document doesn't contain the word at all, Netscape (or Mosaic) gives you an error message. For example, a search for the word *computer* in the Hamlet document results in the error message `"computer" could not be found in this document.`

Saving Documents Retrieved from the Web

When you retrieve a document that you find useful for a paper, you will want to be able to save it. There are really two different approaches to saving documents with Web browsers (and both methods apply to all browsers already discussed, both graphical and nongraphical). The first method is to save the text of a retrieved document to your local disk (or to your UNIX account if you are using Lynx). You then have the text of the document available to you, perhaps for importing into a word processing document or sending in an e-mail message. The second method is to save a pointer to the location of the document (in the form of a URL for the document). This second method is generally called creating a bookmark to the document (in Lynx and Netscape) or adding a document to your hotlist (in Mosaic).

Each method has disadvantages and advantages, of course. Saving the document to a local hard disk or to a floppy disk gives you a permanent copy of the document at a particular time. (Remember that Internet-based documents can and do change!) You have this copy even if the Web site on which the document is located disappears. However, creating a bookmark to a document is more compact and potentially more up-to-date. A bookmark takes up a lot less disk space than the document itself; whenever you use a bookmark to retrieve a document, you always retrieve the most current version.

The next sections show you how to save a document locally, using both Lynx and Netscape. The discussion of bookmarks is in Chapter 4, where bookmark management is covered more thoroughly.

Saving a Document with Lynx

To save a document with Lynx, you first retrieve the document so that it is the one displayed. To save a document, you need to tell Lynx to "print" the document (although this may seem counterintuitive). The reason for this is that Lynx construes printing very broadly, as something like "sending the text of a document somewhere." As you will see shortly in the Printing Options page, that "somewhere" can be a printer, a file, the screen, or an e-mail message. Follow these steps:

1. Type **p** to bring up the Lynx Printing Options page, as shown in figure 3.8.

Figure 3.8

The Lynx Printing Options page.

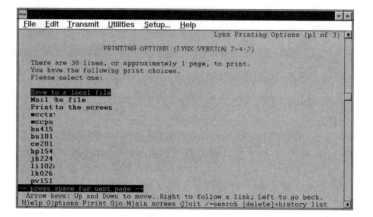

This screen offers several options. You can save the current document to a local file, e-mail the document to yourself, print the document to the screen, or print the document to a printer that has been set up for your system. To save the document to a local file, you choose the Save to a local file option.

2. Use the up- and down-arrow keys to move the cursor to the Save to a local file option. Then press Enter.

The computer prompts you for a file name for the document to be saved. A file name is suggested, usually the name given to the file when it was created on the Web server. For the *Hamlet* example, Lynx might display this prompt:

```
Please enter a file name: Hamlet.dp.html
```

Note that the suggested file name sometimes ends in .html, which can be very misleading. Ending a file name with .html is a Web convention which indicates that the document is marked up in the hypertext markup language (HTML). However, when you save a document to a local file with Lynx, you aren't saving it in HTML form—instead, you are saving it in standard text form. You can either accept the file name suggested, or backspace over it and use whatever you want the name to be, pressing Enter to save the file.

3. Backspace over the name Hamlet.dp.html and type **Testfile**. Then press Enter.

   The document is saved as a UNIX file, called Testfile, in your local UNIX account and can be manipulated with standard UNIX commands.

Saving a Document with a Graphical Web Browser

Saving documents with a graphical Web browser is extremely easy. When the document you want to save is displayed, choose the Save <u>A</u>s option from the <u>F</u>ile menu (with the Macintosh or in Windows). You are then prompted to provide a file name for the resource to be saved. You also have a choice of saving the file as either Text or Source. If you save the file as Text, you lose any graphics and font information. However, you can then import the document into a word processor and work with the text there. If you save the file as Source, you must use your Web browser to view the document if you want to look at it again (which you undoubtedly do, if you are saving it).

The question of whether to save documents directly or to create bookmarks for them is a thorny one. My advice is generally to save documents locally whenever you want to use a full document, or even a piece of a document, in a paper. That way, if your instructor questions you about it, you can always produce the material you used in writing the paper. However, if you simply find a Web site or a document generally useful, and you expect that Web site to be updated frequently, you might prefer to create a bookmark to that document, and then refer directly to the "live" version of the resource whenever you want to look at it. Of course, you take the risk that the document won't be there or will have changed when you retrieve it again—because you have no control over the remote site where the resource is located.

Printing Documents Retrieved from the Web

Printing Web documents can be simple, if you have the appropriate printer connected to your computer. Generally, printing is easy if you are using one of the graphical browsers. If you are using Lynx, though, there are a number of different ways to connect the printer to the computer, depending on your version of UNIX and many other variables. If you are using Lynx, you should ask your computing services department or computer lab assistant how to set up Lynx to print to your printer.

Printing a Web Document with Lynx

To print a Web document with Lynx, you need to go back to the Printing Options page, using the p command (refer to figure 3.8). Follow these steps:

1. With the current document as the one you want to print, type **p** to go to the Printing Options page.

   The Printing Options page tells you how many lines of text are in the document to be printed, along with the approximate number of pages the printed document will require. In the Hamlet example, the document has 98 lines and will require about 2 pages. This information can be quite useful, perhaps preventing you from unintentionally sending a 200-page document to a slow printer!

   From here, you will need to have some information about your local setup. The printer defined in the earlier example is named HPLaserPrinter. However, you will almost certainly see something else (or you may not see anything at all—if your local system administrator hasn't set up any printers for you). Also note that Lynx works well for printing to printers on a network but isn't as good at printing to printers attached to your local computer (primarily because of the archaic UNIX printing architecture that Lynx relies on). For this example, however, you can select HPLaserPrinter as the printer to which you will send the document.

2. Using the up- and down-arrow keys, move the cursor to HPLaserPrinter, or whatever your particular printer is. (If you don't have one, you can always practice by choosing the Print to the screen option.) Then press Enter.

   The document is printed to the local printer or to the screen, depending on which one you chose. Unfortunately, because of the limitations

of a nongraphical Web browser like Lynx, the document you print
will not contain all the graphics, and the text will not be in different
fonts and font sizes. To get the benefit of a more "printed" look, you
need to move to a graphical Web browser, which prints the graphics,
fonts, and formatting along with the text.

Printing a Web Document with a Graphical Web Browser

Printing a document with a graphical Web browser like Netscape or Mosaic
is even simpler than with Lynx, assuming that you have the appropriate printer
connected to your computer. To print the current document from a graphical
Web browser, you just choose Print from the File menu. You then see the
appropriate dialog box for the type of system and printer you are using.
Usually, you just click OK, and your document will be printed, graphics
and all!

Retrieving Non-Web Resources with a Web Browser

One of the nicest benefits to using a Web browser as your tool of choice on the
Internet is its inclusiveness—a Web browser allows you to access resources
created under several other technologies, such as Gopher resources, Usenet
newsgroups, and files available for FTP. All Web browsers, including Lynx,
offer this benefit. Thus, it is often unnecessary to have a Gopher client at all,
because Web browsers are capable of retrieving Gopher-based resources.
Although retrieving Gopher resources with a Web browser is similar to
retrieving the same resources through a Gopher client, providing a simple
example here is instructive. This time, you will be connecting to the National
Science Foundation Gopher server (the URL is `gopher://gopher.nsf.gov`),
using a graphical Web browser. Follow these steps:

1. With your graphical Web browser (Netscape, in this example), go to
   the URL of the National Science Foundation Gopher by choosing
   Open Location from the File menu.

2. Type **gopher://gopher.nsf.gov** in the space provided. Then press
   Enter.

   Figure 3.9 shows the results. Although you are using a Web browser,
   you are connected to a Gopher resource. You can probably see hints
   of both technologies here. The top of the screen tells you that you are
   viewing a Gopher menu, and you see a list of items on-screen, items
   presented to you by the Gopher server. However, these items look

very much like Web hypertext links. In fact, they *are* Web hypertext links—you can follow them to go to the appropriate resource, just as you can select the appropriate items with a Gopher client to connect to the resource.

Figure 3.9

National Science Foundation Gopher server using Netscape.

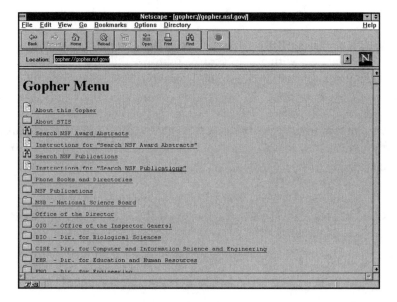

The icon to the left of the menu item indicates the type of resource to which the menu item points. The most common icons are the following:

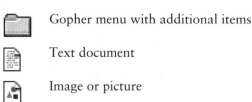 Gopher menu with additional items

Text document

Image or picture

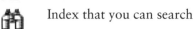 Index that you can search

Now look at one of the text documents—in this case, the first one, which is About this Gopher.

3. Click the mouse on `About this Gopher`, either on the text icon to the left of the link or on the link itself (both are actually links).

The text of the About this Gopher document is retrieved, which you can then print or save if you like.

4. Click the Back button (left-arrow icon) to go back to the main menu of the National Science Foundation Gopher server.

Everything you have just done here will work with Lynx as well; the items will look just a little different. Figure 3.10 illustrates how Lynx accesses the same Gopher server.

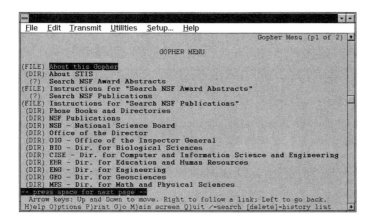

Figure 3.10

National Science Foundation Gopher using Lynx.

Instead of using icons to indicate what type of resource the links are pointing to, Lynx uses an abbreviation, within parentheses, for the type of resource. The most common abbreviations are the following:

(DIR)   Gopher directory or menu of other resources. (DIR) corresponds to the folder icon in the preceding list.

(?)   Index that you can search. (?) corresponds to the binoculars icon in the preceding list.

(FILE)   Text file. (FILE) corresponds to the text document icon in the preceding list.

(IMAGE)   Image that can be retrieved although usually not viewed directly. (IMAGE) corresponds to the image icon in the preceding list.

Now that you have covered the basics of retrieving information with World Wide Web browsers, you need to make the most of this information. The next chapters show you how to find resources that are useful in your studies.

4

How to Find it Again: Bookmarks

Objectives

After reading this chapter, you will be able to

- Understand the concept of using bookmarks to mark good Internet resources so that you can easily get back to them

- Use bookmarks with Web browsers

With all the addresses and Uniform Resource Locators (URLs) for resources being bandied about, you may wonder how you are ever going to remember where everything is. If you find a great resource on the Internet in your searching (which you probably will, time and time again), you will want to know how to mark that site so that you can go back to it later. Fortunately, all Web browsers give you this ability—to mark a site so that you can go back to it. This feature goes by at least two names: bookmarks and hotlists.

The Basics of Bookmarks

The idea behind a bookmark is simple: When you find a good resource that you want to be able to come back to, you create a bookmark for that site. That site is then stored in your bookmark file, and you can go on and do other things, even quit your programs. (Usually, both the title of the resource and its location or URL are stored—some Web browsers even let you add comments about the resource.) When you want to go back to that site, you just go to your bookmark file and select from it the resource that you want to go back to. The Web browser automatically retrieves the appropriate resource.

Many Web browsers provide additional features. For example, many enable you to customize the titles of the bookmarks. Many also allow you to add comments to a bookmark, so that you have more identifying information about the site when you go back to the bookmark. Finally, many clients let you subdivide your bookmark file into hierarchical categories and subcategories. These features can be extremely useful, especially as you start marking more Internet resources. Bookmark management is expected to become a major area of development and innovation for new versions of Web browsers. However, the basic function of bookmarks is very easy: The bookmark enables you to get back to a resource you find useful.

In the following examples, you learn how to create a bookmark to a resource and retrieve the bookmark by using two different Internet programs: Netscape for Windows and Lynx for UNIX. Although the terminology may vary in these programs (the bookmark file is called the *hotlist* in Mosaic), the basic procedures hold for other Web browsers and for the Macintosh as well.

JARGON ALERT!

A bookmark is used by Web browsers to mark resources on the Internet that you would like to return to. If you find a site that you like, you can save it as a bookmark. Then you don't have to remember the address of the site—you can just choose the bookmark from your client's bookmark menu. Many browsers also have additional features that allow you to sort and anno-tate your bookmarks.

In the early days of Web browsers, bookmarks were sometimes called hotlists. *Mosaic still refers to them as hotlists. Other-wise, a bookmark list and a hotlist are the same thing.*

Creating Bookmarks with Netscape

In this section, you use Netscape to retrieve WebElements, a very complete and useful reference to the chemical elements and to the periodic table of the elements. You mark WebElements with a bookmark so that you can find it again. Follow these steps:

1. Using Netscape, go to the WebElements page, at location `http://www.shef.ac.uk/~chem/web-elements`. This page is shown in figure 4.1.

Figure 4.1
The WebElements home page.

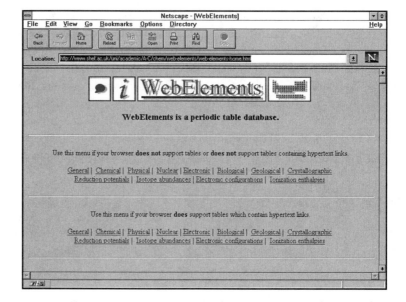

If you are a student of chemistry, this resource is quite useful, so you will probably want to mark it. (Even if you aren't a student of chemistry, you should still do this for the purpose of the exercise.)

2. To mark the resource, select the option **A**dd Bookmark from the **B**ookmarks menu.

You have created a bookmark to this resource. Now, just for fun, move on to something else.

3. Click the Home button to go back to the home page that is configured as the default for your browser.

You should now be looking at some other page. Next, you want to go back to the WebElements page. You could type the URL of that resource again. However, because you created a bookmark, you can go right to the bookmark instead. Your **B**ookmarks menu should look something like that in figure 4.2.

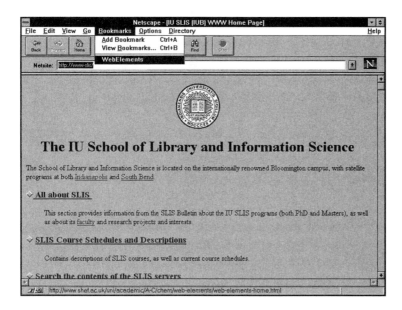

Figure 4.2

The Bookmarks menu with WebElements added as a bookmark.

4. From the **B**ookmarks menu, choose the WebElements bookmark.

You are back at the WebElements page. Nothing could be easier.

Netscape provides features for adding comments to your bookmarks, deleting and editing them, and adding more bookmark levels. For example, you could create a Chemistry Resources bookmark, containing a submenu of individual bookmarks to useful chemistry resources. You can access all these features by choosing the View **B**ookmarks option from the **B**ookmarks menu. This window, which enables you to use these features to edit your bookmark list, is shown in figure 4.3.

Figure 4.3

The window for editing your bookmark list.

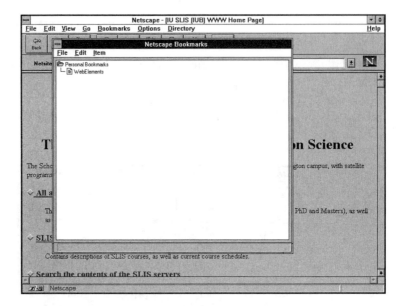

Creating Bookmarks with Lynx

Lynx doesn't offer nearly as rich a set of tools for working with bookmarks. However, Lynx still performs the basic function of bookmarks: to mark a site so that you can get back to it in the future.

Try creating a bookmark with Lynx now. In this example, you want to go to the Project Gutenberg home page. Project Gutenberg provides public-domain literary texts in electronic form over the Internet, for free downloading and use. Project Gutenberg is available from the location **http://jg.cso.uiuc.edu/PG /welcome.html**. To create a bookmark with Lynx, follow these steps:

1. Make sure that you are in Lynx (if you are not, type **lynx** at the UNIX prompt).

2. Type **g** to go to a location.

3. Type **http://jg.cso.uiuc.edu/PG/welcome.html,** the URL of Project Gutenberg.

   Then press Enter. You are now at the Project Gutenberg home page, as shown in figure 4.4.

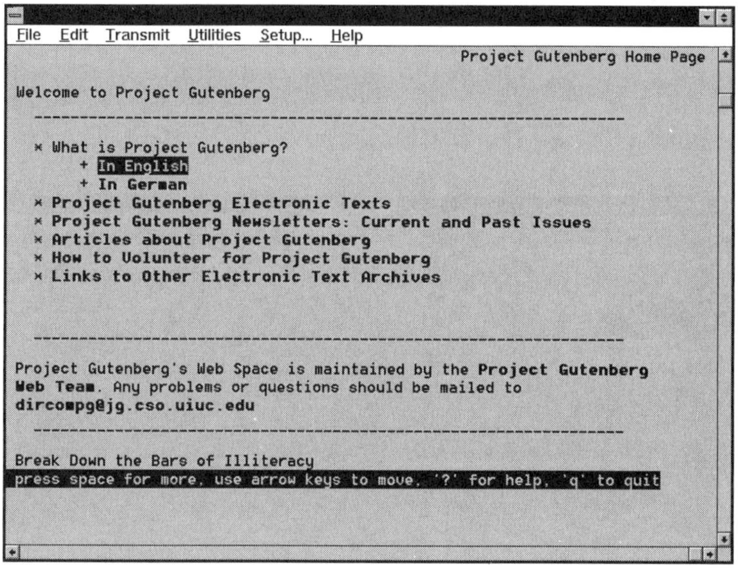

Figure 4.4
The Project
Gutenberg
home page.

59

Because this is a good site, you will want to create a bookmark to it
so that you can get back to it easily.

4. To create a bookmark to the Project Gutenberg home page, type **a**
   (for Add Bookmark).

   Lynx asks you to Save Document (D), Link to bookmark file (L), or
   Cancel (C). If you choose Save Document, you are creating a bookmark to the current document you have retrieved (in this case, the
   Project Gutenberg home page). If you choose Link to bookmark file,
   you are creating a bookmark to the link where the cursor is located
   (in this case, the In English description of Project Gutenberg). You
   can also cancel, if you don't want to create a bookmark at all.

5. Type **d** to save the bookmark to the Project Gutenberg home page
   itself.

   The bookmark is now saved.

6. Now type **m** to go back to the main screen (the default home page for
   which your copy of Lynx is configured). Answer yes (Y) when Lynx
   prompts you to confirm.

   You should be back at your default home page. Now you want to use
   your bookmark to go back to the Project Gutenberg home page. The
   v command, for View Bookmarks, gives you the list of bookmarks.

7. Type **v** to go to your list of bookmarks (labeled Bookmark file).

My list is shown in figure 4.5. Yours may differ slightly if you have already created some bookmarks. I also have another bookmark to the Indiana University WWW Home Page.

Figure 4.5

A list of book-marks in Lynx.

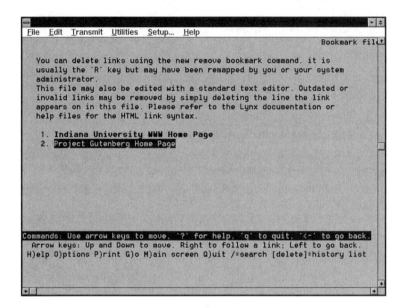

8. Move the cursor to the bookmark that you want to go to—the Project Gutenberg Home Page bookmark.

9. Press Enter.

You should now be back at the Project Gutenberg home page. Note that you can also delete bookmarks from the Bookmark file page by moving the cursor to the bookmark you want to delete and then typing **r** (for Remove Bookmark).

You can easily get lost on the Internet because you are always jumping from link to link. Bookmarks, however, provide you with tools to combat this problem. With them, you can mark the sites or resources that you find useful, and then easily return to those sites later. Use bookmarks often, marking anything that you might find interesting. Also mark items as you find them—you may not be able to find them again if you don't. Remember that you can always go back and delete bookmarks if you decide later that you don't want to use the resource. However, you should actively maintain your bookmark list, going through and organizing the bookmarks, and deleting those that aren't of use. In the meantime, the developers of Internet tools will no doubt come up with interesting new ways of managing your own lists of bookmarks.

5

Using FTP to Retrieve Information from the Internet

Objectives

After reading this chapter, you will be able to

- Use FTP to transfer files from one computer to another

- Log in to an FTP site anonymously

In this book, the three "tools"—the World Wide Web, Gopher, and FTP—are presented in reverse order from how they are usually taught. (Purists would probably argue that the World Wide Web and Gopher are really more architectures than tools.) Generally, the lower-level, older, and more difficult technologies are taught first. Then the more modern tools are presented. This approach is unfortunate. Many students, especially those with a touch of technophobia, turn off as soon as FTP is taught, so that by the time they've moved to the World Wide Web, they are so frustrated and confused that they no longer find it worth their while to use the Internet in their studies. This book's approach is different in that you are not bombarded with unnecessary technical details. Those can come later, if you want to learn them.

FTP is a tool for transferring a file from one computer to another. It is mostly used to retrieve files from shared central repositories, where such files are deposited in order to be shared. These repositories are often called *anonymous FTP servers*. The files retrieved by FTP can be of any type. They can be files that contain only text (ASCII files), or they can be software programs, images, or sounds (binary files).

JARGON ALERT!

FTP (File Transfer Program) *is software on the Internet used to transfer files from one computer to another (from an FTP client to an FTP server). An anonymous FTP server is a computer that allows you to retrieve information from it through FTP, even though you don't have an account or user name on the computer. Usually, you use the user name* anonymous *to log in and retrieve information from the server.*

TIP *When you use FTP, the distinction between binary files and ASCII files is important. With FTP, there is a difference between the two types, and if you try to transfer an ASCII file as binary, or a binary file as ASCII, your file transfer can fail.*

FTP Clients

The FTP client is the software program that you use to connect to the FTP server and to transfer the file. FTP client software is available for almost every type of computer. For example, the most popular FTP programs for the Macintosh are called Fetch and X-Ferit. The most popular programs for the PC include NCSA FTP, RapidFiler, and WinQVT. In UNIX, the most common program is simply called ftp.

Retrieving a File with FTP

In the following example, you use the UNIX version of ftp because it is the most generic. Macintosh- and Windows-based FTP programs may look completely different, but again, the underlying concepts are the same.

Your goal in using FTP is simple: You want to "download" files that you have heard about. That is, you want to transfer them from a remote computer, where they are stored, to your own computer so that you can look at them. To do this, you use the UNIX version of ftp to find and download electronic texts from the Project Gutenberg archive at the University of Illinois. The address of the computer where these texts are located is **uiarchive.cso.uiuc.edu**. Follow these steps:

1. Make sure that you are logged in to your UNIX account and are at the UNIX prompt. (Mine looks like %, but yours may look different.)

2. Connect to the Gutenberg archive computer by typing the following:

    ftp uiarchive.cso.uiuc.edu

    You will see something like the text shown in figure 5.1.

Figure 5.1

Logging in with FTP to the Gutenberg archive computer.

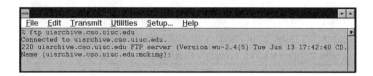

```
 File  Edit  Transmit  Utilities  Setup...  Help
% ftp uiarchive.cso.uiuc.edu
Connected to uiarchive.cso.uiuc.edu.
220 uiarchive.cso.uiuc.edu FTP server (Version wu-2.4(5) Tue Jun 13 17:42:40 CD.
Name (uiarchive.cso.uiuc.edu:mckimg):
```

This information tells you that you are connected to the computer at the address **uiarchive.cso.uiuc.edu**, you are using FTP, and you are being prompted to log in. Just as you had to log in when you were connecting to a remote computer through Telnet, you have to log in when accessing a remote system through FTP. Usually, however, you won't have an account with the computer that you are connecting to with FTP and from which you want to download files. In that case, you use a generic user name, as you did with Telnet. In the case of FTP, though, the standard generic user name to use is anonymous.

3. Type **anonymous** at the prompt and press Enter.

    The computer displays something like the following:

    ```
    331 Guest login ok, send your complete e-mail address as
    password.
    ```

    Normally, the computer now asks for your password. However, when you log in as user anonymous, you don't have a password on the computer. Instead, you should provide your full Internet e-mail address.

4. Type your full Internet electronic mail address and press Enter.

Notice that the computer doesn't display anything when you type your e-mail address. The reason is that the computer is accepting the e-mail address as a password, and computers almost never display passwords on-screen for security reasons. Typing your own Internet e-mail address when you use FTP to download files anonymously is considered a courtesy to the people maintaining (free of charge) the FTP archives from which you are transferring files. Providing this information helps them track how and how often their equipment is being used. You will now see the FTP login message from the computer you connected to, as shown in figure 5.2.

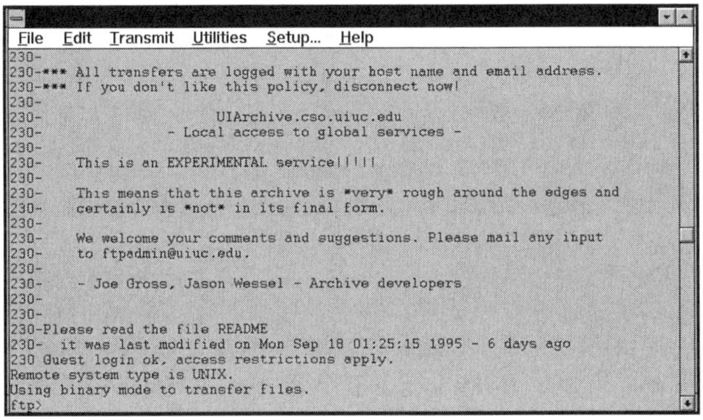

Figure 5.2
A sample FTP
login message.

This is a particularly long "welcome" message. Not all are this long. However, this welcome message gives some introductory material about what is available on the computer, as well as the fairly typical disclaimers about the service being experimental (which means that it can change frequently). The ftp> at the bottom of the screen means that you are logged in and can start typing ftp commands.

The first command that you should try is the dir command. It gives you a list of the files available for downloading to your computer.

5. Type **dir** and press Enter. Your screen should look similar to figure 5.3.

You will probably groan when you see this screen. However, you need to pay attention to only a couple of pieces of information. Look at the last column on the right. The names appearing in this column are the names of the files and directories (collections of files) available to you, such as README, pub, and licensed. Look also at the leftmost character on the screen (in this case, either *d* or -). This character tells you whether the file name on the right is a single file or a directory (collection) of files. The *d* stands for *directory*. In this case, bin, etc, licensed, local, pub, tmp, usage.stats, and usr are all directories.

Figure 5.3

Displaying a directory through FTP.

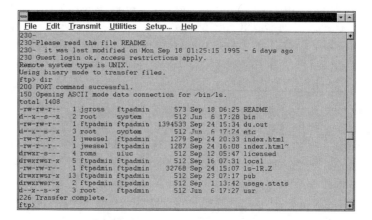

Most of these files and directories are not accessible to you, and not meant for you. Almost universally, the files available for public access and downloading are available in a directory called pub. Thus, the next thing you do is move into the directory called pub and check what is available.

6. Type **cd pub** and press Enter.

The cd command means "change directory." You just told ftp to take you into the pub directory. Figure 5.4 shows the computer's response.

Figure 5.4

The list of directories within the pub directory.

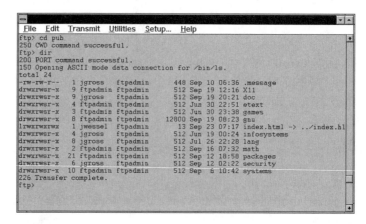

This screen is very helpful, giving you a list of directories within the pub directory. Not all computers are as helpful, though. With many computers, you would have to type another dir command to find out what is in the pub directory.

Because you are looking for Project Gutenberg electronic texts, you use the cd command again to move into the etext directory, the one that contains Project Gutenberg texts.

7. Type **cd etext** and press Enter.

In this case, all you get is 250 CWD command successful, which tells you that your request to change directories to etext worked. However, now you have to request explicitly that the computer tell you which files are available in this directory.

8. Type **dir** and press Enter. You see the display shown in figure 5.5.

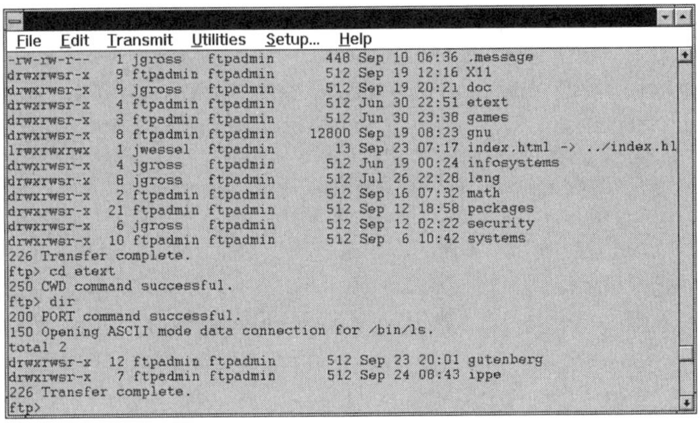

```
 File  Edit  Transmit  Utilities  Setup...  Help
-rw-rw-r--    1 jgross   ftpadmin      448 Sep 10 06:36 .message
drwxrwsr-x    9 ftpadmin ftpadmin      512 Sep 19 12:16 X11
drwxrwsr-x    9 jgross   ftpadmin      512 Sep 19 20:21 doc
drwxrwsr-x    4 ftpadmin ftpadmin      512 Jun 30 22:51 etext
drwxrwsr-x    3 ftpadmin ftpadmin      512 Jun 30 23:38 games
drwxrwsr-x    8 ftpadmin ftpadmin    12800 Sep 19 08:23 gnu
lrwxrwxrwx    1 jwessel  ftpadmin       13 Sep 23 07:17 index.html -> ../index.hl
drwxrwsr-x    4 jgross   ftpadmin      512 Jun 19 00:24 infosystems
drwxrwsr-x    8 jgross   ftpadmin      512 Jul 26 22:28 lang
drwxrwsr-x    2 ftpadmin ftpadmin      512 Sep 16 07:32 math
drwxrwsr-x   21 ftpadmin ftpadmin      512 Sep 12 18:58 packages
drwxrwsr-x    6 jgross   ftpadmin      512 Sep 12 02:22 security
drwxrwsr-x   10 ftpadmin ftpadmin      512 Sep  6 10:42 systems
226 Transfer complete.
ftp> cd etext
250 CWD command successful.
ftp> dir
200 PORT command successful.
150 Opening ASCII mode data connection for /bin/ls.
total 2
drwxrwsr-x   12 ftpadmin ftpadmin      512 Sep 23 20:01 gutenberg
drwxrwsr-x    7 ftpadmin ftpadmin      512 Sep 24 08:43 ippe
226 Transfer complete.
ftp>
```

Figure 5.5

The directories within the etext directory.

You have two directories available: gutenberg and ippe. You know that you want gutenberg, so go ahead and change to that directory.

9. Type **cd gutenberg** to change to the Project Gutenberg directory.

Again, the computer offers little information.

10. Type **dir** and press Enter to find out what is in the gutenberg directory.

Now you see a large number of files, as shown in figure 5.6.

Figure 5.6

The contents of
the gutenberg
directory.

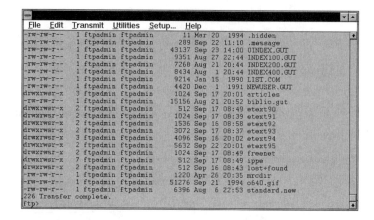

```
 File   Edit   Transmit   Utilities   Setup...   Help
-rw-rw-r--   1 ftpadmin ftpadmin       11 Mar 20  1994 .hidden
-rw-rw-r--   1 ftpadmin ftpadmin      289 Sep 22 11:10 .message
-rw-rw-r--   1 ftpadmin ftpadmin    43137 Sep 23 14:00 0INDEX.GUT
-rw-rw-r--   1 ftpadmin ftpadmin     9351 Aug 27 22:44 INDEX100.GUT
-rw-rw-r--   1 ftpadmin ftpadmin     7268 Aug 21 20:44 INDEX200.GUT
-rw-rw-r--   1 ftpadmin ftpadmin     8434 Aug  1 20:44 INDEX400.GUT
-rw-rw-r--   1 ftpadmin ftpadmin     9214 Jan 15  1990 LIST.COM
-rw-rw-r--   1 ftpadmin ftpadmin     4420 Dec  1  1991 NEWUSER.GUT
drwxrwxr-x   3 ftpadmin ftpadmin     1024 Sep 17 20:01 articles
-rw-rw-r--   1 ftpadmin ftpadmin    15156 Aug 21 20:52 biblio.gut
drwxrwxr-x   2 ftpadmin ftpadmin      512 Sep 17 08:49 etext90
drwxrwxr-x   2 ftpadmin ftpadmin     1024 Sep 17 08:39 etext91
drwxrwxr-x   2 ftpadmin ftpadmin     1536 Sep 16 08:58 etext92
drwxrwxr-x   2 ftpadmin ftpadmin     3072 Sep 17 08:37 etext93
drwxrwxr-x   3 ftpadmin ftpadmin     4096 Sep 16 20:02 etext94
drwxrwxr-x   2 ftpadmin ftpadmin     5632 Sep 22 20:01 etext95
drwxrwxr-x   2 ftpadmin ftpadmin     1024 Sep 17 08:49 freenet
drwxrwxr-x   7 ftpadmin ftpadmin      512 Sep 17 08:49 ippe
drwxrwxr-x   2 ftpadmin ftpadmin      512 Sep 16 08:43 lost+found
-rw-rw-r--   1 ftpadmin ftpadmin     1220 Apr 26 20:35 mrcdir
-rw-rw-r--   1 ftpadmin ftpadmin    51276 Sep 21  1994 o640.gif
-rw-rw-r--   1 ftpadmin ftpadmin     6396 Aug  6 22:53 standard.new
226 Transfer complete.
ftp>
```

Where to start? Unfortunately, there isn't an easy answer. If you already know which file you want, you can go right to that file and download it. However, if you don't know exactly what you want, you pretty much have to take a guess, based on the names of the files. Often, there will be a file called README (or READ.ME or README.DOC) that provides introductory information. In this case, no such file exists. At least two files look promising, though: NEWUSER.GUT and 0INDEX.GUT.

Frequently, you will see a file with the string INDEX in its name, which provides an index of the files available. In this case, the maintainers of the archive put a 0 (zero) in front of the word INDEX to make that item appear first in the alphabetic list of names. For the sake of this example (and because you are a new user), go ahead and download the file NEWUSER.GUT and take a look at it. To download a file, you use the get command.

First, however, you have to decide whether to transfer the file as ASCII (text only) or binary (such as a program or an image), and set FTP's transfer mode accordingly. Because NEWUSER.GUT looks as if it is intended as an introduction (because of its name), it is probably a text file that introduces the service. Therefore, you can take a guess and transfer it as an ASCII text file. If you are wrong, you can always try again.

11. Type **asc** to tell the FTP program that the next files to be transferred are ASCII.

   If you wanted to transfer the file as a binary file, you would type **bin** instead.

12. To download the file NEWUSER.GUT, type **get NEWUSER.GUT**. The get command is case sensitive, so you need to make sure that you type it in lowercase and that you type the file name NEWUSER.GUT in capital letters, which is how the file appears in the directory.

   Within a few seconds, the file is downloaded to your UNIX computer (although not actually to your personal computer). Next, you want to look at what is in the file. However, the FTP software doesn't enable you to look at files directly. Instead, you need to get out of FTP temporarily and go back to the UNIX prompt in order to look at the file.

13. Type **!** (an exclamation point) and press Enter.

   You are now back at the UNIX prompt. However, you haven't quit FTP—it is still there waiting for you to back to it.

14. To look at the file NEWUSER.GUT, type **more NEWUSER.GUT**. Again, this command is case sensitive, so you have to type it exactly as shown. Figure 5.7 shows the computer's response—the contents of the NEWUSER.GUF file.

   The UNIX more command is used to display a text file on the screen, one page at a time. The bottom line of the screen tells you that you have seen only 27 percent of the entire document. To go on to the next page, you can press the spacebar.

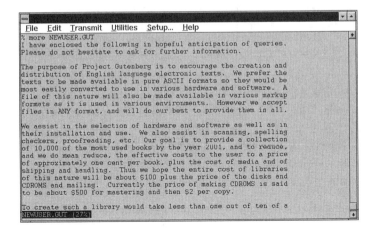

Figure 5.7

The display after you use the UNIX more command.

15. Press the spacebar to move to the next screen of text.

    This document describes the philosophy of Project Gutenberg. To exit the more command, you have two options: You can either keep pressing the spacebar until you are finished with the text, or you can exit the more command.

16. Type **q** to exit the more command.

    You should be at the UNIX prompt again. Now you want to go back to where you were, in the ftp command. To do this, you can use the exit command.

17. Type **exit** and press Enter to go back to the ftp> prompt.

    You are now back in the FTP program, at the ftp> prompt, where you left off. You are still connected to the Project Gutenberg archive computer at the University of Illinois!

18. To quit FTP, type **quit** at the ftp> prompt. This logs you off the remote computer and quits the FTP program.

    You are now back at your UNIX prompt.

> **TIP** *When you are using FTP to transfer files from a remote computer, log in with the user name* anonymous. *When the computer asks you for a password, type your full Internet e-mail address, such as* mckimg@indiana.edu.

To put things in perspective, what you just did was to retrieve and look at the document with the URL `ftp://uiarchive.cso.uiuc.edu/pub/etext/gutenberg/NEWUSER.GUT`. You used the FTP program to connect to the computer with the Internet address `uiarchive.cso.uiuc.edu`. You then went into several directories and subdirectories: first the pub directory, then the etext directory, and then the gutenberg directory. Finally, you retrieved the file NEWUSER.GUT.

Now you understand the basics of how to retrieve information when you know where it is, and which tool to use to get it. Your next task is a much more interesting one—and more closely related to why you want to use the Internet. In Chapter 6, you learn techniques for searching and finding information resources on the Internet.

6

Finding Information on the World Wide Web: Indexes and Searching

Objectives

After reading this chapter, you will be able to

- Understand the components of searching for information on the World Wide Web

- Use several search engines to perform your Internet searching

- Understand the difference between searching and browsing

- Understand the difference between full-text indexing and controlled-vocabulary classification

In previous chapters, you learned about the fundamental tools of the Internet—the technologies you use to access Internet information, such as Telnet, FTP, Gopher, and World Wide Web browsers, as well as the data formats used in Internet information. This chapter focuses on the details of searching for and retrieving information on the Internet, particularly the World Wide Web.

One of the first questions almost every user asks when confronted with using the Web is, Where is the table of contents? Compared to the relatively stable and well-understood print world, which is indexed in *Readers' Guide to Periodical Literature* and organized in library catalogs, the world of the Internet seems chaotic and disorganized. Many people (very reasonably) become frustrated with this lack of order. Before you go any further, you need to understand an important point: *There is no one central index or catalog of all Internet information.*

Searching for information on the Internet is and, for the foreseeable future, will remain very much an art, involving many sources of varying quality. New sources of information appear and disappear almost every day, faster than any one person (or any one organization) can keep track of. But even though the Internet may seem like madness, there is definitely method in it.

Fortunately, searching for information on the Internet is a craft that you can learn with just a bit of instruction and practice, a craft that will pay off quickly in the quantity and variety of resources you can use in your papers, as well as in the convenience of not having to go to a library to look up information in books. Once you understand this principle, you can begin to make effective use of the many incomplete but still useful directories and catalogs of Internet resources.

Be aware that the realm of Web searching is a rapidly emergent one. In the early days of the Web, the most frequent complaint was not about its difficulty of use (although this was a frequent complaint about many earlier Internet technologies). Instead, the most frequent complaint was about the perceived chaos of the information available through the Web—the complete lack of any organization or table of contents. As with earlier Internet technologies, the availability and location of resources were discovered through word of mouth or browsing. Gradually, various groups and individuals began to compile lists of resources, providing simple "road maps" to resources of interest. The National Center for Supercomputing Applications (NCSA), which developed the Mosaic product, included with Mosaic a pointer to several NCSA-developed lists of resources.

Search Engines on the Web

Eventually, others began to write programs to assist in organizing and retrieving Internet information. Such programs enabled users to type pieces of information they would like to find on the Web, and then to retrieve the appropriate information (or pointers to that information). These programs, usually referred to as *search engines*, are now a major growth industry on the Internet. Although most were originally developed by individuals for their own edification or research, many search engines (such as Yahoo, WebCrawler, Lycos, and InfoSeek) have become commercial. These have been improved considerably in their usability, reliability, coverage, and quality.

The discussion of searching and retrieval on the Internet spans several chapters in this book. This chapter introduces the critical components of searching for information: indexes, classification, and Boolean searching. A couple of search engines are used here as examples. This chapter, then, focuses on the process of searching itself. The next chapter deals with the details of using many of the search tools available on the Internet.

Searching and Browsing

Most people do research in two different ways: searching and browsing. Searching is what you do when you know approximately what you want. Searching often involves knowing the author, title, or subject of the material you are looking for. Suppose that you are looking for a resource that contains the text of a bill recently passed by Congress. Because you know exactly what you want—a resource or multiple resources containing the text of the specific bill—you would probably do some kind of search involving the name of the bill or the name of the congressperson sponsoring the bill.

Browsing, however, tends to be less focused. Perhaps you want to do a paper on biotechnology and need to know some of the key areas of research and development in the field. In this case, your need for information isn't very focused. You know what subject area you are interested in, but not much more than that, and certainly not enough to be looking for specific articles, titles, or authors. You will probably want to browse the resources available on biotechnology, hoping that something you see will spark your interest and lead to a more focused search for information. Serendipity, the discovery of information not planned for, is always one of the hopes of a researcher browsing for information. For this reason, many search systems still provide the capability to browse, even though searching seems more efficient and more effective as a way of finding information.

Focused searching and unfocused browsing are integral parts of doing research, and each has its own advantages and disadvantages. The following section discusses some methods and sources for doing focused searching for information on the Internet. The last section of the chapter discusses browsing in some detail.

JARGON ALERT!

A search engine *is a piece of software that gives you the ability to search for Internet resources. Search engines are usually accessed through Internet client software like Web browsers. Each search engine provides different searching options and has its own individual look. Search engines also differ greatly in the number of resources they allow you to search.*

Searching *involves looking for a resource when you know essentially what it is that you are looking for. Often you will use a search engine to search for documents by a particular author or documents that contain a particular keyword or phrase. Searching can be distinguished from browsing.*

Browsing *involves exploring lists of resources, particularly when you aren't looking for a certain resource. You hope that browsing will bring to your attention a resource that you aren't already familiar with, or will at least spark new ideas and lead you in new directions. Search engines like Yahoo provide excellent browsing capabilities.*

Indexes and Indexing

You are already familiar with indexes that appear in the back of a book. An *index* is simply a list of keywords, concepts, and people, along with an indication of where each is mentioned in a particular book. If you are reading a book on genetics and want to find out information about the contributions of Barbara McClintock, you would look in the index for *McClintock*, which would tell you on what pages to look for information about her.

Indexes can go beyond the individual book, however. Many subject areas have had indexes of materials created that cover many books, journal articles, and other materials on the subject. For example, *Humanities Index* provides an index to materials in the humanities, and *PsychLit* provides indexes to materials on Psychology. To use one of these indexes, you look up the concept you are researching, and the index tells you the location of the resource (its book title, periodical title, and so on). The index that you may be most familiar with is *Readers' Guide to Periodical Literature*, which directs you to articles in a large number of general-interest magazines and journals.

Of course, the use of computers has made searching such indexes even easier. Instead of manually looking up each term you want to search for, you can just type the term, called the *search term,* and have the computer do the searching for you. Computers are especially good at this kind of repetitive searching, and computer indexes usually let you combine search terms to produce more sophisticated searches than are possible with paper indexes. More will be said about combining search terms in the next chapter.

Searching on the Internet depends on indexes. Of course, the indexes are not of books and periodicals; the indexes are of Internet resources, such as home pages on the Web, Gopher sites, and files on FTP servers. Instead of just looking through the indexes, as you would with a back-of-the-book index, you must access most (but not all) Internet indexes through search engines. These programs are accessed through the same Internet tools used to access any other resource: Web browsers such as Netscape, Mosaic, and Lynx for search engines on the Web.

A search engine does two things: (1) creates indexes of Internet resources behind the scenes, often at night or during odd weekend hours; and (2) provides a user interface that you can use to search the indexes created by the search engine. A common misconception, though, is that a search engine goes out and searches the Internet at the time you submit a search query to the search program. But when you search with a search engine, you are actually searching the indexes that the search engine created at some point in the past. Thus, for the sake of currency of the information, you certainly hope that the index has been re-created recently.

A number of search engines are on the Internet (with new ones coming out fairly often), and all of them differ in one or more ways. The search engines and their differences are discussed in more detail in the next chapter. In the next sections, you practice using indexes with several popular search engines. The search engines that you use in these sample searches are WebCrawler, Yahoo, and the WWW Virtual Library.

For the first search, you use the WebCrawler search engine, located at `http://webcrawler.com`, the URL of WebCrawler.

Doing a Sample Index Search with WebCrawler

In this search, you want to find resources on the Human Genome Project, one of the largest research projects in the history of science. This project involves the cataloging and mapping of the genetic information of a human being. The amount of information involved is so large that the catalog can never appear in print and, thus, has to be maintained electronically. For this reason, you are assured of finding lots of Internet-based resources on the project. To do a search for information on the Human Genome Project, follow these steps:

1. Go to WebCrawler with your Web browser, by retrieving the URL `http://webcrawler.com`.

   You will see the WebCrawler search form, an interface provided by the WebCrawler search engine (see figure 6.1). This search form enables you to enter the terms you want to search for. You want to search for information on the Human Genome Project, so the phrase *Human Genome* seems as good as any to use as a search query.

Figure 6.1

The WebCrawler search form.

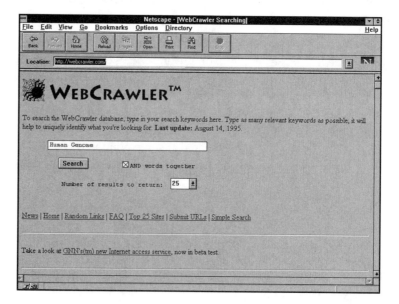

2. Type **human genome** in the box.

   Note that you didn't use the word *project* in your search query. The word *project* is so common that it wouldn't contribute any additional information to your search. Think of it this way: If you are looking for a document on the Human Genome Project and it has the words *human* and *genome* in it, you are probably interested in the document. The word *project* itself doesn't have any bearing on whether you are interested in the document. A good part of searching for electronic information (or print-based information, for that matter) is figuring out which words to use. You may have already guessed that WebCrawler is not case sensitive; it doesn't matter whether the word is spelled *human* or *Human*.

3. Make sure that the box marked AND words together is checked.

   Checking this box tells WebCrawler that you want to find only those resources containing both *Human* and *Genome* in the same resource. If you don't check this box, WebCrawler gives you all resources that contain either *Human* or *Genome* but not necessarily both. You would get lots of irrelevant resources, particularly with the word *Human*. The concept of AND in these kinds of queries is discussed further in the next chapter, covering Boolean logic.

   Note the number 25 in the box marked Number of results to return. Even if more than 25 documents indexed by WebCrawler contain both the words *human* and *genome*, only 25 will be given to you. (Of course, if fewer than 25 resources with the searched-for terms exist on WebCrawler, then only that number will be returned.) Providing a limit prevents the search results from becoming overwhelming if you choose a topic that is too broad.

4. Click the Search button. Nothing will happen until you click this button. The Search button sends your query to WebCrawler, which then looks up your query in its index and returns some results.

   The results of this query are shown in figure 6.2. Your results, of course, may look somewhat different; for example, some new resources may appear, and others may have been eliminated.

The query Human Genome found 722 documents and returned 25. The results appear in the form of a list of links to the resources returned. You can see that this method is a major improvement over a paper-based index. With a paper-based index, once you have looked up a term and found the references, you still have to go find the references yourself. With a Web search engine like WebCrawler, you can go right to the resources returned by the query.

Here is a summary of what just happened:

1. You typed some words (*human* and *genome*) that you thought would appear in the text of resources related to the Human Genome Project.

Figure 6.2

The results of the
WebCrawler
search.

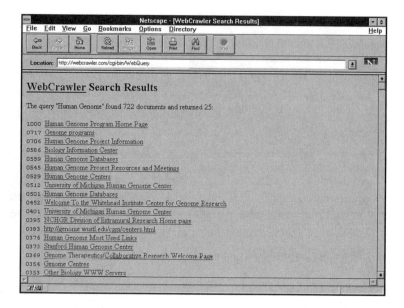

2. You submitted this query to the WebCrawler search engine, which is the WebCrawler software running on a computer somewhere on the Internet.

3. WebCrawler strips out any words that are too common to index or that wouldn't contribute anything useful to the content of a search. Often many of these common words, called *stopwords*, are ones that you wouldn't think of looking up in a back-of-the-book index. Examples are *a*, *an*, *the*, *why*, and *which*. However, many other words qualify as stopwords. For instance, *www*, *web*, and *home page* are usually stopwords. Because so many Internet-based resources contain these words, using them in searches would make little sense.

> **TIP** *In your searches, don't use words that are too common. If you do, your query may retrieve too many results. Think of narrower words to search for, so that the number of resources retrieved by your search is manageable.*

4. WebCrawler then makes all search terms lowercase, which means that its searches are not case sensitive. Thus, a search for the brand name *Apple* and a search for the fruit *apple* are the same thing. Like WebCrawler, most Web search engines generally conduct searches that are not case sensitive.

5. WebCrawler looks through all the Internet documents in the index it has built, searching for occurrences of each search term.

6. Because you have the AND box checked, WebCrawler looks in its index for only those documents that contain *all* the search terms. If the AND box weren't checked (that is, WebCrawler was doing an OR query), you would receive all documents that contained any one of the search terms, but not necessarily more than one.

7. WebCrawler presents the results of the search. Instead of giving you the Web documents themselves, it gives you a list of titles of the documents retrieved. You can then click each of these titles and go right to the resource in question.

8. WebCrawler also gives you a bit of additional information, in the form of a number at the left of each title returned from the query. This number is called a relevance ranking.

The *relevance ranking* is an attempt by the search engine to calculate how relevant the retrieved documents are to your query. The assumption is that, although every document that contains your search terms is relevant to your query, documents in which the search terms occur more often are more relevant. Thus, WebCrawler adds up the number of times that each search term occurs in each document, and presents those documents in order, from most occurrences (most relevant documents) to least occurrences (least relevant documents).

In addition, WebCrawler always considers the relevance ranking of the most relevant document (the one in which the search terms occur the most frequently) to be 1000. The relevance ranking of all other retrieved documents is then expressed as some fraction of 1000, depending on the number of times the search terms occurred. For example, a document with relevance ranking 500 has search terms occurring only half as often as they do in the top-ranked document (because 500 is half of 1000).

The assumption that the frequency of occurrence implies relevance, however, is often not a good assumption. For this reason, you should take the relevance rankings with a grain of salt. They can provide useful information only on a very gross level. In other words, the top-ranked document is usually more relevant than the bottom-ranked document, but finer distinctions are often difficult to make.

JARGON ALERT!

A relevance ranking is a score assigned to a document retrieved by a search engine in response to your query. The ranking is an attempt by the search engine software to assess approximately how relevant the document is to your query. Relevance rankings usually take into account how many times the word or phrase you are searching for occurs in the document, as well as whether the word or phrase occurs in the title of the document. WebCrawler and some other search engines provide relevance rankings. Search engines that provide relevance rankings usually sort the documents presented to you in order of decreasing relevance.

Of course, after all of this, you may ask yourself, What exactly are these documents that WebCrawler returned? Where did they come from? These questions aren't that easy to answer, and the answers depend on the search engine you used. Some search engines actively go out and search the Web in a systematic manner and attempt to index every Web-based document encountered. These search engines are often called spiders or robots.

Other search engines index a document only if its author (or anyone else on the Internet) actively submits the URL of the document to the search engine for indexing. WebCrawler belongs to this category. In any case, not all resources available on the Web are indexed by any one of the search engines, and the fact that a resource *is* indexed by a search engine is in no way a guarantee of quality or appropriateness for your research. Chapter 16 deals with evaluation of such Internet resources.

TIP

Indexing Web documents is a time-intensive process, so most search engines do their indexing infrequently and at odd times. Therefore, the search engines are never completely up-to-date. You can expect some lag time (often a week or two) between a document being submitted for indexing and the document being available for searching.

Remember that searching is an art, not a science. Often you will get too many resources. (A query on the word *Internet* found 39,360 resources in the index, although only 50 were returned.) Just as often, you will not get enough resources. More likely, you will simply get resources that aren't relevant to what you are researching. Because words may have more than one meaning, the concept of full-text searching has an inherent defect: A search based on text indexing will return documents that use your search terms in some manner other than you expected.

Generally, one search will not be enough. For most research, you will need to do multiple searches before you find the information you want, refining your search each step of the way, based on the results you get. For example, if your search is too broad, you need to come up with some additional keywords that may narrow the search a bit. If your search is too narrow, you need to take away the keywords that narrow it, or substitute some broader terms. Many times, you will want to use different search engines and compare their results (and you *will* get different results with each search engine).

The cost of additional searches is negligible, so don't be afraid to try your searches several times, refining them each time. (The cost of additional searches is nonexistent if you aren't paying for your Internet connection directly.)

As suggested earlier in the chapter, not all search engines are alike. Being aware of the differences in search engines will help you understand the different results of multiple searches.

> **TIP** *Unless you are searching for a particular resource, try searching with more than one search engine.*

Full-Text Indexing versus Title-Only Indexing

One issue that definitely affects the results of a search with a particular search engine is whether the actual *text* of the documents is indexed (and therefore searched when you submit a query to the search engine), or whether only the *titles* of the documents are indexed. For example, the Yahoo search engine indexes only the titles of the resources (and a short comment or description about each resource). Lycos, TradeWave Galaxy, and WebCrawler index the entire text of the documents being indexed.

Free-Text Indexing versus Controlled-Vocabulary Classification

The type of indexing that has been discussed so far is often known as *free-text indexing*. The words that are found in the index are the exact words that appear in the documents indexed by the search engine (minus the stopwords, of course). In the search example with WebCrawler, the keywords that are indexed are taken from the documents themselves. That is, if the word *genetics* appears in the resource document, then the word *genetics* will be in the index, and you can retrieve the document on that word.

Another type of indexing, called *controlled-vocabulary indexing*, doesn't rely on keywords from the document itself. Instead, a person looks at the document and comes up with appropriate words to describe it, whether or not those words actually appear in the document. This type of indexing is often called *controlled-vocabulary classification*. It is similar to what a librarian does when assigning subject classifications to a book.

Controlled-vocabulary classification has advantages and disadvantages. A disadvantage is that a person must spend some time and effort to come up with appropriate terms to describe a document. With over 1.5 million potential authors (and with more Internet-based resources coming on-line every day), this approach is simply not feasible. An advantage is that controlled-vocabulary classification enables you to retrieve a document using standard terminology.

To understand this advantage, imagine that you were searching for documents about Shakespeare. Using one of the search engines, you could do a query on the term *Shakespeare*, and you would retrieve documents containing that word. But suppose that a certain document about Shakespeare never uses the word *Shakespeare* at all. Perhaps the author always refers to him as the Bard or "the immortal Bard of Stratford upon Avon." If the index that was being searched was based entirely on keywords in the text, you would not retrieve this document. However, if someone were applying controlled-vocabulary classification to the documents, the person would see that the Bard document was really about Shakespeare and would index the document under *Shakespeare*. Although this example is a bit far-fetched, you can see how controlled-vocabulary classification might be useful when your search terms are different from the terms used by the author.

Doing Sample Directory Searches with Yahoo and the WWW Virtual Library

In this section, you take a look at the search engines Yahoo and the WWW Virtual Library, which apply some controlled-vocabulary classification to Internet resources. (Another search engine that does some controlled-vocabulary classification is TradeWave Galaxy.) Note that such search engines are often called directories or libraries. In fact, *directory* is a good word to use because this kind of search engine is very much like a directory.

You can grasp the concept of controlled vocabulary better by thinking of the Yellow Pages. All the names of businesses are put into a fixed classification system devised by the editors of the Yellow Pages, whether or not the words actually appear in the names or descriptions of the businesses. For example, a business called Southern Indiana Ford doesn't have the word *automobile* in its name. However, the editors determined that Southern Indiana Ford is actually an automobile dealership, and therefore classified Southern Indiana Ford under the heading *Automobile, Dealers*.

This brings you to the subject of browsing—and how it differs from searching. The idea of controlled-vocabulary classification is fairly useless unless you already know the vocabulary terms the classifier used. Studies of information retrieval systems have shown that one of the biggest problems of such systems is that different people use different names for the same thing. The words that a classifier uses to classify a resource are not necessarily the same words that would come to your mind if you wanted to search for a resource, particularly if you were unfamiliar with the subject area. The librarians who do controlled-vocabulary classification alleviate this problem by arranging the controlled vocabulary itself in a hierarchy that can be browsed.

The Web environment (in which programmers, students and computer professionals usually do the controlled-vocabulary classification) makes it particularly easy to present these hierarchies in a form that is handy to browse. Thus, you don't need to know in advance which term was used by a classifier; you just need to be able to pick out the term from a list on-screen (usually with multiple levels). For example, you might not know that the Human Genome Project is classified under Genetics. However, if you saw a list containing Humanities, Social Science, and Science as items, you would recognize that Science is the correct heading for Human Genome Project. From there, if you saw a list with Biology, Chemistry, and Physics as items, you would probably recognize that Biology was the correct heading. From there, you could pick Genetics out of a list of subcategories of Biology.

The following exercises demonstrate this kind of browsing through a list of resources categorized with controlled vocabulary. You do two browses, using these directories:

Yahoo

`http://www.yahoo.com`

WWW Virtual Library

`http://www.w3.org/hypertext/DataSources/bySubject`

To find some Internet resources on sign languages and signing, using the Yahoo directory, follow these steps:

1. Use your Web browser to access the Yahoo search engine, located at `http://www.yahoo.com`.

2. You see a list of broad subjects to choose from, as shown in figure 6.3. These categories (including Arts, Business and Economy, and Science) are shown in a larger font, and subcategories are shown in a smaller font. For example, Literature, Photography, and Architecture are subcategories of Arts. Note that the subcategories aren't complete; they are only a sampling. By following the broader category as a link, you can go to a complete list of subcategories for that category.

   Because Sign Languages is part of language, this topic would probably fall into the category of Linguistics (although a case could be made for it to be under Education as well). Of course, Linguistics is itself a subcategory of Social Science, so you can choose Social Science and from there choose Linguistics, or you can simply choose Linguistics directly from the Yahoo home page. Click `Linguistics` to get the list of Linguistics resources.

3. Now you get another list of categories and resources under the category Linguistics and Human Languages. Click `Sign Languages`.

4. Here you see a list of resources related to Sign Languages. You can take a look at any of these resources and use them as necessary.

   Note that often you can get at a particular resource in more than one way. For example, if you had chosen Education instead of Linguistics at the top level, you would have the option of choosing Languages under Education, which would have led you back to the Sign Languages resources.

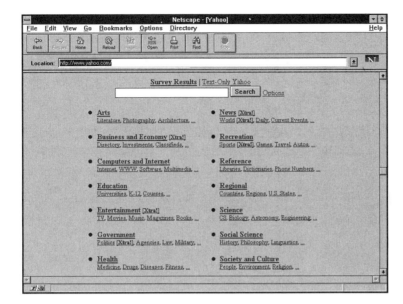

Figure 6.3
The Yahoo home page.

Now suppose that you want to find some Internet resources on Russia and Russian studies. Using the WWW Virtual Library directory, follow these steps:

1. Use your Web browser to access the World Wide Web Virtual Library, located at `http://www.w3.org/hypertext/DataSources/bySubject.`

   Figure 6.4 shows the WWW Virtual Library home page. The top part of the page contains administrative miscellany as well as a list of newly developed categories. At the bottom of the screen, however, and continuing far beyond it, is a long list of browsable subject categories under which Web resources are organized.

2. Scroll through this list to become familiar with the way the subject categories are organized. Note that they are listed alphabetically.

   Because you are looking for information about Russia, scroll down until you see a category in which you think resources about Russia might fit. As with almost any topic, more than one category might be appropriate. For example, Political Science might have some resources of interest, depending on your need. However, the category Russian and East European Studies is probably the closest fit (see figure 6.5).

Figure 6.4

The WWW Virtual Library home page.

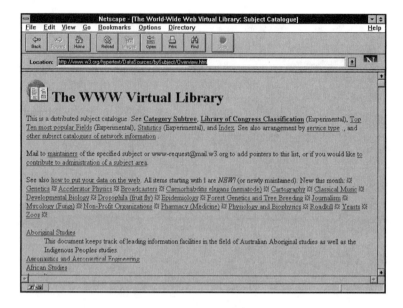

Figure 6.5

A list of subject categories in the WWW Virtual Library.

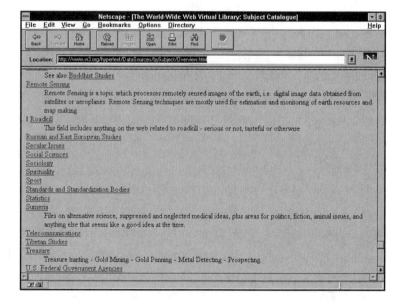

3. Click the Russian and East European Studies link to go to the home page for Russian and East European Studies (see figure 6.6).

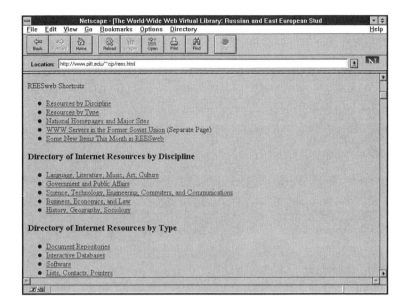

Figure 6.6

The Russian and
East European
Studies home
page.

87

> **NOTE** *Notice in the Location box the URL for the Russian and East European Studies home page. This resource is not located in the same place as the WWW Virtual Library catalog. This difference illustrates the virtualness of the library. Resources are brought together in a single, unified, and organized catalog, yet the resources themselves can be located on computers anywhere in the world.*

The Russian and East European Studies home page is an attempt by its creators (who aren't necessarily the same creators of the other home pages in the WWW Virtual Library) to organize information resources about Russian and East European Studies. As figure 6.6 shows, these resources have been organized by academic discipline (such as Language, Literature, Music, Art, Culture, History, Geography, and Sociology) and by type of resource (such as Document Repositories and Multimedia). Now take a look at the Language, Literature, Music, Art, and Culture resources.

4. Click the link Language, Literature, Music, Art, Culture.

    Figure 6.7 shows a portion of the resulting document. Instead of being presented in list form, as the previous documents were, these resources are presented as links in several paragraphs of text. Typically, you will see both forms—lists of links as well as links within text—in the WWW Virtual Library.

Figure 6.7

A sample resource list from the Russian and East European Studies home page.

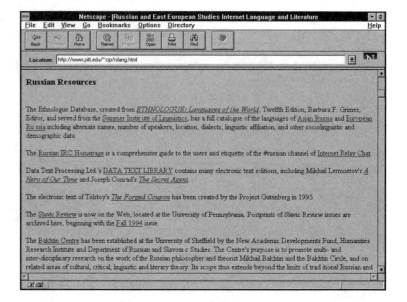

Classifying resources according to controlled vocabulary is a fundamental component of the work that librarians and information specialists do, and such classification is just beginning to come together on the Internet. The best-known controlled-vocabulary classification scheme is the Library of Congress Subject Headings system, used to classify all books published in the United States. There has even been a limited attempt to use the Library of Congress Subject Headings to classify Internet resources in the Virtual Library; the link to that project is available at the top of the WWW Virtual Library home page (refer to figure 6.4).

You are now familiar with the search engine programs that perform searches on the Internet. In this chapter, you saw how to interact with search engines and how to distinguish between free-text indexing and controlled-vocabulary classification. You used a couple of search engines to perform sample searches and browse for information. In the next chapter, you consider methods for refining your searches, using a scheme known as Boolean logic.

7

Refining Internet Searches: Search Engines and Boolean Logic

Objectives

After reading this chapter, you will be able to

- Combine search terms to refine your searches

- Use Boolean AND queries to restrict your searches and make them more specific

- Use Boolean OR queries to expand your searches and incorporate synonyms for words

- Use Boolean NOT queries to exclude resources from your searches

- Understand the concept of truncation and how it affects the results you get from a search

In the preceding chapter, you learned how to do searches based on simple, single terms. This kind of searching, however, is limited in both coverage of the material and accuracy. Most search engines enable you to combine search terms in different ways to produce more sophisticated, and presumably more accurate, searches for resources. These search engines use a system known as *Boolean logic* (named after George Boole, the mathematician who developed it) to enable you to combine search terms.

Although Boolean logic can become quite complex, it allows you to combine search terms in three different ways: using AND, OR, and NOT queries. In short, AND queries allow you to restrict searches so that they retrieve documents that contain more than one search term; OR queries let you expand searches so that they retrieve documents that contain any one of a number of search terms. With NOT queries, you can exclude particular terms from consideration in searches. The following sections briefly discuss these three types of queries.

AND Queries

Assume that you are writing a paper on the history of mathematics. You are going to want to look for documents that contain both the word *mathematics* and the word *history*. If a document has only *mathematics* or *history* in it, the document is probably not relevant to your topic. In this case, you would want to perform a Boolean AND query to search for documents that have *mathematics* AND *history* in them.

The query you did earlier for *human genome* with WebCrawler was actually a Boolean AND query; you were searching for documents that contained *human* AND *genome*. As you can see, AND queries are used for restricting searches. The number of documents returned from an AND query will be fewer than the number of documents returned from either of the two terms by itself. In other words, the number of documents with *human* AND *genome* in them is fewer than the number of documents with *human* in them.

Queries don't always look the same on all search engines, however. For example, you didn't actually type the word AND in your query to WebCrawler; instead, you checked a box labeled AND. Although the Boolean logic is the same on all search engines that use it, each search engine may implement this logic in a different way. To see some of these differences, do another sample

AND query with another search engine. This time, you use the TradeWave Galaxy search engine, whose URL is `http://www.einet.net`.

Suppose that you want to find some resources about a famous petroglyph (rock carving) made by the Anasazi Indians around the year 900. (In case you're wondering whether this search is too contrived, it is a real one that I performed myself after returning from a vacation in the Southwest. After having seen this petroglyph, I decided to find out more about it.) Follow these steps:

1. With your Web browser, go to the URL for the TradeWave Galaxy search engine (`http://www.einet.net`).

2. When you see the TradeWave Galaxy home page, choose the `Search` link, which takes you to the search screen.

   The interface to this search engine is a bit more complicated than the interface to WebCrawler. With TradeWave Galaxy, you need to be concerned about the following elements: the search query itself (the term or terms you want to search for), the maximum number of "hits" to retrieve (the maximum number of documents retrieved by the query to display), and the actual collection of documents to search.

3. Leave the maximum number of hits at the default of 50. (You wouldn't expect this query to retrieve more than 50 documents anyway.) Click the World Wide Web option to do a full-text search of all the text on the Web documents indexed by TradeWave Galaxy.

4. Type **supernova and anasazi** in the search box.

   When you used the WebCrawler search engine to perform an AND query, you simply made sure that the AND box was clicked (which it was by default) and that all the search terms were combined with an implicit AND query. In TradeWave Galaxy, however, the default is to perform an OR query. Thus, if you typed just the keywords **supernova anasazi** in the search box, you would retrieve a list of all documents related to supernovae (containing the word *supernova*), and all documents related to the Anasazi people (containing the word *anasazi*).

5. Click the Search button to perform the search.

   Figure 7.1 shows the results of the query. The query `supernova and anasazi` returned one hit.

Figure 7.1

The results of the query supernova and anasazi with TradeWave Galaxy.

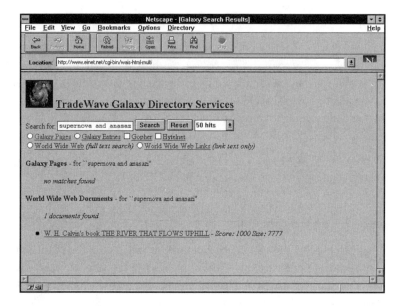

6. As usual, the results of the query are in the form of links to documents. To go to a document, just click the link.

In this case, only one hit was returned, but it was indeed a travel narrative that had a chapter on the supernova seen by the Anasazi.

JARGON ALERT!

The word hit *is often used in the field of information retrieval to indicate a document retrieved by a query. If you submit a search query to a search engine and it finds 29 documents that contain the terms you are searching for, your query returns 29 hits.*

OR Queries

Although AND queries are used to restrict a query, OR queries are used to expand the search. OR queries retrieve documents that have *either* the first term *or* the second term, or both (but not necessarily both). In the sample search earlier, the query human or genome would be inappropriate because it would retrieve documents that contain the word *human* (such as a document on human rights) but have nothing to do with the Human Genome Project. Instead, OR queries are useful when a concept can be expressed in two or more ways, and you want to make sure that you search for both.

The difference between AND and OR queries is often a source of confusion for many people. Note the following points:

- AND queries retrieve only the documents that contain *both* terms that you are searching for. AND queries result in fewer documents being found.

- OR queries retrieve only the documents that contain *either* term that you are searching for *or* both terms. OR queries result in more documents being found.

Now do a sample OR query. In this example, you want to discover Internet resources on films. You could try any of a number of search engines, using *film* as the search term. However, some resources relating to films may not have the word *film* in them. You probably realize that *movie* is a common synonym for *film* and that any query about films, to be complete, should include the word *movie* as well. Because you want to retrieve documents that have either *movie* or *film* (or both) in them, you should use a Boolean OR query.

Fortunately, the TradeWave Galaxy search engine allows full Boolean searching, so you can use this search engine to search for resources about films. Follow these steps:

1. With your Web browser, go to the URL for the TradeWave Galaxy search engine (`http://www.einet.net`).

2. Click the `Search` link to go to the TradeWave Galaxy search engine. This search form was displayed in figure 7.1.

3. Type the query **film or movie** in the search box on the TradeWave Galaxy search form.

4. Click the World Wide Web option so that your search includes all the World Wide Web pages indexed by the TradeWave Galaxy search engine.

5. Click the Search button to execute the search.

   Figure 7.2 shows the query results. Although you left the "maximum hits" setting at the default of 50, the query retrieved 49 documents—ones that contain *movie* or *film*, or both.

Of course, your results might be slightly different because the resources indexed with TradeWave Galaxy may have changed. For comparison, if you searched on *film* only, you would retrieve about 432 documents; if you searched on *movie* only, you would retrieve about 660 documents.

Figure 7.2

The results of the query `film or movie`.

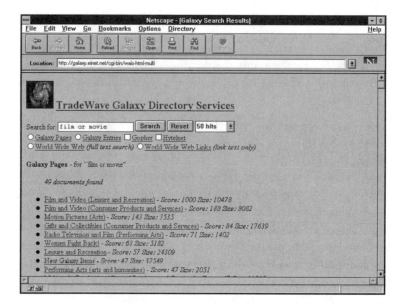

In general, OR queries are most useful when you are using terms that have one or more commonly used synonyms, such as *inheritance* and *heredity*, or *footnote* and *citation*.

NOT Queries

NOT queries are less useful than AND and OR queries, but NOT still has many uses. NOT queries are exactly what they sound like—queries that *exclude* a term rather than include it. For example, if you are searching for resources on stars but want only materials that are related to astronomy—and *not* materials on movie stars—you might define your query conceptually as *stars* NOT *movie*. This query means "first find all resources that have the word *stars* in them (in the titles or the text, depending on the search engine), and then remove all resources from this group that have the word *movie* in them."

NOT tends to be used a lot less than AND and OR. In fact, many search engines provide support for only AND and OR queries. One search engine that does provide support for the NOT query is TradeWave Galaxy. You can do a sample search with NOT on TradeWave Galaxy by following these steps:

1. With your Web browser, go to the TradeWave Galaxy home page (URL **http://galaxy.einet.net**).

2. To go to the search form for TradeWave Galaxy, click the Search link. You see the same search form that was shown in figure 7.2.

3. To search the full text of the Web documents the Galaxy indexes, click the World Wide Web option.

4. Type **stars not movie** as your search query.

   The results are shown in figure 7.3. You have retrieved a list of re-sources that contain the word *stars* but *not* the word *movie*.

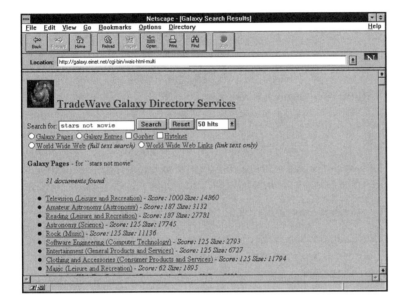

Figure 7.3

The results of the query stars not movie with TradeWave Galaxy.

Theoretically, then, the documents returned by this query will be closer to your needs than those retrieved by a query using just the word *stars*. However, in reality, you will still retrieve a lot of irrelevant material.

> **TIP** *Irrelevant material isn't always a bad thing. You may use it to learn new things and to take your thinking in new directions. In fact, serendipity, or the making of an unexpected and pleasant discovery, is one of the great benefits of using the Internet to do research.*

Combining Boolean Queries

Conceptually, the three types of Boolean queries (AND, OR, and NOT) can be combined to refine your searches even further. Suppose that you want to find resources on astronomy and space, but realize that much of the material on space on the Internet is about *Star Trek*. You might want to combine Boolean queries to produce something like astronomy or space not star trek. This query would retrieve documents that contained either the word *astronomy* or the word *space* (or both), but not the phrase *Star Trek*. Generally, these types of combined queries are evaluated from left to right: the astronomy or space part of the query is performed before the not star trek part. But there are other ways in which these longer queries can be interpreted (for example, AND is often evaluated before OR). The order is usually search-engine specific.

The TradeWave Galaxy search engine supports combined Boolean queries, so try such a query now. Follow these steps:

1. With your Web browser, go to the TradeWave Galaxy home page (URL **http://galaxy.einet.net**).

2. To go to the search form for TradeWave Galaxy, click the Search link. You see the search form shown previously in figure 7.2.

3. To search the full text of the Web documents indexed by the Galaxy, click the World Wide Web option.

4. Type **astronomy or space not star trek** as your search query.

   The results are shown in figure 7.4. You have retrieved a list of resources that contain either the word *astronomy* or the word *space*, but not the phrase *star trek*.

Although you can create complex combined queries that are theoretically more accurate, you may find that such queries are only marginally useful and not worth the complexity involved. You are more likely to succeed if you try a few simple queries on several search engines, collecting your resources that way, instead of trying to come up with a single complex query.

Truncation

Now that you have examined the main elements of Boolean searching (AND, OR, and NOT queries), another concept, truncation, is worth mentioning. *Truncation*, which is sometimes called *substring searching*, is a feature that is built into most Internet search engines. Although you don't have to know the name, you do need to be aware of the effects of truncation.

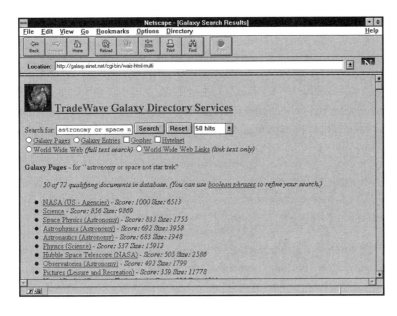

Figure 7.4
The results of the query astronomy or space not star trek with TradeWave Galaxy.

Imagine that you want to search for resources on computing. You could do a search on *computing*, using any of a variety of search engines. However, such a query would ignore documents that contain only the word *computer* or *computational* or *compute*—all of which may be relevant to your quest for resources. What you might do in that case is to notice which part of the word is common to all these words. In this example, all of them contain the string *comput*. Therefore, instead of searching on *computing*, you might search on *comput*. If truncation is implemented on the search engine you are using, this query would retrieve documents that contain *compute, computing, computer, computational, computing, computerese, computerphobia,* and so on.

With truncation, queries on a particular word actually search for that word anywhere in the document, even if the word occurs at the beginning of another word. This automatic truncation of search queries is interesting because non-Internet-based search-and-retrieval systems (such as those used by most CD-ROM database products) tend to work in the opposite manner; you usually have to tell them explicitly to do a truncation search. Otherwise, a query just returns documents that contain the word searched for as a word itself. For example, on H. W. Wilson–based CD-ROM products (such as *Social Science Index* and *PsychLit*), if you want to do a search for documents on computing (including words like *computers* and *computation*), you would have to search for *comput**. On SilverPlatter-based products, the query would be *comput:*. However, on most Internet-based systems, truncation is implicit and automatic.

On most Internet search engines, though, truncation works only when the word you are searching for occurs at the beginning of a word. A query for the word *bat* would retrieve *bat*, *bats*, *batsman*, *BatMan*, and *Batavia*. It would not retrieve *abatement*, *abate*, or *probate*. Although this technique isn't perfect, it is pretty logical when you think about it. Overall, words that begin with your search term are much more likely to be relevant to your need than words that contain your search term in the middle or at the end. Thus, on the whole, automatic truncation of search terms will produce more relevant documents without retrieving significantly more unwanted documents.

JARGON ALERT!

Truncation *refers to the capability of search engines to search for a particular string within other words in a document. For example, using a search engine that supports automatic truncation, a query for the word* bio *would retrieve documents that contain* biology, bioethics, biome, biometrics, *and* bio. *A search engine that doesn't support automatic truncation would retrieve a document only if it contained the word* bio *by itself.*

Beyond Boolean: Relevance Rankings

Although Boolean logic is not the perfect way to retrieve the information you are interested in, its use permeates computer applications at a deep level, and at the moment, it is the most commonly used scheme for refining and perfecting your searches for documents on the Internet. However, other schemes have been developed (and are still being developed) to enable you to retrieve the exact resources you want, and to exclude those you don't want. Relevance ranking has shown some promise.

You learned in the last chapter that relevance ranking is an attempt to have the computer determine not only whether a document fits a query (as Boolean logic attempts to do) but also to what degree the document fits your needs. Relevance ranking is based on the principle that the more often the search terms appear in a document, the more appropriate the document is. Search engines that use relevance rankings assign relevance scores to retrieved documents and present them in ranked order, from highest relevance to lowest relevance.

The WebCrawler, Lycos, and InfoSeek search engines use relevance rankings. Lycos and InfoSeek even enable you to modify the way their engines calculate relevance. For example, you can say that you want a certain word to be included in your query but that you want it to be considered less important than another word you want included. The jury is still out on whether relevance rankings and search techniques that use them are useful to the end users, however.

WAIS Databases

A term that you may encounter as you use the Internet is *WAIS* or *WAIS databases*. Many older books on the Internet spend much time discussing such databases. WAIS stands for Wide Area Information Server, a technology whose purpose is to create and provide indexes to databases (collections) of information.

You can obtain WAIS client programs—with such names as MacWAIS, SWAIS, xwais, and waisq—that allow you to search WAIS databases. However, with the growth of Gopher and the Web, this kind of client software is no longer necessary because Web and Gopher clients allow you to search WAIS databases. In fact, you have probably already searched WAIS databases without realizing it—many of the search engines *are* WAIS databases. The Gopher or Web client simply gives you the opportunity to search, so you don't have to know that the underlying technology used to do the search is WAIS.

JARGON ALERT!

WAIS, *or* Wide Area Information Service, *is a type of Internet information server that you use to retrieve text (or other types of information) from multiple databases. WAIS generally involves full-text indexing of documents and data. Although WAIS clients are available, you actually search WAIS databases through other clients such as Web browsers and Gopher clients. In fact, when you search on the Web, you may be using a WAIS index and not even know it!*

In the next chapter, you look at some of the most useful search engines on the Internet. As you examine these programs, you'll see to what degree Boolean queries are supported by each of them.

8

Search Engines for Searching on the Internet

Objectives

After reading this chapter, you will be able to

- Find and use some Web search engines, including Yahoo, WebCrawler, InfoSeek, Lycos, TradeWave Galaxy, Magellan, and the WWW Virtual Library

- Find and use VERONICA to search the titles of Gopher-based resources

- Understand the differences in these search engines

In the previous two chapters, you considered some general issues that pertain to searching on the Internet. You saw how Boolean logic can be applied to searches, and you learned the differences between free-text indexing and controlled-vocabulary classification, as well as the differences between searching and browsing.

In this chapter, you examine some of the most useful Web search engines, including Yahoo, Lycos, WebCrawler, TradeWave Galaxy, the WWW Virtual Library, and InfoSeek. You also take a look at the Gopher-based search engine VERONICA. You have already encountered several of these search engines in earlier examples; this chapter provides more detail about each of these search engines.

How Search Engines Differ

Many search engines are available on the Internet, and new ones seem to appear every week or so. However, you certainly don't need to learn how to use each of them. Familiarity with several of the best search engines, along with an understanding of their differences, will serve you well as you look for Internet information to use in your research. You will also undoubtedly develop personal favorites and will learn through experience which search engines work best for which areas.

The following questions illustrate the areas in which search engines are likely to differ:

1. Does the search engine enable you to browse the resources or search by querying (or both)?

2. Does the search engine index the full text of documents or just the titles and URLs?

3. Does the search engine enable you to refine your search by using Boolean queries or other schemes like relevance ranking?

4. Does the search engine use free-text indexing, or does it apply some sort of controlled-vocabulary classification?

5. Which resources does the search engine index?

The rest of this chapter describes some of the most useful search engines and provides answers to these questions, if applicable, for each search engine.

Web Directories of Resources

Some Web search engines are primarily lists of resources that have been put into categories. These resources are generally accessible both by browsing and by searching the appropriate categories. Generally, when you search the categories, you are searching only the titles (and often descriptions) of the resources, rather than the full text itself. These categorized lists of resources are often called *directories*, which are analogous to telephone directories and other types of directories that list resources.

Yahoo

The whimsically named Yahoo is one of the newer Web search engines and one of the most popular. Originally started by a couple of students (self-proclaimed "yahoos") at Stanford University, this simple directory of Internet resources gained fame when Netscape built a link to Yahoo into the menus of their Web browsers. Suddenly Yahoo became one of the most popular sites on the Internet. Since then, the students, with the aid of venture capital funding, created their own company, Yahoo, Inc., and they now support the Yahoo search engine/directory with advertising dollars. (If you use Yahoo, you will see these advertisements in their full hypertextual glory.) Many features have been added to the original product, so it is now a top-notch research tool.

Location: `http://www.yahoo.com`

Yahoo is also available from the Netscape browser menu directly. You choose the Internet Directory option from the Directory menu, and you access the same search engine. Netscape simply provides an easier way to get to it.

TIP	*If you use Netscape, you can get access to Yahoo, as well as other browsable search engines, by choosing the Internet Directory option from the Directory menu. This is also a great way to learn about new directories of Internet resources—Netscape will generally add them as they appear!*

Resources indexed: Yahoo currently indexes over 60,000 Web resources. Yahoo staff members search Internet resources continually and add them to the Yahoo directory. In addition, users can use the Yahoo search form to submit the URLs of their own resources, which can then be added to the Yahoo directory. The creators of Yahoo provide some editorial filtering as well, so Yahoo resources are often of slightly higher quality than those found in some other search engines. Of course, the trade-off is in comprehensiveness—Yahoo doesn't list as many resources as do some other search engines (which may provide access to millions of resources).

Controlled vocabulary versus free text: Yahoo is essentially a controlled-vocabulary search engine, although the titles of the resources are also free-text indexed (but *not* the text of the documents themselves). Yahoo staff members, or the users who submit resources to be listed in Yahoo, assign a category to each resource. Once the resource is available in Yahoo, it can be retrieved by category term, as well as by the words that appear in the resource's title.

Browsing versus searching: Yahoo allows both browsing and searching. However, you can search only on the title of a document indexed, as well as on the brief comment associated with that document.

Search language/interface: The Yahoo interface, shown in figure 8.1, enables you to do searching (through queries you enter in the empty box next to the Search button) and browsing (through the list of categories on-screen). The categories are listed on two levels. The top-level categories in boldface (such as Arts, Business and Economy, Computers and Internet, and Education) are the broadest categories, and the categories in smaller type (such as Literature and Photography) are subcategories. You can browse the broad categories or the subcategories by clicking the appropriate category name.

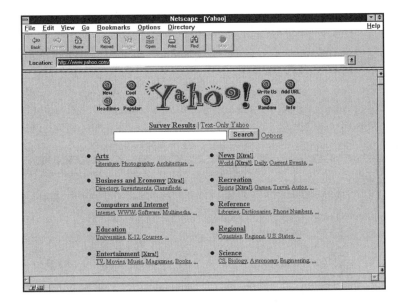

Figure 8.1
The Yahoo interface.

When you search with Yahoo, it considers all the terms that you enter to be connected by an implicit AND (the default). However, by clicking the Options link next to the Search button, you can refine your queries to be more precise.

Figure 8.2 shows the options screen, illustrating the degree to which you can refine your queries. The following are the highlights of the Yahoo query language:

- By default, queries are not case sensitive. For example, *Biology* is the same as *biology*.

- By default, all searches are of titles, URL names, and comments about the resources. You can, however, "uncheck" any of the boxes in the options screen to restrict the search to just one or two of these types of information.

- As noted, all query words are connected by an implicit AND. This means that a document is retrieved if, and only if, all the query words are present in the document. You can change the AND query to an implicit OR query, in which a document is retrieved if *any* of the query words are present. To change an AND query to an OR query, you select the button labeled At least one of the keys (boolean or).

- By default, all query terms are automatically truncated; that is, the term *bio* retrieves *biology*, *biomechanics*, and so on. You can turn off this feature by clicking the Complete Words button.

- The default number of retrieved documents to display is 100; that is, even if the query retrieves 1,000 documents, only the first 100 are displayed. You can change this number by pointing to the number 100, holding down the left mouse button, and selecting another number from the list.

Figure 8.2

The Yahoo options screen.

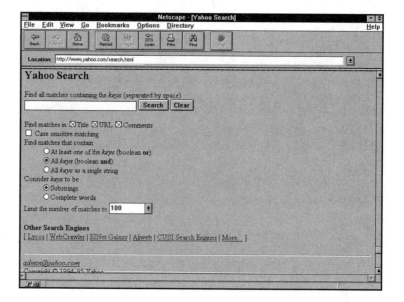

Sample search: In Chapter 6, you used Yahoo to browse, so do a sample search this time. To discover resources about the chemical elements, follow these steps:

1. With your Web browser, open the Yahoo home page, located at
   `http://www.yahoo.com`.

   In this example, try *elements* as your search query.

2. Type **elements** in the search box and click the Search button.

   Yahoo searches the titles of the resources it indexes, as well as the brief comments associated with the resources. It then displays the links to the retrieved resources.

   Figure 8.3 shows the results of the query. Note that there were 48 documents retrieved. This means that 48 documents had the word *elements* in the title or description of the resource. You can browse these documents to get an idea of what kinds of resources they are. To get a better grasp of the full set of resources available on this topic, try another query, using different search terms. You know that chemical elements, as a group, are usually referred to as the Periodic Table, so do a search on *periodic table*.

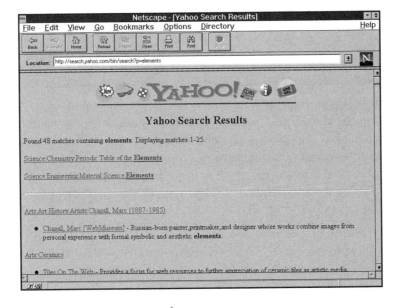

Figure 8.3

The results of the elements query.

> **TIP** *When you are doing searches on the Web, try to think of synonyms that might be used to represent the concepts you are researching. In this example, you use the terms elements and periodic table to try to find information about the elements.*

3. Type **periodic table** in the search box and click the Search button.

   Figure 8.4 shows the results of your second query.

Figure 8.4

The results of the periodic table query.

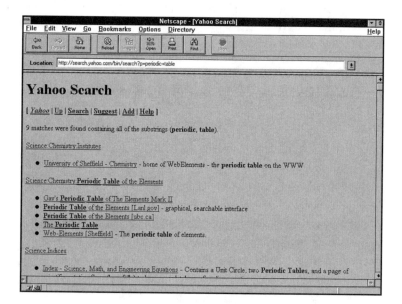

Note that the second query retrieved some new resources, and both sets of resources may be relevant to your search. As this example shows, you should consider using not only the first term that comes to mind, but also related terms that other people might use to describe a resource. Although controlled-vocabulary systems are helpful (by classifying resources into easily recognized categories), they aren't perfect. Therefore, you should think broadly about the terms you might use in retrieving the resources you want.

General comments: Yahoo is usually the first tool that I use when beginning a search for information. I usually browse first, if I can make an educated guess about the subject category in which a resource might be classified. If, through browsing, I don't find what I want (or even if I do), I then try a Yahoo search. Sometimes Yahoo retrieves a resource even if it is classified in a category that hasn't occurred to me.

TradeWave Galaxy

TradeWave Galaxy, run by TradeWave, Inc., is a search engine that provides controlled-vocabulary classification (along with the capability to browse the resources classified by category). This search engine is also a free-text search facility.

Location: `http://www.einet.net`

Resources indexed: TradeWave Galaxy provides indexes to several categories of resources, all selectable from the TradeWave Galaxy search form. These categories include the following:

- The full text of subject-specific guides to other resources. These guides make up the Galaxy itself and are created by subject experts, so-called "guest editors" invited by TradeWave to maintain the pages.

- The titles of the Galaxy subject-specific resource guides.

- Specially selected Gopher-based resources, referred to as Gopher Jewels.

- HYTELNET resources (library-catalog-related resources, which are discussed in Chapter 10).

- The full text of almost all the Web resources referred to by the Galaxy subject-specific resource guides.

These categories range from very narrow (only the Galaxy resource guides themselves) to very broad (the full text of all the resources referred to in the resource guides of the Galaxy).

Search language/interface: Figure 8.5 shows the TradeWave Galaxy home page. From here, you can browse various topics (such as Arts and Humanities, Engineering and Technology, and Reference Information) as well as subtopics (such as Astronomy, Biology, Chemistry, and Geosciences). Following a main topic link (such as `Arts and Humanities`) takes you to pages with additional subtopic listings. Following a subtopic link (such as `Astronomy`) takes you to resource guides associated with disciplines related to the subtopic. If you follow the `Astronomy` link, for example, you are given a guide to Internet resources on astronomy. All the resource guides are maintained by TradeWave (although they are developed by guest editors), so they all have a similar organizational structure and appearance, unlike the resources in the WWW Virtual Library.

Figure 8.5

The TradeWave Galaxy home page.

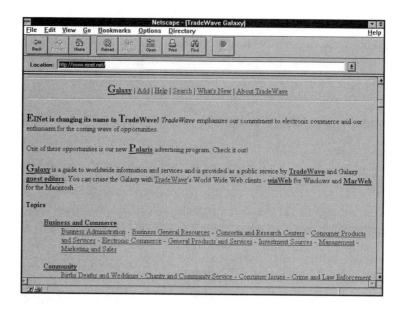

Besides letting you browse the resource guides, the Galaxy provides the capability to search the indexes just described. You obtain the search form, shown in figure 8.6, by following the Search link on the Galaxy home page.

Figure 8.6

The TradeWave Galaxy search form.

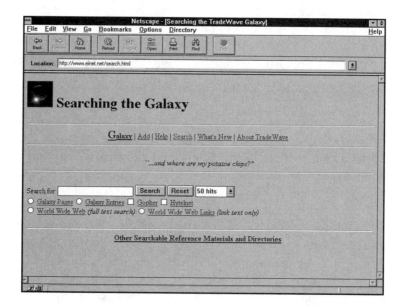

The Galaxy search form provides several options:

- The search box, where you type your query, accepts Boolean AND, OR, and NOT queries. These are evaluated from left to right, in the order that you put them in a query.

- You use the small squares and circular buttons to select which indexes to search. You cannot search all the indexes at the same time, but unfortunately, you can't tell from the interface which ones you can search simultaneously. To select an index, you click the button next to it. The available indexes include the following:

Galaxy Pages	The full text of the subject-specific resource guides that are specially selected and created
Galaxy Entries	Only the titles of these specially selected resource guides
Gopher	The index of Gopher Jewels, a collection of many of the best resources available through Gopher
Hytelnet	The database of library catalog information
World Wide Web	The full text of Web resources referred to in the Galaxy Pages resource guides
World Wide Web Links	Only the titles of Web resources referred to in the Galaxy Pages resource guides

- The box containing 50 hits indicates the maximum number of documents to be displayed by your query.

Sample search: In this example, you use TradeWave Galaxy to retrieve information about the Swahili language, a commonly studied African language of the Bantu family of languages. Follow these steps:

1. With your Web browser, go to the TradeWave Galaxy home page, at URL http://www.einet.net.

2. To obtain the Galaxy search form, follow the Search link.

3. Type **swahili** in the search box.

4. For the largest possible index coverage, click both the Galaxy Pages button and the World Wide Web button.

5. Click the Search button to execute the search.

The results of the search, shown in figure 8.7, show that documents were retrieved from both sets of indexes (Galaxy Pages and World Wide Web). At the top of each of the two lists are the documents calculated by the search engine to be the most relevant (they aren't always, though); these documents are assigned a relevance ranking of 1000. Even though the relevance ranking isn't perfect, you should probably look at these documents first, as they are more likely to be relevant. Now look at the first of the World Wide Web documents retrieved, the document entitled Karibuni Kamusi.

Figure 8.7

The results of the search.

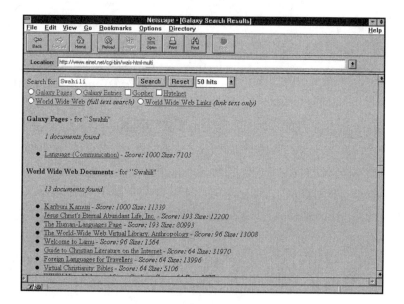

6. Follow the link Karibuni Kamusi.

This link takes you to the Kamusi home page, the Internet Living Swahili Dictionary, an online, collaboratively built Swahili-Swahili and Swahili-English dictionary that is quite useful.

Just to see the wide variety of resources retrieved, notice the next document after the Karibuni Kamusi document. Although the Karibuni Kamusi document has a relevance ranking of 1000, the next document, Jesus Christ's Eternal Abundant Life, Inc., has a relevance ranking of only 193, significantly less than that of the first document. This second document, in fact, mentions your search term only to say that a tract is available in Swahili.

General comments: I get mixed results when I use the Galaxy. Although both searching and browsing are available, I tend to find the browsing features more useful. The number of documents indexed by the Galaxy is much more restricted than those indexed by many other search engines. For browsing subject areas, however, the Galaxy can be a highly effective way to examine the resources available.

WWW Virtual Library

The World Wide Web Virtual Library is one of the oldest, yet still one of the best, sources of information on a variety of academically oriented topics of interest to students. Providing a controlled-vocabulary classification of subject-oriented Web pages, the Virtual Library is about as close as the Web comes to an actual library.

Location: `http://www.w3.org/hypertext/DataSources/bySubject`

Resources indexed: The WWW Virtual Library provides access to over 150 subject-oriented guides to Internet resources, almost entirely on academic or regional subjects and disciplines, ranging from Aboriginal Studies to Zoos. Each subject area available through the Virtual Library is maintained by a different person or group; these subject-oriented guides are usually located on different computers on the Internet.

For example, the maintainers of the Archaeology page of the Virtual Library are located at the University of Connecticut, whereas the maintainers of the Environmental Law page are at Indiana University. Because of this arrangement, the structure of each subject page is completely different from the others. The page is usually organized in some manner appropriate to the discipline, although the quality and clarity of organization vary from subject to subject and from page to page.

Search language/interface: Figure 8.8 shows the Virtual Library home page, consisting of the list of subject categories developed by the creators of the Virtual Library. Each subject category is a link to a subject-specific home page for that category. The page also announces all new subject categories added to the Virtual Library during the current month.

Figure 8.8

The WWW
Virtual Library
home page.

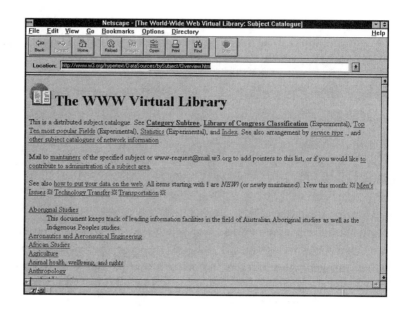

Also available is a new and experimental organization of these same subject-specific pages, classified by Library of Congress Subject Headings (the best-known subject-oriented document classification system). To access this new organization, you follow the link `Library of Congress Classification`. However, the new organization is useful only if you are familiar with the Library of Congress classification system; otherwise, you might as well stay with the original WWW Virtual Library classification system.

Sample search: In this example, you browse part of the WWW Virtual Library, looking for Internet resources on philosophy. The Philosophy page is a fairly typical subject page by Virtual Library standards. Follow these steps:

1. With your Web browser, go to the Virtual Library page at URL
   `http://www.w3.org/hypertext/DataSources/bySubject`.

2. Scroll down until you locate the category that seems to describe best the subject of the resources you want to browse. In this case, Philosophy is probably the most appropriate category, so you should follow the `Philosophy` link.

   The category that you want won't always be as obvious as this one. For example, economics resources are found in the category Political Science and Economics, and geology resources are split between the Earth Sciences and Geophysics categories.

As noted, the Philosophy page is typical of those available through the Virtual Library (see figure 8.9). Resources are arranged by type, such as resource guides, journals, electronic texts, philosophy departments, and electronic discussion groups. Other subject pages in the Virtual Library have their subjects organized differently, such as by geographical location or disciplinary division.

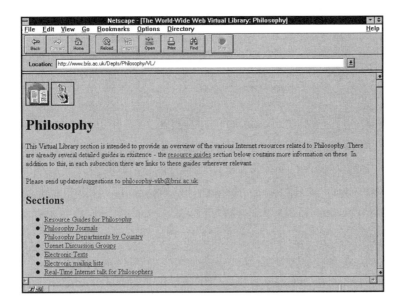

Many of the resources pointed to by the Philosophy page are resource guides or pointers to *other* resources (which may consist of pointers to still other resources). This display is an unfortunate consequence of the hypertextual nature of the Internet. Sometimes finding any content at all is difficult; you can get stuck following reference after reference, each leading to more references. To continue the search, go ahead and take a look at some of the electronic texts available in philosophy.

3. Follow the Electronic Texts link.

You now see a list of electronic text resources in the area of philosophy. Take a look at the hypertext repository of philosophical texts.

4. Follow the link Hypertext repository of philosophical texts.

You are now looking at the Philosophers page. This page is a repository of philosophical texts maintained in hypertext form at the University of Idaho. The top part of the page provides access to the works of a number of philosophers. Spanish philosopher Jose Ortega y Gasset is often quoted in the field of information organization and library usage, so take a look at his works now.

5. Place your mouse pointer on the box labeled Aristotle and hold down the left mouse button until a list of other philosophers appears.

6. Click Ortega y Gasset, Jose (see figure 8.10).

Figure 8.10

The Philosophers page.

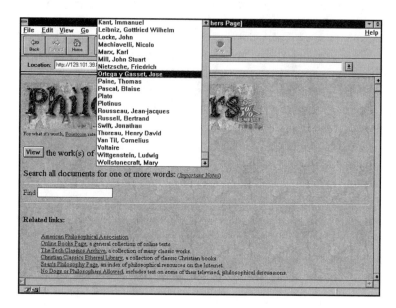

7. Click the View button to view the works of Ortega y Gasset.

You should now see a list of the works by Ortega y Gasset that are available in hypertext form on this site. You can browse these works at your leisure.

General comments: The WWW Virtual Library is clearly a tool meant for browsing rather than searching. This tool is most useful when you know what subject or discipline you are interested in, or when you can pick the discipline from a list.

Magellan

Magellan is another browsable directory of Internet sites. Its distinguishing characteristic, though, is its editorial board: The company who runs Magellan, The McKinley Group, hires writers and subject experts who review and rate

Internet sites for inclusion in Magellan. Although not every Internet site available through Magellan has been evaluated and rated, many have, and thus Magellan can provide you with some guidelines as to which Internet resources are worth looking at.

Location: `http://www.mckinley.com`

Magellan is also available through Netscape (with the Internet Search option from the Directory menu).

Resources indexed: Magellan allows you to search the title and description information for several million Internet resources. The ratings have been applied only to about 50,000 resources, which can also be browsed by category, but new ones are being evaluated every day.

Resources in Magellan are rated on a scale from zero to four stars. The original criteria, which were used by Magellan to rate most resources, were completeness of coverage, organization, whether the resource is up-to-date, and ease of access. Magellan has recently implemented a new rating system in which sites are rated in three areas: depth, ease of exploration, and net appeal. Eventually, Magellan also plans to start evaluating newsgroups, LISTSERVs, and other mailing lists as well as Web sites.

Search language/interface: Magellan permits both searching and browsing by category. The search language is quite complete, allowing standard AND, OR, and NOT Boolean queries, as well as a number of other search commands, including ones that let you retrieve a site only if a certain search term appears within a certain number of words of another search term. The Magellan home page provides a link to Help, which gives details on all these search options.

Perhaps the most interesting aspect of Magellan, though, is the summary information it provides for each resource evaluated. Once you have done a search, you can look at the summary information for the resource. The summary includes a description of the resource, the producer and producer address, whether the resource is commercial, and the intended audience, as well as an actual link to the resource and the rating given to it by the Magellan evaluators.

Finally, all the resources evaluated by Magellan can also be browsed with a fairly standard set of subject categories (Arts and Music, Business and Economics, and so on).

General Comments: Magellan is undoubtedly one of the most exciting new Web resources available to you. It combines the capability to browse through subject categories with the capability to search, and it offers a very good rating and evaluation system. I've found myself using it more and more, especially as its resource base grows to equal those of some of the other search engines.

Web-Based Search Engines

Now that you have covered a couple of Web-based directories, you learn in this section about several Web-based search engines. Although there are many more Web-based search engines that won't be covered, the ones described here are among the most useful.

WebCrawler

WebCrawler is maintained by America Online and provided free as a service to the Internet. This tool is one of the most reliable and useful search engines on the Web.

Location: `http://www.webcrawler.com`

Resources indexed: WebCrawler has indexed the full-text contents of over 250,000 Web documents. This search engine is aware of almost two million Web documents that it hasn't yet been able to index, but that can still be retrieved by the URL or links. WebCrawler generally indexes documents as they are submitted to it. A significant lag time between submission and indexing is evident; the reason is that the WebCrawler not only indexes documents submitted to it, but also indexes all documents that these documents have links to. Thus, you can see how the WebCrawler index can become extremely large.

Controlled vocabulary versus free text: The resources in WebCrawler have full-text indexing, with no controlled-vocabulary classification.

Search language/interface: Figure 8.11 shows the interface to the WebCrawler search page. Notice how simple the interface is. You don't have to type complicated Boolean queries; in fact, WebCrawler won't even process ANDs, ORs, and NOTs (although it does provide a similar way to combine search terms, described a bit later). WebCrawler is also not case sensitive; you can type your queries in upper- or lowercase, and the results will be the same. You can change two parameters:

- Whether the search terms you type are automatically combined into a Boolean AND query

- How many of the retrieved documents to display

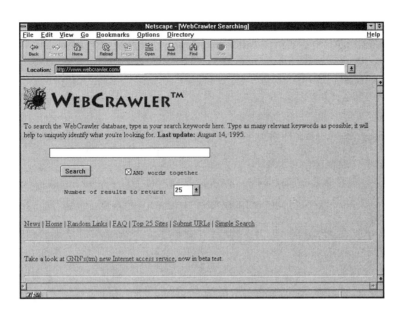

Figure 8.11
The WebCrawler interface.

The first parameter, labeled AND words together, is checked by default. If you leave this box checked and then use search terms like *Halley's comet*, the search retrieves only the documents that contain both *Halley's* and *comet* (although not necessarily side by side). If you uncheck this box and submit the same query, you get documents that contain either *Halley's* or *comet,* or both. This query will probably yield a much larger number of documents than the first query.

The second parameter, labeled Number of results to return:, puts a cap on the number of retrieved documents to be displayed. This option serves two purposes: (1) Having a limit on the number of displayed documents is more manageable for you; and (2) Setting a limit reduces the burden on the computers that run the WebCrawler server software, so that they don't have to retrieve and send huge lists of resources.

Sample search: In this example, you search for information on African-American history. Because *African-American* and *History* are words that might be used to retrieve appropriate resources, use both terms in your query. Follow these steps:

1. With your Web browser, go to the WebCrawler search form, at URL `http://webcrawler.com`.

2. Type **African-American History** in the search box and click the Search button.

Figure 8.12 shows the results of the query, a list of the top 25 documents (in terms of relevance rankings) of the 398 documents retrieved. You can now explore these documents and the other documents they point to, as you continue to find the most appropriate resources for your search.

> **TIP** *If you use Netscape, you can also get to WebCrawler, as well as to many other search engines, by choosing the Internet Search option from the **D**irectory menu. As new search engines are developed and introduced, they are added to this page, so this is a great way to keep up with new search engines!*

Figure 8.12

The results of the African-American History query.

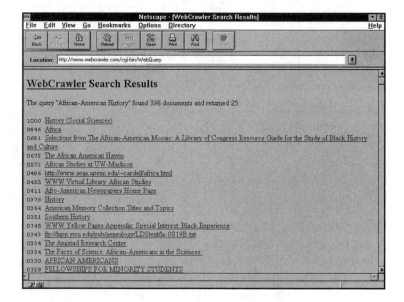

General comments: Although WebCrawler doesn't necessarily contain a significant number of resources that aren't included in other search engines, it can still be quite useful. WebCrawler is often one of the faster search engines, and its simple and uncluttered interface, as well as its simple and uncluttered display of results, makes it desirable when you want quick results. I often use WebCrawler to get a "quick and dirty" overview of the Internet resources available on a particular topic. I then use other search engines to refine my queries.

InfoSeek

InfoSeek is different from the other search engines discussed in that it is commercial and its full use requires a fee. Although many other search engines are subsidized or maintained by commercial entities (such as Yahoo by Yahoo, Inc., Lycos by Microsoft, and WebCrawler by America Online), these search engines are generally supported by advertising revenues, not by direct-use fees. For the money, however, InfoSeek provides more than just an index to freely available Web documents, as do many other search engines; InfoSeek provides an index to documents from a number of commercial publications, including the Computer Select database of computer magazines, and several business newswires. InfoSeek also enables you to retrieve these documents.

With InfoSeek, you get free access to a demo search engine with limited capabilities; for example, the commercial periodicals are not included, and each search returns only up to 100 documents. Even though this version has limitations, it is still quite useful and is included here in the sample search.

Location: `http://www.infoseek.com`

This is the address of the InfoSeek home page. From here, you can access the free search engine by selecting the link `Search the web for FREE!` (don't come to InfoSeek if you expect understatement), or you can sign up for commercial accounts.

Resources indexed: In its free version, InfoSeek provides the capability to search several hundred thousand Web pages. In its commercial version, InfoSeek can also search some commercial newswire services; business databases; and Computer Select, a large and complete database of computing journals and magazines.

Search language/interface: Figure 8.13 shows the free-access search form. The form is deceptively simple, presenting a single box in which you type your query, along with a series of words and phrases you can search. However, InfoSeek has some subtleties in its search language:

- InfoSeek does not support Boolean queries directly. It supports a system of relevance ranking, returning documents in order of decreasing relevance.

- Because searching is case sensitive, you should capitalize names, titles, and other appropriate words in your query. For example, use *Einstein* instead of *einstein*.

- Phrases that you want to search for should be enclosed in quotation marks or connected by hyphens. For example, if you want to retrieve documents that contain the words *DNA testing* only when these words appear together, you should type either **"DNA testing"** or **DNA-testing**.

- Words that you want to be considered less important in searching for documents should be preceded by a minus sign (-). Thus, if the word appears in a document, that document will automatically have a lower relevance ranking. Using this technique has a somewhat similar effect to using a Boolean NOT query on other search engines.

- Words that you require to be in the retrieved documents should be preceded by a plus sign (+). The relevance ranking is automatically raised for any document that contains the word preceded by +.

Figure 8.13

The InfoSeek free-access search form.

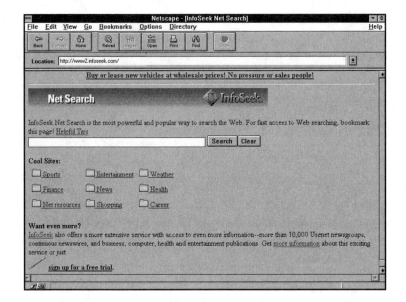

Sample search: Now do a sample search for resources related to DNA testing. Follow these steps:

1. With your Web browser, go to the InfoSeek home page at URL `http://www.infoseek.com`.

2. To access the free demo search engine, click the link `Search the Internet for FREE!`

   You now see the search form for the free demo InfoSeek search engine. If you want more information about the specifics of the query language (described in the preceding list), as well as examples and answers to frequently asked questions (FAQs), you can click the link `Helpful Tips`.

3. Type **DNA-testing** in the search box.

Because you capitalized *DNA*, InfoSeek searches only for the capital letters. Because *DNA* and *testing* are connected with a hyphen, InfoSeek searches for *DNA testing* as a phrase, retrieving only those documents that contain these words together.

4. Click the Search button.

Figure 8.14 shows the query results, a list of the top 10 documents retrieved. InfoSeek doesn't actually tell you how many documents were retrieved, but simply displays the top 10. The relevance ranking that InfoSeek assigned to each document is displayed in square brackets, such as [682] for the first resource retrieved.

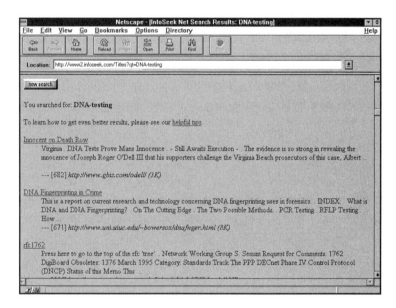

Figure 8.14
The results of the
DNA-testing
query.

Notice that InfoSeek also provides a brief abstract, constructed from the first couple of lines of the document, as well as a link (a short description) to the resource itself. The provision of these items is one of the reasons why InfoSeek is so useful; you can often tell (although not always) whether a document is relevant to your search just by reading the abstract and the short description.

From the abstract for the second resource, DNA Fingerprinting in Crime looks as if it may be of use, and probably contains links to other resources on the subject. To retrieve the document, just click the link DNA Fingerprinting in Crime.

Lycos

Lycos, whose name is the first five letters of the Latin word for the wolf spider, is perhaps the most complete and sophisticated of any Web search engine. Developed at Carnegie-Mellon University, Lycos has indexed and can search almost 8 million Web documents (it is estimated that Lycos has indexed 91 percent of the entire Web!), and it uses sophisticated computer techniques to search that many documents in a short time. Of course, being the most complete and sophisticated does not necessarily mean being the simplest. Lycos is most useful when you need to search or retrieve a large number of documents, or when one of the other search engines fails to retrieve enough relevant documents.

Location: `http://www.lycos.com`

Resources indexed: Lycos makes systematic attempts to traverse the Internet, indexing any documents it finds, including those available through Gopher or FTP. As mentioned, Lycos has already indexed almost 8 million documents, and it indexes more every day. Besides making sweeps of the Internet, Lycos will index a particular resource if you tell it to do so. The link for submitting (and deleting) a resource for indexing is available on the Lycos home page. Lycos is undoubtedly the most complete search engine available (although it does not include everything, of course).

Search language/interface: The search options for Lycos are quite sophisticated (and some are fairly technical). Lycos provides you with the ability to control the number of search terms, the number of results displayed, the amount of information displayed for each result, and the "strictness" with which Lycos interprets your search query.

Figure 8.15 shows the Lycos search screen, which is also the home page. To search Lycos, you simply type your search terms in the box and click the Search button. Lycos does not directly support Boolean queries, and it retrieves documents based on a calculated relevance ranking. The search screen itself tells you a little about how Lycos processes your query. Lycos ranks documents highest that meet the following criteria:

- *The document matches more of your words.* For example, if you search for documents containing *liver disease*, Lycos ranks documents that contain both *liver* and *disease* higher than documents that contain only one of these words.

- *The document matches more of the word itself.* For example, if you search on *analog*, Lycos retrieves documents that contain either *analog* or *analogy*, but ranks documents that contain *analog* higher.

- *The document contains the search terms earliest in the document itself.*

Figure 8.15

123

The Lycos search screen.

Lycos does not process phrases directly and therefore cannot retrieve documents *only* when the search terms appear side by side. Because of this shortcoming, the relevance calculation is quite different from that of other search engines. The documents retrieved as "most relevant" to your query may differ significantly from those found "most relevant" by other search engines. For this reason, you should always try queries on multiple search engines.

Sample search: In this example, you use Lycos to try to find information about Yasser Arafat. Follow these steps:

1. With your Web browser, open the Lycos home page at location `http://www.lycos.com`.

2. Type **Arafat** in the search box and press Enter.

   There probably aren't many Arafats out there, so you don't need to use the first name to limit the search. If you were searching for someone named Smith, you would want to use additional search terms, including the first name and possibly the subject area of interest.

   Figure 8.16 shows the results of your query. The Lycos search results screen is undoubtedly the most complicated, but also the most informative, of all the search engines.

Figure 8.16

The results of the
Arafat query.

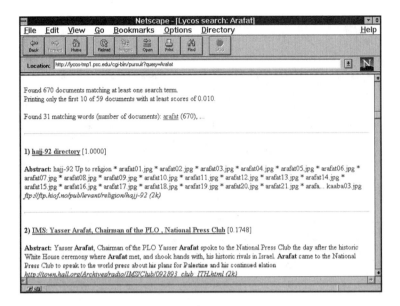

The following is a brief key to some of the information you see on-screen:

- The first two lines tell you that your query on Arafat found 670 documents that contained the word *Arafat*. Printing only the first 10 of 59 documents with at least scores of 0.010 tells you that Lycos, in the interest of lowering network and server traffic as well as information overload, is presenting only the top 10 retrieved documents (in terms of relevance rankings). The phrase with at least scores of 0.010 tells you that Lycos will return only the documents with a relevance ranking of at least 0.010. Theoretically, documents of marginal relevance to your query will not be presented.

- The next section, beginning Found 31 matching words lists the words in the document that match your query. Because Lycos truncates automatically and is not case sensitive, the Arafat query finds documents that contain *arafat*, *arafats*, and *arafatz*. Note that Lycos found 31 different words that match this query. However, Lycos automatically displays only the word that matches the query the most times. To find out what other words match your query (such as *arafats*, *arafat's*, and so on), you must click the ellipsis (...), which is actually a link. In any case, what this line is telling you is that the word *arafat* occurred 670 times, but there were 30 other words (probably containing *arafat*) that also matched your query.

This information can be useful because you often may need to know whether a document matches your query term exactly, or simply contains your query term as part of a longer word.

- Information about the first 10 retrieved resources is displayed next. This information includes the title, a relevance ranking (in brackets), an abstract of the resource containing your search terms, the URL of the resource (at the bottom of each section, in italics), and the size (in kilobytes) of the resource, in parentheses.

- The title of the document is actually a link to the document itself. (For example, the second document's title is "IMS: Yasser Arafat, Chairman of the PLO, National Press Club.") This link works just like any other link; to retrieve the resource, you just follow the link.

General Comments: Lycos is the most comprehensive search engine on the Web, indexing an estimated 91 percent of the entire Web. Thus, Lycos is really the best search engine to use, when comprehensiveness is essential (which it isn't always) or when you need to find a fairly obscure resource that might not be available through Yahoo or some of the other search engines. I find myself most often alternating between Yahoo for general searches of high-quality subject resources and Lycos for specific documents or for people's individual home pages. Lycos is particularly useful when I know that a document is out there somewhere (that is, I've seen it before) but don't remember how to get to it.

A Gopher Search Engine

Thus far, you have looked at search engines used primarily for World Wide Web resources, although TradeWave Galaxy does provide access to some Gopher-based resources. This emphasis on Web-based resources has been intentional. Although Gopher has its devotees and will probably exist in the future, its use is dwindling, while use of the Web is growing at a fantastic rate. Therefore, the most useful and sophisticated search engines—those most likely to provide access to resources that researchers and students would want—are available through the Web. Nevertheless, many useful resources are available through Gopher only. For this reason, VERONICA, the primary search engine for Gopher-based resources, is included here.

Like many other Internet tools, VERONICA is an acronym that was selected before the words for which it stands were selected. The name VERONICA was chosen in honor of an earlier, FTP-based search engine called "archie." But the creators of VERONICA now claim that it stands for Very Easy Rodent-Oriented Net-wide Index to Computerized Archives.

Location: Several VERONICA servers are available, containing essentially the same information. However, the update schedules may vary; and occasionally some resources may not be available for indexing outside a particular country or site, so they may appear on one VERONICA server but not another.

The primary reason for having multiple VERONICA servers available is that VERONICA is frequently overloaded and therefore unusable. In fact, to get a query to work, you may have to try more than one VERONICA server, especially during the day. Fortunately, some Gopher pages provide a menu of different VERONICA servers so that you can easily try one after the other, until you succeed.

The best of the VERONICA pages is probably the one from UNR, located at

```
gopher://veronica.scs.unr.edu:70/11/veronica
```

This page provides access to the VERONICA servers at NYSERNET, University of Koeln, University of Bergen, PSINet, and others.

The University of North Carolina provides a similar page of VERONICA servers, located at

```
gopher://gopher.tc.umn.edu:70/11
/Other%20Gopher%20and%20Information%20Servers/Veronica
```

Resources indexed: Much of the popularity of VERONICA lies in its comprehensiveness. VERONICA is estimated to provide access to more than 99 percent of all Gopher servers on the Internet—a number that translates to 15 million resources. However, VERONICA indexes only the titles of the Gopher resources (as well as the titles of all non-Gopher resources pointed to by Gopher servers), not the full text of the documents themselves.

Some VERONICA servers enable you to search only what are called "Gopher directories"—Gopher items that consist of a list of other Gopher resources. The reason for this service is to help users avoid retrieving many individual documents from the same source on the same topic, when all they want is the reference to the overall Gopher site that contains all these documents.

Both types of VERONICA servers are available from pages like the one shown in figure 8.17. The first type of search (the search through titles of all Gopher resources) is labeled Search GopherSpace by Title word(s) or Simplified veronica: find ALL gopher types. The second type (the search through titles of Gopher directories) is labeled `Find GOPHER DIRECTORIES by Title word(s)` or `Simplified veronica: find Gopher MENUS only`.

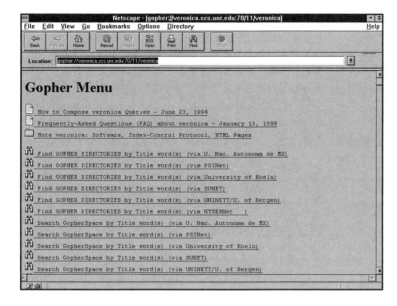

Figure 8.17

127

The Veronica home page.

Search language/interface: The page shown in figure 8.18 enables you to choose whether to pick your own VERONICA server, such as `Find GOPHER DIRECTORIES by Title word(s) (via University of Koeln)` or `Find GOPHER DIRECTORIES by Title word(s) (via NYSERNET)`. Or you can elect to use the UNR simplified VERONICA, which automatically picks a VERONICA server for you. I highly recommend using the simplified VERONICA, which will automatically move onto another VERONICA server if the first one is busy. You must also choose whether you want to search the titles of all Gopher resources, or just the titles of Gopher directories of other resources. Because VERONICA queries often generate large numbers of responses, you may want to search Gopher directories first; if that doesn't work, you can then search all Gopher resources.

Figure 8.18 shows the search interface for the VERONICA server. You just enter your search terms and press Enter.

The query language for VERONICA is fairly simple, although it offers some complex options that enable you to search only certain types of Gopher resources (such as images, sounds, Telnet sessions, and Gopher directories). Here are the highlights of the Gopher query language:

Figure 8.18

The University of
North Carolina
VERONICA
server page.

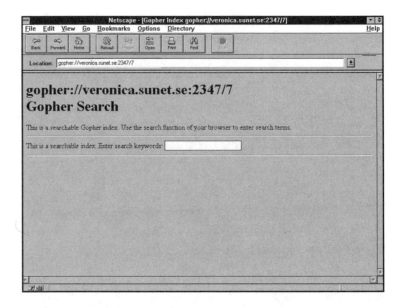

- Searching is not case sensitive. For example, *Clinton* retrieves the same documents as *clinton*.

- The order of search terms does not matter. A query for *Darwinian evolution* retrieves the same documents as *evolution darwinian*.

- All search terms are connected with an implicit AND statement. A query for *paper mill* retrieves only documents that contain both *paper* and *mill* in the title.

- By default, a maximum of 200 of the retrieved documents is displayed. To increase this number, you can use the -m parameter. For example, the query `internet -m2000` returns the first 2,000 documents with the word *internet* in the title—probably not a useful query for you to perform!

- Boolean AND, OR, and NOT queries are permitted. You use *and*, *or*, and *not* in your queries. For example, the query `Belgian and Congo` retrieves only documents that contain both *Belgian* and *Congo* in the title. Of course, this query is the same as querying for *Belgian Congo*, because Gopher assumes a Boolean AND query if words are listed one after another.

  The query `astronomy or cosmology` retrieves all documents that have either *astronomy* or *cosmology*, or both, in the title. Use OR queries sparingly, as they increase VERONICA's tendency to retrieve too many documents.

Finally, the query `engineering not civil` retrieves all documents that have *engineering* but not *civil* in the title.

- You use the -t option to retrieve documents of a specified Gopher type. For example, the query `comet -tg` retrieves only GIF images with the word *comet* in the title (because *g* is the Gopher abbreviation for the GIF image type). The following list indicates all the Gopher types that you can use with the -t option in VERONICA queries:

0	Text file
1	Directory
2	CSO name server
4	Mac HQX file
5	PC binary
7	Full-text index (Gopher menu)
8	Telnet session
9	Binary file
s	Sound
I	Image (other than GIF)w
M	MIME multipart/mixed message
T	TN3270 session
g	GIF image
h	HTML (HyperText Markup Language)

Sample search: For this example, you want to use VERONICA to retrieve Gopher documents about the history of Civil Rights. Follow these steps:

1. Go to the location **gopher://veronica.scs.unr.edu:70/11/veronica** with your Web browser. If you don't have a web browser, go to the location **veronica.scs.unr.edu:70/11/veronica** with your Gopher client.

2. You want to search the titles of all Gopher resources, so click `Simplified veronica: find ALL Gopher types` to let the computer choose which VERONICA server to use.

   Figure 8.18, shown earlier, shows the VERONICA query screen. The words *civil* and *rights* are quite good to use as search terms in this example. They are general enough to retrieve any documents on the topic, fairly unambiguous (because documents on civil rights usually have those words in the titles), and specific enough to exclude irrelevant documents. However, the word *history* would limit the scope of the query unnecessarily, because a document that discusses the history of civil rights may not use that word in its title.

3. Type **civil rights** in the VERONICA search box and press Enter.

Figure 8.19 shows the results of the query. Unfortunately, you can't tell clearly from this screen how many results were returned by the query. If more results are returned than the maximum number that VERONICA will display (200 by default), the last result line tells you how many documents were retrieved but not displayed. You can then retry your query using the -t parameter.

Figure 8.19

The results of the civil rights query.

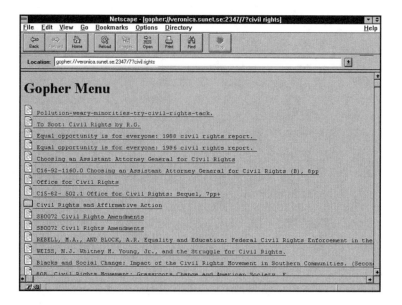

From here, you can browse the Gopher documents returned by the query, determining for yourself whether the query gave you what you wanted. Based on your examination, you can then restrict the query further by adding additional terms, or expand the query by using broader terms.

TIP *You may be surprised to discover that many of the returned documents wind up being duplicates. Although this happens sometimes with all search engines, duplicate titles are common with VERONICA. Such results are simply a consequence of the way VERONICA does indexing: It may index the same menu item several times because that item appears on multiple Gopher servers.*

General comments: VERONICA can be a useful resource but also a frustrating one, because of the large number of resources retrieved. I recommend using VERONICA as a last resort if you aren't able to find resources through other search engines, or if you have access to Gopher clients but not Web browsers. Furthermore, the percentage of resources that are outdated seems higher than with other search engines.

Common Problems of Searching on the Internet

The Internet can be a frustrating place. Every time you access a resource, you are dependent not only on your own equipment functioning properly but also on the equipment that hosts the resource you are accessing, as well as lots of systems in between. Be prepared for frequent roadblocks and system failures—but don't let these failures get in your way. Just try again. The following list describes the most frequent problems that may occur, along with the reasons for them:

1. *Even though a search engine retrieves a resource, that resource may no longer exist.*

   The unfortunate fact of the Internet is that Internet resources come and go. A large number of resources on the Internet, even some very good ones, are not funded. Instead, they are created and maintained by a conscientious or interested librarian, professor, computing-center professional, or student. However, if that person leaves the job or no longer has the time to update the resource, it may go unattended, be moved to another computer, or even disappear.

   Generally, when you search an index with a search engine, you are not searching the Internet itself, but you are searching the index that has been built from resources on the Internet. Although the resource may have existed when the index was created, the resource may have disappeared by the time you do your search. Your search retrieves the resource, but when you attempt to go to that resource (by clicking the link in the Web, for example), you get an error message that the resource no longer exists. When you use Gopher resources and the search engine VERONICA, you are particularly prone to this problem because many Gopher resources are gradually being replaced with Web resources.

2. *You are temporarily unable to connect to the resource.*

The Internet has become a pretty busy place. If you do a search that returns 100 potential resources, chances are that those resources are at 100 different sites, on 100 different computers. Chances are also high that at least one of those computers is down when you want to connect to it, or that the site is temporarily inaccessible because of network failure or congestion. In such cases, you may see error messages like `Can't Connect`, `Unable to connect`, or `This site is busy or inaccessible`.

Don't panic when you see messages like these. Just try again later. Usually, the resource will be accessible again within a few minutes. Occasionally, though, the system will be down for as long as a day. Your best bet then is to go on to other resources at other sites.

3. *Your search returns no results.*

Sometimes your search returns no results at all. This problem may have one of the following causes:

- The search engine may not be working correctly. In that case, try again later.

- Your search terms are too narrow. Try broader search terms that encompass the subject in which you are interested.

- You have a misspelling or a typo in your search query. Fix the problem and search again.

4. *You don't have permission to access documents retrieved by the search engine.*

Sometimes Gopher resources—especially those derived from commercial sources like newswires, online news services, encyclopedias, and journals—are available only from within particular institutions. For example, Indiana University provides commercial databases through Gopher that are accessible only to students, faculty, and staff at Indiana University. VERONICA may index these resources but doesn't allow you to access the resources themselves. If you are using VERONICA, you may get error messages indicating that you don't have permission to access certain resources. You can't do much about this problem, except urge your own institution to provide the same information!

5. *The resource that you are attempting to retrieve has been moved or redirected.*

Occasionally, when you try to follow a link retrieved through a search engine, you get a message indicating that the resource you are looking for has been moved or "redirected." This message is similar to "the number you have dialed has been changed" message you hear when you call a telephone number that has changed. Sometimes resources on the Internet are moved to other computers or even to other sites. These messages are Web or Gopher pages left in place of the original URL to inform people that the location has changed. These pages usually provide a link to the new location. Just follow that link to browse the resource at its new location.

You have just examined the most useful search engines—tools for searching indexes of Internet resources. These search engines often provide the best gateway into the resources of a discipline, enabling you to query for the information you want, and to browse the resources available (if the search engines support browsing and controlled-vocabulary classification).

Search engines, however, will not cover all your information needs. Sometimes you won't know enough about a topic to make effective use of the search engine, or you may not be familiar with the internal organization of the discipline itself. Other times, the search engine will put you right smack in the middle of difficult material, without any sort of introduction or overview. The next chapter discusses some tools that can help make up for these deficiencies. You learn how to use subject-oriented resource guides and lists of frequently asked questions (FAQs), as well as some techniques for finding resources when the other methods fail.

9

Think Globally, Act Locally: Subject Guides to the Internet

Objectives

After reading this chapter, you will be able to

- Find and use subject-oriented guides to Internet resources

- Understand what frequently asked questions (FAQs) are and know how to use FAQ lists

- Recognize the value of the home pages of many information-providing organizations

No matter how much you know about searching on the Internet, you may still find it very difficult to begin a search. If you are unfamiliar with the subject area, you may have trouble just getting started. You may not know, for example, the names of people in the discipline, the names of journals in the area, or the terminology of the discipline. In addition, you probably aren't familiar with the types of Internet resources available in (and frequently used by) a discipline.

Fortunately, a couple of tools can help you become familiar with the Internet resources of a particular discipline. One tool is a resource guide to subject-specific information, and another tool is a list of frequently asked questions (FAQs). Each of these tools is focused on a very specific area of study. However, when you need information about that area, this focus can be a strong asset.

Resource Guides to Subject-Specific Information

Many of the academic users of the Internet have long considered it to be a big, disorganized mess. Some librarians, instructors, and graduate students have attempted to deal with this problem, for themselves and other users. A clear organization of the Internet on a grand scale is, of course, beyond the capabilities of any individual or group. But many people have attempted to create some sort of organization on a small scale, usually on the level of a discipline or a subject area, by offering subject-specific guides to Internet resources.

Taking advantage of these guides is an example of "thinking globally but acting locally." Subject-specific guides can be extremely useful as you begin working with a subject area on the Internet. Even though the Internet as a whole may be disorganized, you can make use of these little pockets of organization in order to learn which resources are available and where you can find them.

The Clearinghouse for Subject-Oriented Internet Resource Guides is a collection of subject-specific guides to Internet resources. It is not a search engine, nor have its maintainers attempted to cover all subjects equally. The Clearinghouse is simply a place for the librarians, professors, and graduate students (or anyone else) interested enough to write subject guides to deposit them for others to access. It is a great place for students who are looking for collections of resources on a specific subject. Until recently, the Clearinghouse was directed to users of Gopher and e-mail distribution lists. Recently, however, a large influx of Web-based resource guides has greatly improved the usefulness of the Clearinghouse.

Figure 9.1 shows the Clearinghouse home page. It presents a simple subject classification used to organize the resource guides. Beyond this page, the resource guides are listed alphabetically by topic, so you don't need to navigate a complicated hierarchical menu system.

Figure 9.1

The Clearinghouse home page.

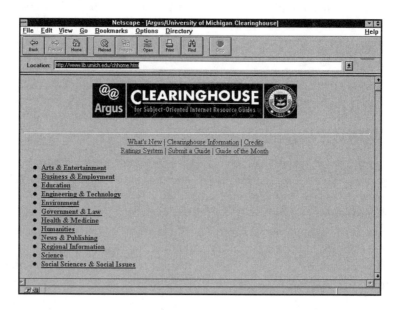

Now take a look at the kinds of subject guides the Clearinghouse makes available, using science as an example. Follow these steps:

1. With your Web browser, go to the URL for the Clearinghouse for Subject-Oriented Internet Resource Guides (`http://www.lib.umich.edu/chhome.html`).

2. Follow the `Science` link to look at subject guides in the sciences.

   As you can see in figure 9.2, the science topics covered by the Clearinghouse run the gamut from the broad (Astronomy and Chemistry) to the specific (Genetic Algorithms and Aluminum). Agriculture, the first item on the list, is a good example that shows the capabilities of these guides, so take a look at that subject guide now.

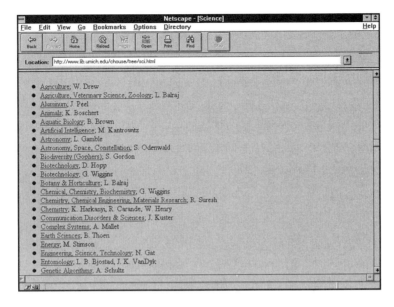

Figure 9.2

A list of subject
guides in the
sciences.

137

3. Follow the Agriculture link to look at the highly regarded Not Just
   Cows guide to agricultural resources on the Internet.

   Figure 9.3 shows the standard Clearinghouse cover page that appears
   before each subject guide. This cover page gives a few administrative
   details about the page, including the full title, the author or editor of
   the resource guide, and a few keywords on which the guide is indexed. The cover page also tells you whether the guide is available in
   hypertext format (with links, formatting, images, and so on) or in
   text-only format (plain text). The Not Just Cows guide happens to be
   available in both formats. Some guides, however, are available only in
   hypertext or in plain text. Now take a look at the hypertext version.

4. Follow the link hypertext to go to the hypertext version.

   Be patient on this one. The guide is very long, although not all guides
   are. Figure 9.4 shows the table of contents for the Not Just Cows
   guide, giving you an idea of the kinds of resources described. The
   resources are organized by resource type, such as library catalogs,
   Gophers, electronic bulletin boards, World Wide Web sites, electronic
   journals, and e-mail-based discussion groups. (Other resource guides
   in the Clearinghouse are organized by subject.)

Figure 9.3

The cover page for the Not Just Cows guide.

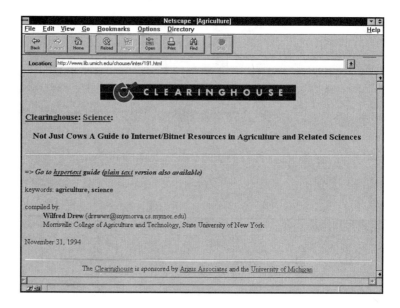

Figure 9.4

The table of contents for the Not Just Cows guide.

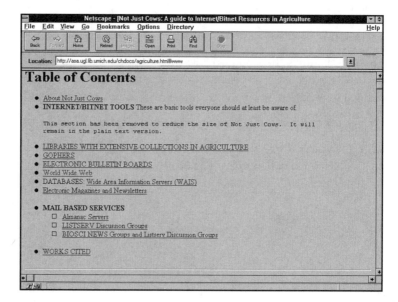

Guides that are available in hypertext format contain links to the resources themselves; guides in text-only format give the addresses to the resources. Some guides, including Not Just Cows, include a short annotation for each resource, giving users a brief evaluation of it.

5. Follow the World Wide Web link to look at the World Wide Web servers described in Not Just Cows.

Figure 9.5 illustrates the kinds of annotations that appear in Not Just Cows and other subject-specific resource guides. These annotations are the primary reason why resource guides can be more useful than search engines; you can get an idea in advance about whether a resource is worth the effort or will add value to your study.

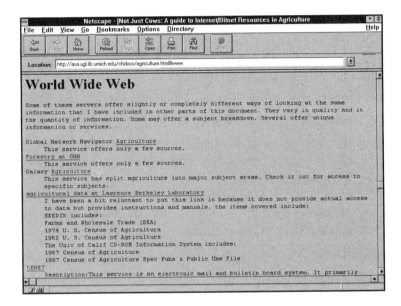

Figure 9.5

Sample annotations for resources described in Not Just Cows.

One promising development at the Clearinghouse that may save even more time in your research is the creation of a ratings system for the subject guides. In the future, subject guides will be rated on four criteria by the maintainers of the Clearinghouse: (1) the level of objective information on resources covered, (2) the level of subjective information on resources covered, (3) the organizational schemes used by the guides, and (4) the level of information provided about the guides themselves.

You can get more information about this ratings system by following the Ratings System link on the Clearinghouse home page. Once the ratings system is applied to the subject guides, it will help students wade through all the useless material on the Internet and find resources that will benefit their research.

You won't always find what you are looking for at the Clearinghouse. Uneven and spotty subject coverage may be noticeable. However, if the specialized topic that you are researching happens to be covered by one of the subject-oriented guides listed in the Clearinghouse, you will have an excellent resource, one that you should not overlook when writing a paper.

Lists of Frequently Asked Questions (FAQ Lists)

After you start to use the Internet to obtain sources for a paper, how do you get a handle on the scope of resources available? How can you find out what all the jargon means, all the terms that everyone else seems to know? How do you get those obvious beginner questions answered? The Frequently Asked Questions list, or FAQ list, as it is usually called on the Internet, is perhaps one of its most enduring features.

Although people who participate on the Internet share information as "equals," they exhibit a wide range of skills in using technical tools and accessing various content areas. Often the technically knowledgeable, content-savvy users get frustrated in answering the same questions from novice users. Because of this frustration, lists of frequently asked questions have evolved. These lists, compiled by expert users and presented in question-and-answer form, are given to new users.

Before you delve into a subject area or begin using a particular tool, be sure to check whether a FAQ list is available. It will save you a lot of time and may save you the scorn of fellow Internet users. No central site exists for FAQ lists (although there is one for FAQ lists associated with Usenet newsgroups), nor is there any individual or company that writes FAQ lists. As an area becomes developed on the Internet, some ambitious or devoted person usually becomes the maintainer of the FAQ list for that area. A good way to find the FAQ list for a particular subject is to use FAQ as a search term when you use a search engine.

> **TIP** *Use FAQ as a search term along with other words that describe your subject. Including FAQ in your search is often a quick way to get the list of frequently asked questions for a subject.*

As with everything else on the Internet, FAQ lists have no fixed schedule of updates, nor is there any guarantee of accuracy with FAQ lists. However, they tend to be more accurate than other Internet resources because they undergo a more thorough peer review. Users who read the FAQ list for an area are usually quick to point out any potential errors to the maintainer of the list.

Home Pages for Organizations

One other source of information is the home pages of organizations. Examples of useful information obtained this way include the following:

- *Government information and statistics from the home pages of various government agencies.* Yahoo and the WWW Virtual Library have good collections of pointers to government agency Web servers. Gems include the Department of Education, the National Science Foundation, National Public Radio, the Library of Congress, and THOMAS (the congressional information service).

- *Information about books, particularly new books, from the home pages of publishers and presses.* Pointers to these home pages can also be obtained from Yahoo. I have found the Macmillan (`http://www.mcp.com`), O'Reilly (`http://www.ora.com`), and MIT Press (`http://www.mitpress.mit.edu`) Web pages to be quite useful. If you know of a publisher that publishes heavily in an area that interests you, check whether the publisher has a home page.

- *Information about products or corporate strategy.* If you are interested in finding information about a company, try visiting its home page. Many corporations, even small ones, are putting up home pages, and more are coming online every day. Of course, the information you get from a corporation's home page will undoubtedly be of a promotional nature, but you may still find it interesting. Yahoo is the undisputed leader in listings of business and corporate home pages.

- *Information about various disciplines from the departments or organizations that study the disciplines.* If you are aware of a university or college department or an organization somewhere that is known in a certain area, try looking at the home page for that department or organization.

TIP *If you know the organization that puts out information of interest to you, you can often guess at the location of the Internet resource. The reason is that an Internet site is usually named for the organization that owns it. Note some examples:*

IBM	`http://www.ibm.com`
WordPerfect	`http://www.wordperfect.com`
MIT	`http://www.mit.edu`
Indiana University	`http://www.indiana.edu`

Sometimes the location of the home page won't be quite as simple as these but will still be guessable. Here are some examples:

Sage Publications	`http://www.sagepub.com`
NPR (National Public Radio)	`http://www.npr.org`
White House	`http://www.whitehouse.gov`
Senate	`http://www.senate.gov`
House of Representatives	`http://www.house.gov`

Of course, you can still always go to Yahoo, but it doesn't hurt to guess!

Strategies for Finding Useful Resources on the Internet

The following strategies can help you find Internet resources that may be of use in your research:

- If you have a person's name that is associated with a resource or you have its title, use that name or title in your queries. This strategy can be especially effective if the name or title is fairly uncommon.

- If you are looking for resources that include acronyms or abbreviations, try searching for the acronyms or abbreviations as well as the phrases for which they stand. For example, you might use both *CIA* and *Central Intelligence Agency* as search terms if you want information on the CIA.

- Try using multiple search engines. They don't all contain the same information.

- Think of which organization might provide the information you want. This organization might be a university center or department, a company, or a government agency. Use the name of the organization in your queries.

- Look for a subject-specific resource guide for the area you are re-searching.

- Ask a librarian for assistance. Librarians are generally skilled in Internet searching and can help you come up with the appropriate terminology to use in your search.

In this chapter, you learned how to use the many subject-oriented resource guides as well as the repositories of such guides so that you now have a place from which to begin your search. Although the subject coverage is very uneven and spotty, some excellent guides are available that can save you a great deal of time and frustration while researching a topic. You also learned about the usefulness of the home pages of various organizations (such as companies, universities, and government agencies). Sometimes it is easiest to go right to the source! Next, the focus of this book moves from directly accessing resources over the Web to accessing the catalogs of books, journals, and other types of materials held by libraries around the world.

10

Using Library Catalogs on the Internet

Objectives

After reading this chapter, you will be able to

- Understand why you might (or might not) want to use a library catalog in your search for Internet resources

- Use a library catalog

- Use HYTELNET to locate library catalogs as well as instructions for their use

Why You May Want to Use a Library Catalog

Despite the wonders of this brave new world of electronic information resources, you may find the best resources in good old-fashioned printed books and journals. For various reasons, books and journals are still considered more accurate and are often written by respected scholars. Many professors will accept only books and journal articles as sources for term papers. The Internet, however, can still be of great help to you, even if the resources you are looking for exist only as printed text.

Through the Internet, you can access almost every college and university library catalog in the country, as well as many catalogs throughout the world. In addition, many large public library catalogs are available over the Internet, and more are coming online every month. You can access all these catalogs from your computer in a public computing lab, in your dorm room, or at home. This capability is especially useful if you are at a small college that doesn't have a large library. But even students at major research universities can benefit from having access to such a large number of library catalogs; invariably, the book you want is the one your library doesn't have.

What an Online Library Catalog Can and Cannot Do

In some ways, library catalogs are similar to the World Wide Web and Gopher search engines you have already examined. Library catalogs enable you to search an index of materials and retrieve a list of documents that match your search query, just as a Web search engine enables you to query and retrieve Web-based documents that match your query. Library catalogs generally provide both free-text and controlled-vocabulary searching, as do many Web search engines. In addition, catalogs usually provide some sort of Boolean searching.

Library catalogs and Internet search engines have some important differences, however. Library catalogs provide an index to materials that are owned by a particular institution (namely, the library) instead of being scattered all over the Internet. When you use a library catalog, you can usually search for only the author, title, or subject of a work—not search the full text of the material itself. Finally, when you query a library catalog, the results that you get are pieces of information about a physical object held by the library, rather than the resource itself. Although many of these differences are slowly disappearing, for the most part, they still stand. (Libraries are now adding some full-text indexing features to their catalogs, as well as pointers to Internet-available electronic resources.)

Finally, library catalogs don't tend to provide indexes to journal articles themselves, only to the titles of the journals. Although a few library catalogs provide indexes to journal articles, these catalogs are usually available only to students and faculty at the university where the catalog is located, not to the general public on the Internet. Thus, if you want to look up specific journal articles, you will probably have to use one of a number of electronic or paper indexes, most of which are not publicly available on the Internet but are still common in libraries. A couple of these electronic indexes are discussed in Chapter 11.

Given these similarities and differences, you will want to search a library catalog for one of three reasons: (1) to search for and locate a book, a journal, or other print material with the intention of checking it out or looking at it; (2) to find bibliographic information about a particular item, such as author, publisher, or date of publication; or (3) to see what books or journals are available on a particular topic or by a particular author. You do not search a library catalog if you want to retrieve the material electronically.

Using a Library Catalog

Although some library catalogs are being put experimentally on the Web or Gopher, most catalogs are accessible only through Telnet. For one reason, library catalogs are usually quite large, which, until recently, prevented them from being used through Web and Gopher servers. Second, library catalogs tend to be integrated with library management applications like billing and purchasing, and these applications were generally not feasible over the Internet. Finally, because library catalogs were originally designed to work with terminals mounted inside the library itself, Telnet was the natural tool to use. (Accessing a resource through Telnet is the same as accessing it by terminal.)

One of the biggest problems with accessing library catalogs is that many types of software are used in the catalogs, and each software package has its own command language. To make matters worse, each institution often modifies the software to reflect the institution's needs, so that even the same program looks different from site to site. Despite these problems, library catalogs are designed to make searching simple in order to accommodate thousands, if not tens of thousands, of people with different levels of computer experience. Thus, with a little guidance and perhaps a help screen or two, you should be able to search most library catalogs with little difficulty.

Accessing an Online Library Catalog

Now take a look at the library catalog at Indiana University, called IUCAT. (Most library catalogs go by similar acronyms and abbreviations.) You access IUCAT by connecting to **infogate.ucs.indiana.edu** with a Telnet client. Follow these steps:

1. With your Telnet client, connect to **infogate.ucs.indiana.edu**. (If you have questions about how to make this connection, refer to Chapter 1.)

   You are asked to log in to the system. If you are affiliated with Indiana University, you type your student ID number, which gives you access to IUCAT as well as a number of other services. A non-IU user is welcome to use the IUCAT library catalog and needs to log in with the user name guest.

2. At the login: prompt, type **guest** and press Enter.

   You see a list of library catalogs that you can search. (Through IU's system, you can search many other library catalogs in Indiana and at other Big Ten schools.) You see also a set of *database labels*, or abbreviations for the catalogs. To search a particular catalog, you just type the name of the database label for the catalog.

3. To search the IU library catalog, type **iucat** and press Enter.

   Figure 10.1 shows the IUCAT search screen, where the search commands are explained. You can search for an item by author, title, or subject. (Searching by subject means the use of controlled-vocabulary subject headings assigned to works by the Library of Congress, specialized medical subject headings, and the call numbers assigned to each work by the Library of Congress.) You can search also by keyword, which means that you can search for any of these types of information. Note that IUCAT provides some examples on-screen (in this case, examples pertaining to Rachel Carson's *Silent Spring*).

Figure 10.1

The IUCAT search
screen.

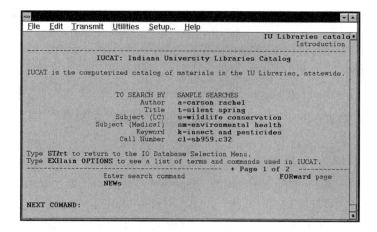

```
 ┌─────────────────────────────────────────────────────────────┐ ▼ ▲
 │  File   Edit   Transmit   Utilities   Setup...   Help         │
 │                                              IU Libraries catalog ▲
 │                                                   Introduction │
 │ ------------------------------------------------------------- │
 │              IUCAT: Indiana University Libraries Catalog       │
 │                                                               │
 │ IUCAT is the computerized catalog of materials in the IU Libraries, statewide.│
 │                                                               │
 │              TO SEARCH BY    SAMPLE SEARCHES                   │
 │                    Author    a=carson rachel                  │
 │                     Title    t=silent spring                  │
 │              Subject (LC)    s=wildlife conservation          │
 │         Subject (Medical)    sm=environmental health          │
 │                   Keyword    k=insect and pesticides          │
 │               Call Number    cl=sb959.c32                     │
 │                                                               │
 │ Type STArt to return to the IO Database Selection Menu.       │
 │ Type EXHlain OPTIONS to see a list of terms and commands used in IUCAT.│
 │ --------------------------------------------  + Page 1 of 2 ------------│
 │                  Enter search command                FORward page│
 │                  NEWs                                         │
 │                                                               │
 │ NEXT COMAND:                                                  │
 │                                                             ▼ │
 └─────────────────────────────────────────────────────────────┘
```

Performing Author and Title Searches

Author and title searches work the same way. Follow these steps:

1. To search the IU library catalog for books by Ernest Hemingway, type

   a=hemingway ernest

   The a= means that you are doing a search by author, and hemingway ernest is the name of the author, with last name first. If you didn't know the author's first name, you could still search for a=hemingway; in that case, you would get a list of all the Hemingways.

2. To search for the book *For Whom the Bell Tolls*, type

   t=for whom the bell tolls

Performing a Keyword Search

The most common types of searches, however, are keyword searches. By using keywords as search terms, you can search everything about the work—author, title, publisher, subject, and so on (well, everything but the text of the work itself). To perform a keyword search, follow these steps:

1. Type

   k=hemingway

You retrieve works by Hemingway (any Hemingway) as well as works about Hemingway, works with Hemingway in the title, and works by Hemingway Publishers.

IUCAT supports Boolean searching for keyword searches only, even though the sample search shown in figure 10.1 doesn't really show how. For example, to find materials that contain either *bicycle* or *tricycle*, you would query

k=bicycle or tricycle

Similarly, if you want to retrieve materials that contain both *Hemingway* and *bell*, you would type

k=hemingway and bell

Although the k= command (for keyword queries) is specific to the software on which IUCAT runs, similar types of queries by title, author, subject, and keyword are available through almost every kind of library catalog software. Next search for books that contain the name *Einstein* and the word *mathematics*.

2. Type **k=einstein and mathematics** to search for works that contain both *Einstein* and *mathematics* in the subjects, authors, titles, or publishers.

   Figure 10.2 shows the results of this query. Although the specific details are unimportant (and include a number of copies of the same work, each owned by a different branch library), you should note several things:

   - You can tell that your query found 44 items containing *Einstein* and *mathematics*.

   - You are viewing only the first 14 items. To go on to the next set, you can type **for** (for forward, as stated at the bottom of the screen).

   - To get more detail on one of these items, you just type the number of the item.

   - The bottom of the screen gives you other actions you can take, including getting other options (OTH), starting over (STA), and getting help (HEL). Every library catalog has some kind of help screen that gives you more information about the commands the catalog provides.

- If you want to try another query, you can simply type your new query at the NEXT COMMAND: prompt.

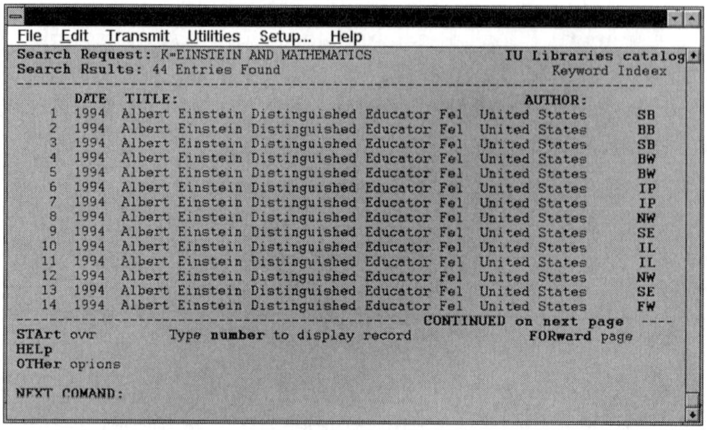

Figure 10.2

The results of the query k=einstein and mathematics.

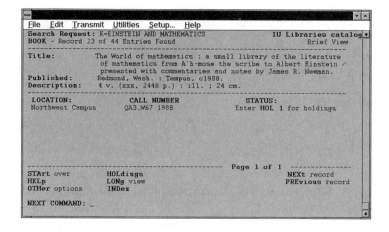

To see what these items look like in more detail, examine one of the items that resulted from your query.

3. Type **for** to go to the next page of items.

   You are now viewing items 15 through 28. Now take a look at item 23.

4. Type **23**.

   Figure 10.3 shows the 23rd item (called the 23rd record) in detail.

Figure 10.3

Detailed information about the 23rd item retrieved by the keyword search.

You can tell that this item is a book, titled *The World of Mathematics: A Small Library of the Literature of Mathematics from A'h-mose the Scribe to Albert Einstein*. Again, the bottom of the screen tells you some of the options available. You use FOR to go forward a page to look at more information on this item (if there is more information), NEX to go to the next record (item 24, in this case), and PRE to go to the previous record (item 22). The IND (index) command takes you back to the list of items retrieved by your query.

Performing a Subject Search

Now try another example. This time, instead of searching by keyword, do a subject search. As mentioned, when you search IUCAT by subject, you are doing a query on a series of controlled-vocabulary subject headings that the Library of Congress assigns to each of the materials in the catalog. For this example, you want to browse the literature on the topic of endangered species. To perform a subject search, follow these steps:

1. Type

   s=endangered species

   as your search query and press Enter.

   Figure 10.4 shows the results of the subject search. As you can see, the results look different from those of the keyword search (which looks just like the author and title searches). What you see now is not a list of books or journals, but instead, you see the Library of Congress subject classifications.

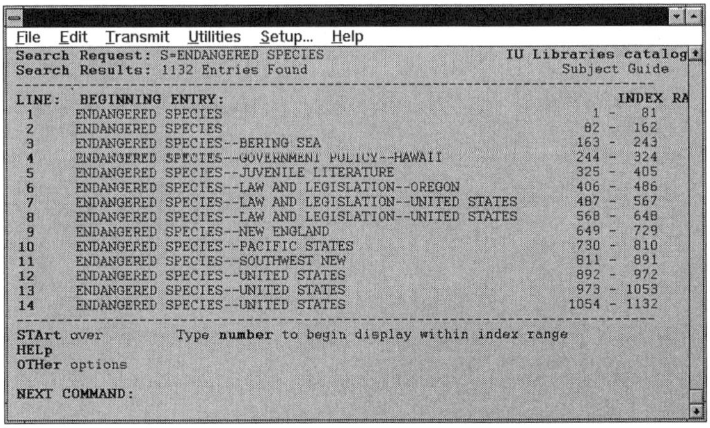

```
 File   Edit   Transmit   Utilities   Setup...   Help
Search Request: S=ENDANGERED SPECIES                IU Libraries catalog
Search Results: 1132 Entries Found                      Subject Guide
-----------------------------------------------------------------------
LINE:   BEGINNING ENTRY:                                       INDEX RA
  1       ENDANGERED SPECIES                                     1 -   81
  2       ENDANGERED SPECIES                                    82 -  162
  3       ENDANGERED SPECIES--BERING SEA                       163 -  243
  4       ENDANGERED SPECIES--GOVERNMENT POLICY--HAWAII        244 -  324
  5       ENDANGERED SPECIES--JUVENILE LITERATURE              325 -  405
  6       ENDANGERED SPECIES--LAW AND LEGISLATION--OREGON      406 -  486
  7       ENDANGERED SPECIES--LAW AND LEGISLATION--UNITED STATES  487 -  567
  8       ENDANGERED SPECIES--LAW AND LEGISLATION--UNITED STATES  568 -  648
  9       ENDANGERED SPECIES--NEW ENGLAND                      649 -  729
 10       ENDANGERED SPECIES--PACIFIC STATES                   730 -  810
 11       ENDANGERED SPECIES--SOUTHWEST NEW                    811 -  891
 12       ENDANGERED SPECIES--UNITED STATES                    892 -  972
 13       ENDANGERED SPECIES--UNITED STATES                    973 - 1053
 14       ENDANGERED SPECIES--UNITED STATES                   1054 - 1132
-----------------------------------------------------------------------
STArt over          Type number to begin display within index range
HELp
OTHer options

NEXT COMMAND:
```

Figure 10.4

The results of the subject search.

At the top of the screen is the broad classification ENDANGERED SPECIES, and toward the bottom are specific classifications, such as ENDANGERED SPECIES—UNITED STATES. Unfortunately, this screen is a bit difficult to interpret. You know from the notice at the top that 1,132 items are about endangered species (including its subcategories), as classified by the Library of Congress. The IU library catalog divides the items according to the number of lines on the screen (14), so that each line represents 81 items. This approach—to divide the items by number instead of by subcategory—is an annoying and illogical feature of the NOTIS software, used in the IU library catalog. For example, you would type 1 to get the first 81 items, 2 to get the next 81 items, and so on.

2. To look at the first 81 items, type **1** and press Enter.

   Figure 10.5 shows the results. The first couple of items listed in the subject search aren't books or journals, but other subject categories related to the one you searched for. To search any of these additional categories, you just type the number of the category (such as 1 to do a search on endangered plants).

Figure 10.5

The first 81 items of a subject search.

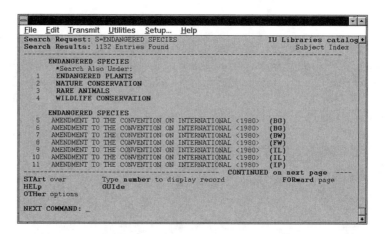

The first 4 items, labeled *Search Also Under:, are actually other subject headings related to the endangered species heading. They aren't actually subheadings but are related headings that might contain items of interest to someone searching for endangered species.

Next, you see that items 5 through 11 are items classified under the subject heading ENDANGERED SPECIES (as are several hundred more on pages that follow). You can use the FOR command to move forward a page of items, and the BAC command to move back a page of items. To go back to the previous screen of subject headings (refer to figure 10.4), you use the GUI (guide) command.

When you do a keyword search, the search is done on these same subject headings—in addition to title, author, publisher, language of publication, and so on. You would do a subject search, like the one in this example, for one of two reasons: (1) you want to browse a number of items on a particular subject, or (2) you want to understand the scope and depth of the materials available on a subject. In either case, subject searching can be much more powerful and effective than keyword searching alone.

The sample searches presented here illustrate the basic capabilities of the Indiana University library catalog, one that is fairly typical of the catalogs you will find on the Internet. From these sample searches, you can see the differences between two types of searches: a keyword search for a particular item and a subject search for browsing the materials on that subject.

What do you do *after* you find one or more items in a library catalog? If you just want to get a feel for the works on a subject or by an author, or if you want to find bibliographic information about an item, your task may be complete. But if you want to obtain the materials you have looked up, you probably won't be able to accomplish this goal on the Internet. You will have to retrieve the material from your library, or, if it doesn't own the material, you will have to ask the library to do an interlibrary loan. Most materials can be obtained through *interlibrary loan*, a cooperative lending system that libraries use. Your librarian will be happy to help you with this system, and it probably won't cost you a dime.

> **TIP** *If you find an item in a library catalog on the Internet and your library doesn't own the item, ask your librarian for help in getting the item through an interlibrary loan.*

Locating Library Catalogs with HYTELNET

Library catalogs can, at times, be difficult to find. You usually have to go to the home page of the college or university and then look for a link to its library catalog. Furthermore, you've learned that each library catalog looks a little different and may have a unique set of commands. You can use a tool, however, that helps bring Internet-accessible library catalogs from around the world into a single directory and provides some directions for using the catalogs. The tool is HYTELNET.

This tool is named HYTELNET because it provides a hypertext-based directory of library catalogs and uses Telnet to access them. HYTELNET is one of the older, most respected Internet tools available. In fact, it was one of the first major tools to use hypertext on the Internet, predating the growth of the World Wide Web. HYTELNET used to come with its own client software, which you would have to download and install on your computer before you could use the directory. Although you can still get the client software, HYTELNET itself is available through the World Wide Web, which is the easiest way to make use of HYTELNET's power.

The HYTELNET information page—with information about updates, client software, and changes—is located at `http://www.lights.com/hytelnet`. However, the World Wide Web version of HYTELNET is located at `http://moondog.usask.ca/hytelnet`.

Figure 10.6 shows the HYTELNET interface. Simple and nongraphical, the Web HYTELNET tool is meant for users with either graphical or nongraphical browsers.

Figure 10.6
The HYTELNET
Web interface.

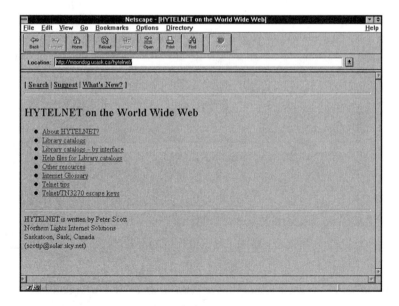

The main menu gives a pretty good picture of what is available through HYTELNET. Notice that several options on the HYTELNET menu provide different types of help information about the resources accessed through HYTELNET:

- `Help files for Library catalogs` provides a summary of the commands available for each type of library catalog software. Usually, you won't need to access help in this way, because you can access help directly from the page that leads you to the catalog you want to search.

- `Internet Glossary` gives you a small glossary of Internet terms and acronyms, focusing on those relevant to online library catalogs.

- `Telnet tips` contains a summary of tips and hints about different Telnet clients.

- `Telnet/TN3270 escape keys` summarizes the keys used to exit from ten different Telnet clients.

The resources themselves are available through the following options:

- `Library catalogs` gives you a menu-based directory of library catalogs arranged first by country and then by library type (such as academic, public, and law). This directory is the most useful feature of HYTELNET and one you will certainly want to use.

- `Library catalogs - by interface` gives you the same list of library catalogs, but arranged by catalog software type. This list isn't very useful because most people don't want to search for library catalogs based on the software used.

- `Other resources` is a list of other non-library-catalog Internet resources, such as Web servers, Gophers, and a variety of other databases. This collection isn't always current, and its coverage of Web sites is weak. The list might be worth browsing, though, for databases that aren't available through other means. For example, the list provides access to a number of community information systems and bulletin boards, as well as to a large number of specific text and graphics databases, including some from NASA.

Using HYTELNET to Access Library Catalogs

Now try using HYTELNET to access a library catalog. In this example, you want to obtain a list of the books written by Douglas R. Hofstadter that are available through the Ohio State University library. Hofstadter is a prominent researcher in the areas of computer science and cognitive science, and the author of the Pulitzer Prize winner *Gödel, Escher, Bach*. Follow these steps:

1. With your Web browser, go to **http://moondog.usask.ca/hytelnet**. You see the page illustrated in figure 10.6.

2. Follow the link `Library catalogs`.

   You then see the first of the geographical groupings (see figure 10.7).

Figure 10.7

HYTELNET library catalogs by region.

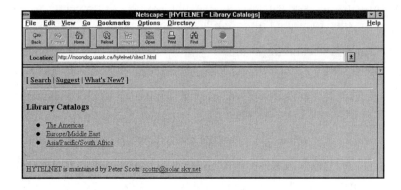

3. Follow the link `The Americas`.

   You now see a list of the countries in the Americas that have library catalogs available through HYTELNET. Note that the list of countries in the Americas gives you the option of viewing the libraries in the United States by state and by type of library.

4. Now go ahead and look at libraries in the United States by following the link `by Type of Library`.

   You see a list of the different types of libraries in the United States. Because the Ohio State University library is an academic library, you want to select from the academic, research, and general libraries.

5. Follow the link `Academic, Research, and General Libraries`.

   You see an alphabetic list of all the academic, research, and general libraries in the country whose catalogs are available over the Internet (see figure 10.8).

6. Scroll down until you find the link `Ohio State University`; then follow that link.

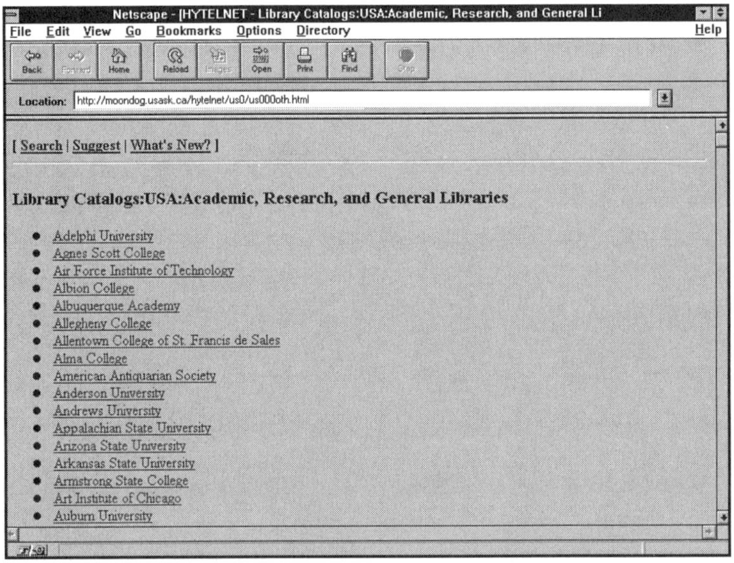

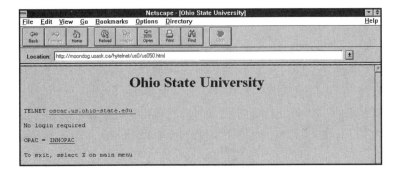

Figure 10.8
A list of academic, research, and general libraries whose library catalogs are available over the Internet.

Figure 10.9 shows the HYTELNET page for the library catalog at the Ohio State University.

Figure 10.9
The Ohio State University HYTELNET page.

This page gives you four pieces of information:

- *The Telnet address that you use to access the catalog.* Telnet addresses are actually links, so if your Web browser is set up correctly, all you do is follow that link, and you will be connected to the catalog.

- *An indication that no user name or login name is required.* Some library catalogs require a login name. The Indiana University catalog, for example, requires you to log in as guest. The HYTELNET page will tell you the appropriate login name to use if one is needed.

158

- *An indication that the library catalog software used at the Ohio State University is INNOPAC. (OPAC stands for Online Public Access Catalog, which is a library catalog.) The INNOPAC link takes you to a page of information about the catalog software, giving a summary of search commands.*

- *The command that you use to exit from the library catalog when you are finished using it.*

You probably want to find out first about the search commands available to you, so you can go to the information page about INNOPAC catalog software.

7. Follow the INNOPAC link to the INNOPAC information page.

Figure 10.10 shows the INNOPAC information page, summarizing the commands available when you access INNOPAC-based library catalogs. As you can see, the commands are similar to those used in the Indiana University catalog, which uses the NOTIS software. The types of searches available (title, author, subject, and keyword) are identical.

Figure 10.10
The INNOPAC information page.

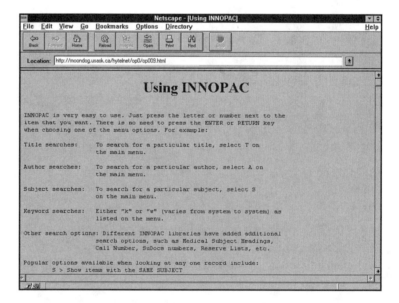

8. Using your Web browser, go back to the previous page, the Ohio State University catalog page.

9. To connect to the library catalog, follow the link to oscar.us.ohio-state.edu.

If your Web browser is set up correctly, the Telnet program should automatically connect to the Ohio State University library catalog. After Telnet makes the connection, the catalog software asks you what type of terminal you are using. In most instances, the option V (for VT100, a brand of terminal) will work for you.

10. Type **v** in response to the request for terminal type.

11. Type **y** to confirm your choice.

    Figure 10.11 shows the Ohio State University library catalog main menu.

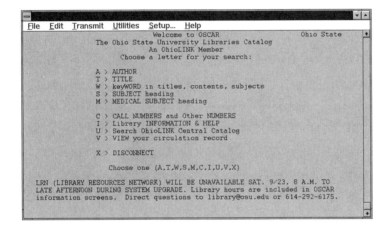

Figure 10.11

The Ohio State University library catalog main menu.

12. You want to search for all the works by Douglas R. Hofstadter, so type **a** to search by author. You then see an introductory search screen, as shown in figure 10.12.

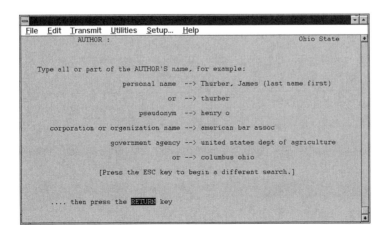

Figure 10.12

The introductory search screen for the Ohio State catalog, with examples.

Next, you type the author's name. The screen gives you some examples of how to enter author names (such as last name before first name).

13. Type **Hofstadter, Douglas R.** and press Enter.

Figure 10.13 shows the results of your query. The Ohio State University library system owns three books by Douglas Hofstadter. The names and call numbers are listed, and you can type the number of the item you are interested in for more information about that item.

Figure 10.13

The results of your query with HYTELNET.

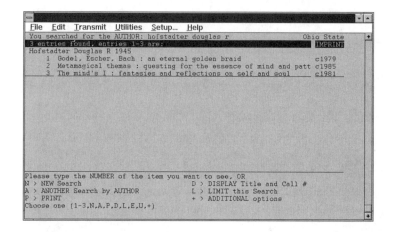

> **TIP** **HYTELNET is updated fairly frequently. For the latest and greatest information on HYTELNET, you might want to check the HYTELNET home page occasionally (located at http://www.lights.com/hytelnet).**

Although using the Internet to find information for your papers is certainly convenient, most of the time you will still have to use books and journals. By using online library catalogs and letting HYTELNET guide you, the Internet can be a great aid to you, even when you need to resort to print materials.

11

Useful Commercial and Government Resources

Objectives

After reading this chapter, you will be able to

- Recognize the range of commercial resources available in your library

- Access the UnCover document delivery system over the Internet

- Understand the capabilities of the LOCIS system and the THOMAS system

In previous chapters, you looked at very general research tools freely available to you over the Internet. In this chapter, you learn about a couple of tools that are commercial in nature but may still be available in your college library. These tools can be extremely useful and may, in fact, be the only way to obtain certain types of information. The services described in this chapter are the CARL network, the UnCover document delivery system, LEXIS-NEXIS, Dialog, and Dow Jones News/ Retrieval.

These commercial resources (with the exception of some features of CARL and UnCover) are not publicly and freely available over the Internet, although with the appropriate passwords, you *can* access them over the Internet. However, most academic libraries will have access to at least some of these resources. Your librarian should be able to tell you which tools are available from your own library.

After becoming familiar with these commercial tools, you learn about a couple of government-sponsored research tools that may also be quite useful in your research.

UnCover: A Document Delivery Service

Document delivery is a term generally used to refer to the electronic transmission of journal articles. Document delivery developed not so much because of its convenience to the user but because of economics. Quite simply, libraries can't afford to subscribe to all the journals that students and faculty might possibly want. Thus, a common strategy is to subscribe to a certain number of core journals and to subscribe to commercial document delivery services that can transmit articles, as requested, from the rest of the journals.

Many of these document delivery services may still seem pretty old-fashioned. In fact, most don't even send the document to you by computer at all. Even though you can request a document by computer, the article is usually faxed to you.

Although a number of such services are available to many libraries, one of the most useful is called UnCover. It began as a service of CARL, a consortium of Colorado libraries, which eventually spun off to become CARL Corporation. CARL Corporation was recently purchased by Knight-Ridder, Inc. UnCover also happens to be available over the Internet, and it can be very useful even if you don't want to pay any money.

With UnCover, you can do the following:

- Browse the tables of contents of several thousand journals in all areas of study

- Search the article titles, journal titles, and names of the authors of these articles (although not the full text of the articles themselves)

- Request that these articles (most of them, at least) be faxed to you, with the help of a credit card and the payment of a fee

The cost per journal article tends to be between $8 and $15, depending on the length of the article and the publisher. Note that most of the cost of the article is the copyright fee, not the actual faxing itself.

> **TIP** *Although UnCover can be useful, cheaper options are often available. Libraries can usually get documents delivered through various interlibrary loan sources free of charge to you, although the process generally takes several days. If you have the time to spare, you can usually save yourself some money. If you don't, you might want to investigate UnCover.*

The CARL home page provides access to the UnCover document delivery service, as well as information about (and access to) many other databases through what is called the CARL network. You need a password to access most of the databases provided through CARL. (Ask your librarian to find out whether the library has a password available for public use; often the use of such a password is automated through the menus of the computers in the library.) You can obtain the CARL home page by going to the location `http://www.carl.org` with your Web browser.

To access the UnCover service, follow these steps:

1. From the CARL home page, choose `Information about CARL and access to the CARL network`.

2. From the subsequent page, choose `The UnCover Home Page`.

   Note that you can follow many other links to obtain more information about the various services available. From the UnCover home page, you can find out more about the UnCover service (see figure 11.1). To connect to UnCover, follow the link `Click here to access the UnCover database`. Telnet is automatically invoked and connects to the UnCover system; you then see the menu shown in figure 11.2.

Figure 11.1

The UnCover home page.

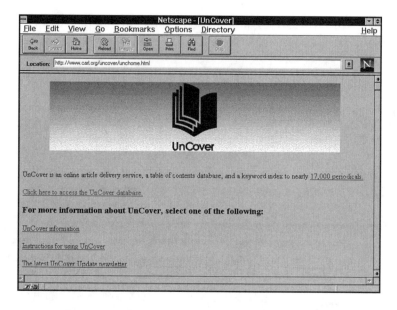

Figure 11.2

The initial UnCover connection screen.

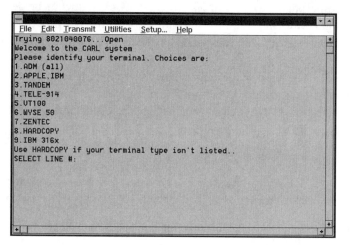

UnCover asks you to choose the type of terminal you are using to access the service. If you are accessing UnCover over the Internet, you are probably using a VT100 (choice 5).

3. Type **5** and press Enter to tell UnCover to go on.

You now see the menu shown in figure 11.3.

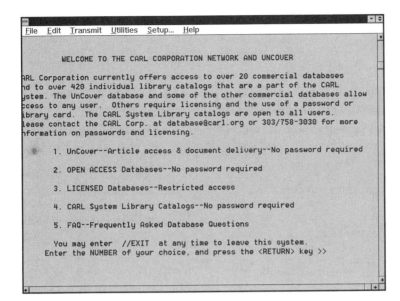

Figure 11.3
The CARL
network and
UnCover database
menu.

165

You can choose from the databases listed. Unfortunately, almost all of them require a password of some sort, so you can access only those databases to which your library subscribes. However, the CARL System Library Catalogs and UnCover are publicly available.

4. Type **1** and press Enter to enter UnCover.

Figure 11.4 shows the next screen you see.

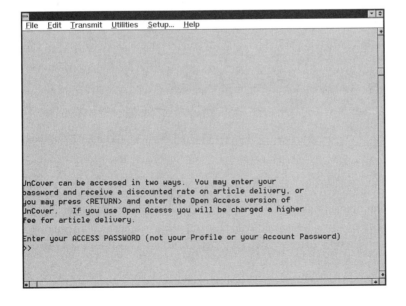

Figure 11.4
The next UnCover
screen.

5. You probably don't have an access password, so just press Enter.

6. Press Enter again to continue. (Going into UnCover can be very cumbersome!)

   You are prompted to enter a profile number, although you probably don't have one now. If you are a frequent user of UnCover, you can set up a profile with your name, your address, and even your credit card number. That way, you don't have to enter this information each time you request that a document be faxed to you.

7. Press Enter to continue.

   At this point, you can set up a profile. For this exercise, just move to the next step.

8. Again, press Enter to continue.

   Finally, you see the UnCover main menu, as shown in figure 11.5.

Figure 11.5

The UnCover main menu.

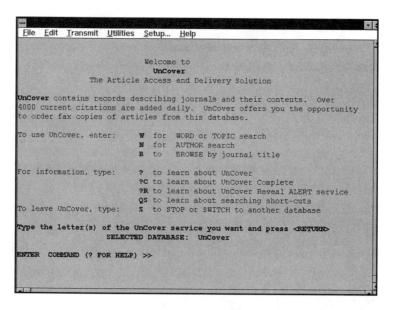

This is the menu from which you do your searches. The W command enables you to search by word in the journal title, article title, or subject area. You use the N command to search for an author's name. You use the B command first to search for a particular journal title, and then to browse the titles and authors of all the issues of the journal you chose to search.

Note that UnCover usually contains back issues to around 1988, and sometimes not that far back. UnCover tends to be most useful for more recent articles.

Figure 11.6 shows the results of a sample browse by journal title. The journal is *Business Week*.

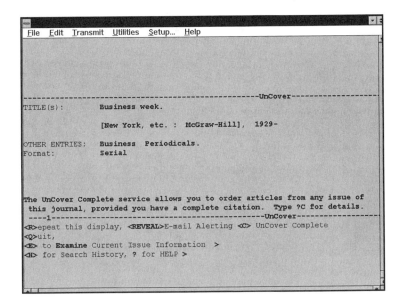

Figure 11.6

Results of a search of UnCover.

The bottom of the screen gives you the options available. Often the meanings of these options aren't entirely clear, and you don't always know which choice is the right one for you. Choice E, which allows you to browse the journal, is the correct choice (even though all it tells you is that you can examine current issue information).

Figure 11.7 shows a sample table of contents listing from *Business Week*. As you can see, this issue is dated 8/21/95. Menu items at the bottom of the screen enable you to mark (M) any of these articles for delivery. If you want more details about the article itself, you can simply type the number of the article (for example, 007 for "Think EDS Is Hot Now? Just Wait"). If you have marked documents for ordering, you can type the letter O, and you will be prompted to enter credit card and addressing information.

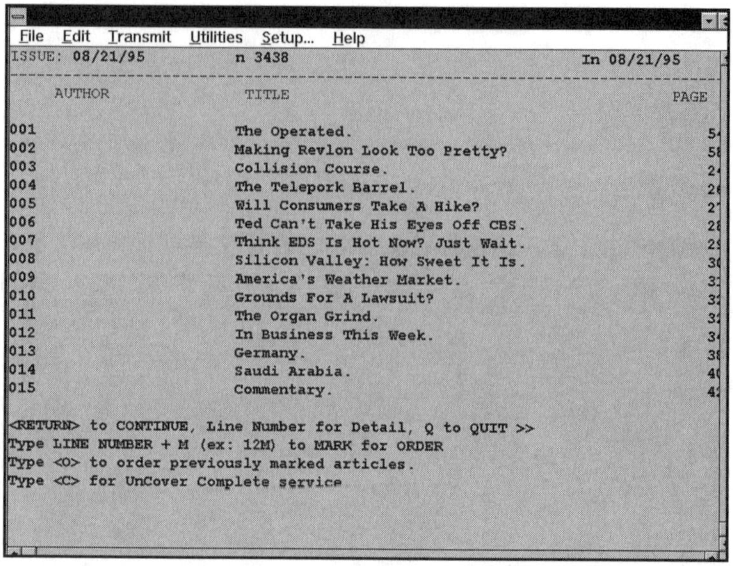

Figure 11.7

The table of
contents of a
journal in
UnCover.

```
File  Edit  Transmit  Utilities  Setup...  Help
ISSUE: 08/21/95          n 3438                    In 08/21/95
---------------------------------------------------------------
     AUTHOR              TITLE                         PAGE
001                      The Operated.                   5
002                      Making Revlon Look Too Pretty?  5
003                      Collision Course.               2
004                      The Telepork Barrel.            2
005                      Will Consumers Take A Hike?     2
006                      Ted Can't Take His Eyes Off CBS. 2
007                      Think EDS Is Hot Now? Just Wait. 2
008                      Silicon Valley: How Sweet It Is. 3
009                      America's Weather Market.       3
010                      Grounds For A Lawsuit?          3
011                      The Organ Grind.                3
012                      In Business This Week.          3
013                      Germany.                        3
014                      Saudi Arabia.                   4
015                      Commentary.                     4

<RETURN> to CONTINUE, Line Number for Detail, Q to QUIT >>
Type LINE NUMBER + M (ex: 12M) to MARK for ORDER
Type <O> to order previously marked articles.
Type <C> for UnCover Complete service
```

> **NOTE** *There is some risk, although slight, in having your credit card number transmitted over the Internet. If you are concerned about this matter, you can contact CARL Corporation and have someone set up a profile over the telephone. Then you won't have to enter your credit card over the Internet; all you do is type your profile number when you enter CARL.*

Remember that you don't have to use the document delivery features of UnCover to benefit from the service. Just searching for journal articles with UnCover can be highly useful and won't cost you anything. UnCover is most useful to me when I remember something about an article but need full bibliographic information so that I can correctly cite the article.

LEXIS-NEXIS

LEXIS-NEXIS, owned by Reed Elsevier, is a high-end, expensive database. It is generally very up-to-date (usually within a few hours of publication) and contains the full text of thousands of newspapers, reports, and journals. The NEXIS part is what you would probably use if you accessed this database in a library. LEXIS is actually a database of legal information, used by law offices and law students for research.

The home page for LEXIS-NEXIS, which provides complete information about the service, is available at the location `http://www.lexis-nexis.com`. You can obtain comprehensive information on which publications are indexed and provided by LEXIS-NEXIS, as well as answers to frequently asked questions (FAQs) about searching LEXIS-NEXIS by following the `Customer Information` link from the home page.

LEXIS-NEXIS works by enabling you to search "libraries" of information, using a search language that provides full Boolean search features for refining your queries. To give you an idea of the scope of these libraries, consider the News library. It is one of several hundred libraries available (and the most frequently used by students), and it contains the full text of over 2,300 newspapers, newswires, newsletters, and broadcast transcripts. Publications provided in the News library include everything from *The New York Times* to *Le Monde* to *Africa News*.

Once you have executed your search on LEXIS-NEXIS, you can display, save, or print your results in a number of ways, from the full text of the articles to the citations of the articles.

Searching with LEXIS-NEXIS tends to be costly, so you probably won't want to subscribe on your own. However, most libraries have access to it, and many will let you do your own searching on LEXIS-NEXIS. Be sure to ask a librarian whether LEXIS-NEXIS is available in your library; you cannot find a more comprehensive source for current news or business information.

Dialog

Dialog is another expensive database of academic and business information. It is also fairly difficult to use; people take entire courses just to learn how to search Dialog. It is sometimes available in academic libraries and is frequently used in the corporate world. The home page for Dialog, which provides information about the service, is located at `http://www.dialog.com`.

Dow Jones News/Retrieval

Dow Jones News/Retrieval is another commercial information service like Dialog and LEXIS-NEXIS. And like Dialog and LEXIS-NEXIS, this service is available over the Internet but is also quite costly. For this reason, you will probably want to access it through your library or college. Although other databases are available through Dow Jones News/Retrieval, its focus is clearly business and financial news.

Besides being the only information service that provides the full text of the *Wall Street Journal*, Dow Jones News/Retrieval contains extensive files of newswire reports, company stock filings, stock and mutual quotes, and company profiles. Unfortunately, both the search language and the interface are rather outdated and ugly. However, for any student doing research in business or corporate intelligence, Dow Jones News/Retrieval is almost a necessity. You would do well to master the system. More information on this service can be found on the Dow Jones home page, located at `http://www.dowjones.com`.

Library of Congress Services

The Library of Congress contains an incredible wealth of resources and should not be overlooked when you are doing research on the Internet. LOCIS and THOMAS, two of the most useful services provided over the Internet by the Library of Congress, are described here. The Library of Congress' home page can be found at `http://www.loc.gov`. This home page provides links to LOCIS and THOMAS, information on how to use these services, and links to many special exhibits.

LOCIS: Library of Congress Information System

LOCIS, the Library of Congress Information System, is really a very large library catalog. It provides information about an enormous array of materials, including books and nonprint materials catalogued by the Library of Congress, federal legislation, copyrighted materials registered with the Library of Congress, braille and audio materials, bibliographies for people doing basic research, and foreign law materials. More information on LOCIS can be found on the Library of Congress Online Services home page, located at `http://lcweb.loc.gov/homepage/online.html`.

Of course, the Library of Congress doesn't actually provide the full text of the materials accessible through LOCIS. Because most of the materials are copyrighted, you still have to purchase them or find them in a library if you want to use them. However, the system is very useful for retrieving information about published works, particularly when you then want to go to a library to locate the material.

Although you can access LOCIS in several ways (including through Telnet), the newest and most user-friendly way is over the Web, using a search system (actually a search standard) known as Z39.50. Don't worry—this method is actually much easier than it sounds! Figure 11.8 shows the search form that enables you to search the LOCIS databases. As you can see, the form provides support for Boolean logic and allows you to search such information as author, title, and subject. You can access this search form at **http://lcweb.loc.gov /z3950/mums.html**.

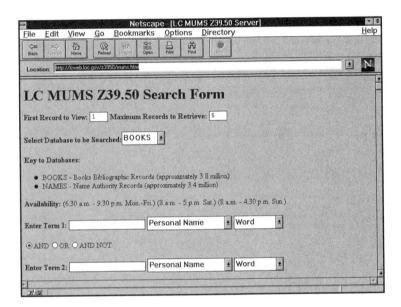

Figure 11.8

The LOCIS Web search form.

THOMAS: Legislative Information on the Internet

THOMAS is one of the newer services on the Internet, and one of the most valuable for any student needing information on legislation. You can reach THOMAS at **http://thomas.loc.gov**. THOMAS provides information about the activities of the U.S. Congress, including the full text of all bills and legislation. This information can be searched and retrieved in a number of ways, including by type of bill and by keyword in the text of the bill. Figure 11.9 shows a form that you can use to search for legislation. Although THOMAS is fairly new, containing legislation back to the 103rd Congress (1992), the service is very up-to-date. It always contains the text of new bills within 48 hours, and often in much less time.

Figure 11.9
THOMAS
legislation search
form.

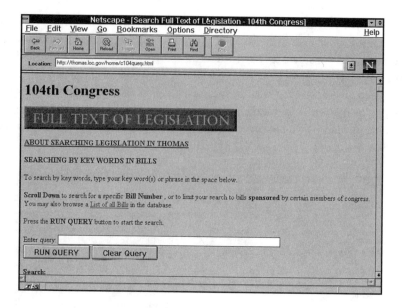

FedWorld

No discussion of research tools on the Internet would be complete without a mention of FedWorld, a Web site maintained by the National Technical Information Service of the U.S. Government. This resource provides links to Internet-accessible reports (and Internet servers) from all agencies of the U.S. Government—from NASA to the military to the National Institutes of Health. FedWorld is useful to students for a variety of research needs, including the need for policy statements or analysis from various agencies; scientific data, such as that provided by NASA; and geological information, such as that provided by the United States Geological Survey.

You can access FedWorld on the Web at `http://www.fedworld.gov`. The information linked to by FedWorld is organized into a set of categories devised by the National Technical Information Service. Figure 11.10 shows part of the FedWorld index of these categories of federal government information. Each category contains links to other government Web servers. FedWorld maintains a uniform system of organization and categorization up to this point. Once you move on and connect to an Internet server provided by one of these government agencies, things will not necessarily look the same; you may have to hunt around a bit to find the exact information you want.

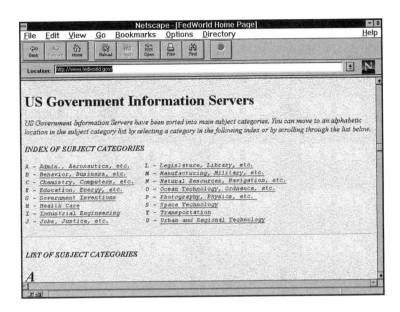

In this chapter, you learned about some resources in the commercial and government domains that may aid you in your studies. The commercial services described generally provide comprehensive, full-text databases of information in the areas they cover:

Uncover	Journals and magazines
LEXIS-NEXIS	Law and news materials
Dialog	Academic and business information
Dow Jones News/Retrieval	Business

These services, however, are not always available from every location. They are often expensive and rarely available to you as a student in your home or residence hall. Government information is a "world unto itself" on the Internet. Although this book has generally stayed away from describing discipline-specific resources, government information is so pervasive, so multidisciplinary, and sometimes so mysterious that most readers can benefit from exploring some of the most useful government information systems like LOCIS, THOMAS, and FedWorld.

12

Using E-Mail on the Internet

Objectives

After reading this chapter, you will be able to

- Understand the basic concepts of Internet e-mail

- Use the PINE e-mail program to send, receive, and reply to messages

- Use PINE to file your messages in folders

- Use PINE to create a personal address-book file to store the e-mail addresses of your colleagues and friends

- Understand the norms of e-mail etiquette

Perhaps no Internet-based tool, not even the World Wide Web, has transformed the college environment the way *electronic mail,* commonly called *e-mail,* has. Instructors now use e-mail to distribute assignments and supplementary material to their students; students use e-mail to turn in homework and assignments to their instructors. E-mail even enables instructors to keep in touch with students at remote sites.

At its best, e-mail removes barriers of time and space. At its worst, e-mail can create misunderstandings and frustration among people not used to communicating in this medium. Particularly when combined with the one-to-many communication of distribution lists (that is, one person can send a message, and many people will automatically receive it), e-mail can contribute significantly to information overload.

There is no way of getting around the fact, however, that electronic mail is here to stay. Fortunately, e-mail can be a valuable resource for students who want to get the most out of the Internet for their research needs.

Basics of Internet Mail

Although dozens of programs are used on the Internet for e-mail, several programs are used widely. One such program, PINE, is rapidly becoming quite common on college campuses. Before learning about PINE, however, you need to understand the basic concepts of Internet e-mail.

In general, you find two different architectures for e-mail on the Internet: POP mail and host-based mail. The POP mail architecture consists of a POP server and a POP client. The POP server is a remote computer (usually a computer running UNIX) that receives, forwards, and sorts e-mail, much like an electronic post office. In fact, POP is an abbreviation for *Post Office Protocol*. The client is a program that runs on your own computer (usually a PC or Macintosh). Periodically, the client program contacts the server computer over the Internet, downloads the mail to the computer on which the client is running, and terminates the connection with the server. Therefore, whenever a user works with mail (sending, composing, reading, and so on), the user is working with a local copy of the mail on his or her own computer and needn't maintain the Internet connection to the server.

The best-known POP mail client is Eudora, available in both Macintosh and Windows configurations (as well as commercial and free versions) from Qualcomm, Inc., at the following address:

```
http://www.qualcomm.com
```

In the host-based mail model, however, the "post office" mail functions (such as sending, forwarding, receiving, and sorting) are handled on the same computer on which the mail client program runs. (The mail client program is the one that you actually use to read, compose, and send your mail.) Usually, this remote host computer also runs UNIX. The most common host-based mail programs are Berkeley Mail (generally just called "mail" in the UNIX environment), VAX mail, elm, and PINE.

POP mail is often used by e-mail users who have their own computer workstations with a direct Internet connection and who seldom use other computers. For this reason, faculty and staff at colleges often use POP mail. However, students who often move from computer to computer—either between home and campus or from computer to computer in a public lab—usually use host-based e-mail.

This chapter focuses on the University of Washington's PINE mail program for the following reasons:

- It has become extremely popular on the Internet, and most sites now provide it.

- It is full featured and flexible enough for almost any user.

- It is available free of charge and runs on almost any variety of UNIX computer.

- It is quite user-friendly. Menus throughout the program tell you exactly what options are available, which frees you from having to learn any commands. (Amusingly, many hard-core computer people don't like PINE simply because it is too user-friendly!)

Comprehensive information about PINE is available from the PINE home page at the University of Washington, which you can access at the following address:

`http://www.cac.washington.edu/pine`

This chapter provides an overview of the use of PINE.

About E-Mail Addresses

Fortunately, you can send messages to and receive messages from another user regardless of which mail program you or the other person uses. Almost every mail system can now receive mail from any other mail system, through the use of *mail gateways*—programs that convert from one mail system to another. Fortunately, you don't need to know about these gateways. All you have to know is the Internet e-mail address of the person to whom you want to send a message. The gateways automatically handle the rest.

These Internet e-mail addresses are unique on the Internet. Internet e-mail addresses are in the following form:

> *username@hostname*

username identifies the user on a particular mail system, and *hostname* identifies the mail system and location. For example, my e-mail address is `mckimg@indiana.edu`. `mckimg` is my user name, and `indiana.edu` refers to the mail system that I use.

You can usually derive some information about the mail system just by looking at the address. For example, the suffix `edu` tells you that my address is at an educational institution. Yours most likely also ends in `edu`. Some other common suffixes are `com` for commercial organizations, `net` for Internet service providers, `org` for nonprofit organizations, `mil` for the military, and `gov` for government institutions. The rest of the host name usually identifies the institution as well. All Indiana University addresses end in `.indiana.edu`, for example, and NASA addresses end in `nasa.gov`. The addresses of mail that originates outside the U.S. may also end in a country code, such as `fr` for France, `ca` for Canada, and `uk` for the United Kingdom.

How do you find out someone's e-mail address? The following are probably the best ways:

- Ask the person to whom you want to send the message what his or her e-mail address is.

- If the person previously sent you an e-mail message, you can reply to that message or simply look at the message for a return address.

If neither of these methods is possible, try looking up the person in one of the many incomplete but useful e-mail directories. Chapter 13 discusses these directories.

A mail gateway is a computer that acts like a post office— reading, sorting, and forwarding electronic mail according to the addresses. Because of gateways, you just have to know the address of the intended recipient of your e-mail; you don't have to know how to get the mail to the recipient.

A user name identifies an e-mail recipient. Generally, the e-mail user name is the same as the name the person uses to log onto his or her own e-mail system. E-mail addresses are in the form username@hostname. *The host name identifies the computer on which an e-mail user receives mail.*

Basics of the PINE E-Mail Program

This section describes the basic operation of the PINE e-mail program. You learn how to start the program and send, receive, read, and file messages with it. If you use an e-mail program other than PINE, you will find the specific commands different; however, the basic operations will be the same.

Starting PINE

The way that you invoke PINE depends on how your institution has set up the program. Usually, you must first use a Telnet program (or another type of communications program) to log in to a computer that runs UNIX. At the UNIX prompt, you type **pine** to invoke the PINE program. However, your institution may have automated the process of running PINE or simply made it a menu choice.

After invoking PINE, you see PINE's main menu, as shown in figure 12.1.

Figure 12.1

The PINE main menu.

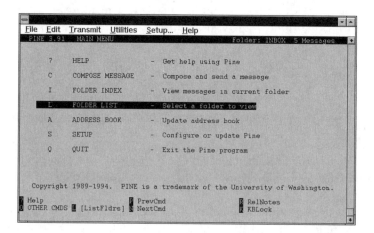

The main menu displays the options available to you. Most of these options are self-explanatory. You will frequently use the following options:

Access Key	Option	Purpose
C	COMPOSE MESSAGE	Writing and sending messages
I	FOLDER INDEX	Reading messages sent to you
L	FOLDER LIST	Working with different folders (collections) of mail

178

You can now send, read, or delete a mail message; file a mail message in a folder; or enter an address in your PINE address book.

Sending a Mail Message with PINE

Sending (or composing) a mail message in PINE is extremely simple. You choose the PINE menu's COMPOSE MESSAGE option. You then see the PINE message compose form shown in figure 12.2.

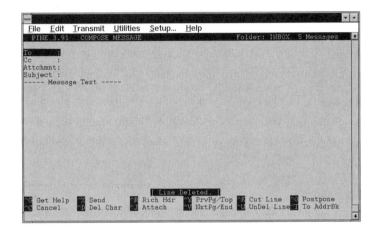

Figure 12.2

The PINE message compose form.

This form looks a bit like an office memo form, with blanks for essential information like To and Subject. To send a message, you must fill in (type in) several of these blanks. To move among the blanks, you press the arrow keys, Tab, or Enter. The most essential blanks to fill in are the following:

- In the blank after the To field, you enter the Internet e-mail addresses of the people to whom you want to send the message. You can type multiple addresses in this field by separating them with commas.

- In the blank after the Cc (carbon copy) field, you enter additional e-mail addresses of people to whom you want to send copies of the message. The Cc field actually works just like the To field—everyone entered in either field receives a copy of the message. However, you usually use the To field to indicate the people to whom you are sending the message directly, and you use the Cc field when you are just informing someone else about some correspondence.

- In the Subject field, you enter a line of text to describe the subject of your message. When the recipient receives your message, the Subject field is often all that he or she will see, so entering something short

180

and descriptive is helpful. (Message is probably a bad entry for the Subject field, but Question about Assignment #2 is better.)

- You can safely ignore the Attchmnt field in this case. This field enables you to send data files other than straight text in your mail message—files that might contain graphics, software programs, or documents created with a word processor like WordPerfect.

- Finally, everything under the Message Text line is the actual body of the message you are sending.

Fortunately, PINE makes it easy for you to figure out what to do next. The bottom two rows of the screen display a menu of the various actions you can take while composing the message. First, you need to understand some of the menu's notations. In PINE menus, the caret (^) indicates a key combination that includes the Ctrl key. For example, the notation ^C means that you are to hold down Ctrl while pressing C. You can use several such key combinations while editing your mail message:

Key Combination	Effect
^Y	Moves the cursor up a screen of text
^V	Moves the cursor down a screen of text
^K	Deletes (cuts) the line of text that you are currently editing
^U	Undeletes (pastes) the line of text that you previously cut by pressing ^K
^T	Runs the PINE spelling checker on the message that you are composing

The other commands at the bottom of the screen are actions you can take with your message. The most important are the following:

Key Combination	Effect
^C	Cancels the message on which you are working
^G	Brings up the PINE Help system
^O	Postpones the current message so that you can return to it later (you learn more about this command shortly)
^X	Sends the message

For some of these commands—particularly those that take actions you cannot undo or revoke, such as Cancel (^C) and Send (^X)—PINE asks you to confirm whether you really want to take the action.

Now send a sample message to yourself by following these steps:

1. Invoke PINE (usually by entering **pine** at the UNIX prompt).

2. From the PINE menu, type **c** to compose a message.

   You should see the PINE message compose form shown previously in figure 12.2. You need to fill in this form, particularly the critical elements: the To and Subject fields and the message text. Your cursor should be next to the To field.

3. Enter your own e-mail address in the To field. (For example, my address is `mckimg@indiana.edu`, so I would type that in the field.)

4. Press the down-arrow key to move the cursor down to the Subject field.

5. In the Subject field, enter **Test message to myself!**

6. Press the down-arrow key again to move the cursor down so that you are editing the message text.

7. Type a sample message to yourself.

   While you are composing a message, you can use all the arrow keys to move the cursor around to edit. You can also insert text simply by using the arrow keys to move the cursor to wherever you want to insert the text, and then begin typing. When you reach the end of a line of text, PINE automatically wraps the last word to the next line; you don't have to press Enter at the end of each line of text.

   Now, for practice, try to postpone the message that you are currently entering.

8. Press ^O to postpone the message.

   PINE displays a message telling you that your message is postponed, and then returns you to PINE's main menu. Although the message on which you were working seems to be gone, it really has been saved for you to continue editing it. In the meantime, you can do other tasks, such as reading and sending other messages, or even quitting PINE and then returning to the program. This feature is quite useful if you are working on a long message and want to stop to do other things.

Now continue editing your message.

9. From the PINE main menu, type **c** to compose.

This time, instead of going right into the message compose form, PINE presents the following question:

```
Continue postponed composition (answering "No" won't erase
it)? (y/n/^C) [y]:
```

If you type **n**, you go to the normal message compose form and can begin a new message. However, for this exercise, you want to continue the postponed composition.

10. Type **y** to continue the postponed message.

PINE returns you to where you were before you postponed the message. You can continue to edit the message for as long as you want. Now type a couple of sentences of text. After typing your message, you want to check its spelling. The ^T command invokes the spelling checker.

11. Press ^T to invoke the PINE spelling checker.

PINE pauses in front of each word that it detects as misspelled, according to its internal dictionary. You are prompted to correct each paused word. (Unfortunately, PINE doesn't suggest a correct spelling; it just tells you whether it thinks the word is misspelled.) You can choose whether to correct the word and then press Enter to continue. When the spelling checker finishes, PINE displays the message Done checking spelling.

Note that PINE's dictionary is limited. It occasionally flags a word as misspelled even if the word is spelled correctly, such as an acronym, a proper name, or jargon.

After checking the message's spelling (and correcting any discovered errors), you want to send the message.

12. When you are finished checking spelling, press ^X to send the message.

PINE asks whether you really want to send the message. If you type **n**, you can continue editing the message.

13. Type **y** to send the message.

You return to the PINE main menu, and your message is on its way. In a few minutes, you should receive a message at the bottom of the screen, indicating that you have new mail.

> **TIP** *In PINE, you can almost always press ^C to cancel whatever action you are performing or command you are executing.*

Reading Mail with PINE

To read mail in PINE, you use the mail index, which you can obtain by selecting FOLDER INDEX (or typing **i**) from the PINE main menu. The mail index is a list of mail messages you have received, including those you have already read (and not filed away) and those you haven't read.

Figure 12.3 shows a mail index. In this example, the index has five messages available to read (that is, five messages are in the user's mail "inbox").

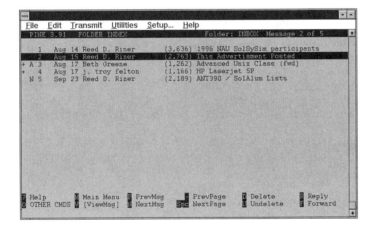

Figure 12.3
A mail index.

The mail index provides several pieces of information about each message. From left to right, the information includes the following:

- The plus sign (+) indicates that the message was sent directly to the recipient—that the message's sender entered the recipient's name in the To field rather than the Cc field.

- An N in front of one of the messages indicates that the message is "new"—that the recipient has not yet read the message. After the recipient reads the message, the N goes away.

- The number (in this case, from 1 to 5) indicates the sequence in which the inbox received each message. The first message received is numbered as 1.

- Next is the date the message was sent.

- Following the date is the name or e-mail address of either the sender or the recipient (depending on the way the message was sent).

- The number in parentheses is the size of the message, in characters.

- The text at the end of the line is the subject of the message, as the sender typed it in the Subject field when sending the message. Because this text is what the recipient sees, be sure to make your Subject field entry useful when you send messages.

Once again, the two lines of text at the bottom of the screen indicate the commands that are available. One other piece of information on the screen is important. Note the phrase Folder: INBOX at the top of the screen. This phrase indicates that you are actually reading mail in your mail inbox. However, there are other collections of mail, called *folders*, from which you can read mail. An upcoming section, "Filing Messages with Folders in PINE," discusses folders in more detail. Finally, from this screen, you can use the arrow keys to move the cursor from message to message.

Follow these steps to read your mail in PINE:

1. From the PINE main menu, type **i** to go to the mail index.

2. Using the arrow keys, move the cursor so that it is on the new message. (Because you just sent a message to yourself, that new message should be waiting for you.)

3. Press Enter to read the message.

   You can now browse the current message by using the up-arrow key or hyphen key (-) to move the screen up, and the down-arrow key or spacebar to move the screen down. When you finish reading the message, you can return to the index by typing **i** again.

4. Type **i** to return to the index.

Note that the N is now gone, because you have read the message. You can go on to read other messages, or you can type **m** to return to the PINE main menu. After you read a message, you can take several other actions: you can reply to the message, forward it to someone else, delete it, or save it to a mail folder.

You don't have to save your messages explicitly, however; if you don't delete your messages, they remain in your inbox.

Replying to a Mail Message

After reading a message, you often want to reply to it, sending a message back to the person who sent you the message. Of course, you can always just compose a new message. However, PINE provides a shortcut that saves you from having to type the address of the recipient of your reply. PINE even gives you the option of including in your reply the text of the message to which you are replying.

Use the following shortcut to reply to the message that you have already sent to yourself:

1. From the PINE main menu, type **i** to go to the PINE index.

2. Move the cursor to the message you sent yourself earlier.

3. Press Enter to read the message.

4. Type **r** to reply to the message. (The menu at the bottom of the screen gives you this option, in case you forget the command.)

   PINE asks whether you want to include the original message in your reply. Including at least part of the text of the original message is useful, so that your message's recipient has an idea of the context of your reply. By answering yes in response to this question, you tell PINE to insert the text of the original message into your reply.

5. Type **y** to include the original message.

   You can probably see that you are back in the message compose form. However, there are a couple of key differences: the recipient of the message (the blank next to To) is filled in with the e-mail address of the person to whom you are replying; the Subject field is filled in with the subject of the message to which you are replying (with the prefix Re, meaning *regarding*, inserted before the subject); and the text of the original message is inserted into the message body with the greater-than character (>) at the beginning of each line. The > character is a fairly standard Internet convention for indicating text that is being quoted or included from another document, instead of being composed in the current message.

In this form, you can continue to edit the reply—you can cut existing text by using the ^K command to delete text line by line. Quite often, when you include the text of the original message, you must cut some of the text to avoid sending a message that is too long and confusing. Figuring out how much original message text to include and how much to delete often requires a delicate balance.

6. When you finish editing your reply message, press ^X to send the message, and type **y** when PINE asks you to confirm that you really want to send it.

> **NOTE** *Before you send a reply to a message, always check the To and Cc fields to see who the actual recipients of your reply are. When working with messages received from a LISTSERV or e-mail distribution list, you can easily reply to the whole distribution list, instead of replying only to the person who should get the reply. This accident can be very embarrassing, so check these fields before you send your message!*

Deleting Messages in PINE

You don't always want to keep every message you receive, so you may need to delete PINE messages. To delete a message in PINE, you must be reading the message or at least be in the message index. Follow these steps to delete a message:

1. Go to the message index by typing **i** from the PINE main menu.

2. Move the cursor to a message you want to delete (perhaps to one of the messages you just sent yourself).

3. Type **d** to delete the message, as indicated by the menu at the bottom of the screen.

   The letter D now appears to the left of the message, indicating that you have marked the message for deletion. PINE hasn't actually deleted the message, however. In fact, PINE doesn't delete the message until you quit the program. Until then, you can undelete the message by moving the cursor to the message and typing **u**. In that case, the D next to the message disappears.

4. With at least one message marked for deletion, type **q** to quit PINE.

   PINE asks whether you really want to quit.

5. Type **y** to confirm that you want to exit PINE.

   PINE now asks whether you want to expunge the one deleted message from the inbox. *Expunge* is the rather odd word that PINE uses to denote the actual deletion of the messages marked for deletion. If you confirm that you want to expunge the deleted messages, PINE deletes them. If you don't, the messages remain marked for deletion and are still in the inbox (although still marked for deletion) the next time you go into PINE.

6. Type **y** to expunge the deleted message from your PINE inbox.

   You are now out of PINE.

Filing Messages with Folders in PINE

If you receive only a few messages, you may decide to leave all of them in your inbox. However, your e-mail can be a valuable resource for your research. For this reason, as you start accumulating e-mail, you will want to file away your messages so that you can retrieve them later.

PINE provides a facility for filing away your e-mail in different collections, called folders. You can use the folders however you want; you can create an unlimited number of folders, and you can give the folders any names you like.

To see how to use this feature, create a folder in which to file one of the sample messages you sent yourself:

1. Go into PINE (enter **pine** at the UNIX prompt if you aren't already in PINE).

2. From the main menu, type **i** to go into the PINE index.

3. Move the cursor to the sample message you sent yourself, and press Enter to read the message.

4. To file this message in a folder, save it by typing **s**.

   PINE now asks in which folder you want to save this message. Depending on how PINE is configured, it might even suggest a default folder name. If you want to accept the default folder name that PINE gives you, just press Enter. Otherwise, type a folder name and press Enter. If the folder doesn't already exist, PINE prompts you to create the folder.

5. To save your message to a folder called learning-pine, type **learning-pine** and press Enter.

   This folder doesn't exist, so PINE asks whether you want to create the folder.

6. Type **y** to create the folder.

   PINE creates the folder named learning-pine, saves a copy of the current message in the folder, and marks the copy in your inbox as deleted. Of course, PINE doesn't actually delete the copy until you quit the program and expunge the message.

Working with messages in other folders is quite simple. Working with other folders is just like working with the inbox, which, as you might have already guessed, is really just another folder.

To work with the messages in the learning-pine folder, follow these steps:

1. From either the PINE main menu or the folder index, type **l** to go to the list of folders that are available.

   Figure 12.4 shows the folder-selection screen. In this case, the screen shows 11 folders available. (Your screen will show a different number of folders, of course.) From this screen, you can move the cursor to any of these folders and look through it by pressing Enter. The menu at the bottom of the screen also provides some other options, including the capability to create (add), delete, and rename folders.

Figure 12.4
PINE's folder-selection screen.

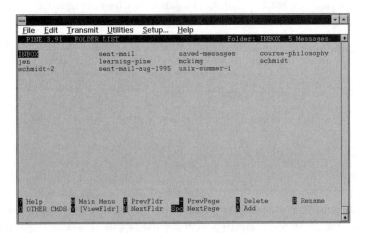

2. Move the cursor to the learning-pine folder and press Enter.

   You are now in what looks like the folder index. In fact, it *is* a folder index—an index of the learning-pine folder rather than the inbox. The folder indicator at the top of the screen now shows that you are viewing the learning-pine folder (it reads `Folder: learning-pine` instead of `Folder: INBOX`). You can browse, read, delete, and reply to any messages in the learning-pine folder, just as you could when you were in the inbox folder index.

3. To return to the inbox, type **I** again to go to the folder-selection screen.

4. Move the cursor to `INBOX` and press Enter.

   You are now back in the index of the inbox.

The more messages you save, the more important it is to put some thought into how you create your folders, and to devise a good classification scheme for your messages. As you have already discovered by examining the different search engines, classification of information resources is a fundamental aspect of information management and retrieval. You should consider your own e-mail messages valuable information resources worthy of thought and consideration. You may be glad that you saved them, especially when the time comes to write your papers.

> **TIP** *PINE automatically provides a folder, called sent-mail, that contains a copy of each mail message you have sent. Because sent-mail works like any other folder, you can browse, read, print, and even reply to these copies of messages already sent.*

Tips on Filing Messages

Here are some tips on filing your messages:

- Think of the context in which you will want to retrieve the message later. Will you want to retrieve it by sender or topic? Create your folders appropriately. For example, if you think that you will want to retrieve a message using the sender's name, you might want to save the message, along with other messages by that sender, in a folder named for the sender.

- Avoid generic folder names like saved-messages, listserv, and messages.

- Avoid using abbreviations that you are unlikely to remember later.

- Use folder names that are long enough to have some meaning to you later. Although you cannot use spaces in the names of folders, you can use underscores (_) and hyphens (-). Therefore, you can create folders with such names as microbiology-class or about-internet.

- Use enough folders so that each one is distinguished by content and no folder contains an unmanageable number of messages.

- PINE enables you to have folders within folders. However, setting up folders within folders is extremely cumbersome. If you want to file by category and subcategory, use both the category name and the subcategory name in the folder name, separated with a hyphen. For example, you might file your messages about different Internet tools by tool name, as in internettools-telnet, internettools-gopher, and internettools-web. I file messages about the UNIX courses that I teach by semester, as in beginningunix-spring95, beginningunix-fall95, and advancedunix-summer95. By using such a folder-naming system, you can have more control over exactly how you categorize your messages.

- When PINE asks which folder you want to file your message in (after you type **s** from the message index menu), you don't actually have to type the name of the folder in which you want to save the message. Instead, you can use the ^T command (labeled as ^T To Folders in the menu at the bottom of the screen) to bring up a list of folders you have created, and then choose a folder in which to file your message.

Address Books in PINE

Internet e-mail addresses of people can be difficult to remember, particularly if the address isn't the person's name. For example, the e-mail address of an old colleague of mine is **bill02@zombie.uc.edu**. PINE, however, provides a feature for keeping track of your e-mail addresses: the address book.

The address book enables you to collect e-mail addresses so that you can paste them into messages. This feature enables you also to create *aliases* for e-mail addresses, so that you merely have to type the alias for an e-mail address, rather than the e-mail address itself, in the message compose form. For example, I have **bill** set as an alias in my address book for **bill02@zombie.uc.edu**, so I just need to type **bill** in the To field. PINE then automatically substitutes **bill02@zombie.uc.edu** before my eyes.

JARGON ALERT!

An alias is something that stands for something else. In the context of e-mail, an alias is a short name that you can create to avoid having to remember a long e-mail address. Once you have created the alias, you can use it in place of the actual e-mail address in e-mail messages.

Try putting your own address in your PINE address book, and then use that address in a new message. Follow these steps:

1. Go into PINE.

2. From the main menu, type **a** to go into the address book (or select A - ADDRESS BOOK from the main menu).

   Once again, the menu at the bottom of the screen indicates what you can do.

3. To add a new address to the address book, type **a**.

   PINE asks for the full name (in the form *Last, First*) of the person whose e-mail address you are adding. You are adding yourself, so use your own name.

4. Type your name and press Enter.

   PINE now asks for a nickname for this address. This is the alias referred to earlier. You can type the alias instead of the e-mail address when you are composing a message. In this example, you are adding yourself, so use *me* as an alias.

5. Type **me** and press Enter.

   PINE next prompts you for the e-mail address itself.

6. Type your e-mail address and press Enter.

   Your address has now been added to the address book. Figure 12.5 shows your address book as it exists now (although your name and e-mail address will be different, of course).

   The menu at the bottom of the screen in figure 12.5 enables you to edit, delete, or add new addresses to your address book. The CreateList (S) option might be particularly useful to you as you become a PINE user. With this option, you can create distribution lists of addresses and add them to your address book. Then, if you enter the alias of the distribution list when you compose a new message, PINE automatically sends the message to everyone on the list.

Figure 12.5

A sample address book.

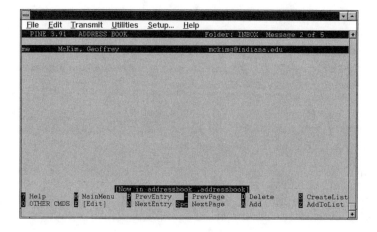

7. Type **m** to return to the main menu.

    Now you want to compose a new message to yourself.

8. Type **c** to go into the message compose form.

9. This time, instead of entering your own e-mail address in the To field, type **me** and press Enter.

    Before your eyes, the me that you typed disappears and is replaced with your e-mail address, as you entered it in the address book. However, suppose that you forgot your alias and want to refer to your address book. You can use the address book to look up your address again and put it in the carbon copy (Cc) field.

10. Make sure that the cursor is on the Cc blank. Press ^T (or select ^T To AddrBk from the menu at the bottom of the screen) to go to your address book.

    You now see your address book again.

11. To choose the address to which you want to send your message, move the cursor to the appropriate address and press Enter.

    PINE automatically pastes in the Cc field the address you just chose. You can do this for as many addresses as you want. Now you can go on to finish your message.

E-Mail Etiquette

Although e-mail has been around for many years, it is still a relatively new medium for most people. For this reason, many people are unsure of how to behave while using e-mail. It is much easier to offend people through e-mail than through other media. For example, recipients are unaware of nonverbal cues and the context in which the sender wrote the message. In addition, it's easier to be nasty when you are typing messages to an anonymous screen than when you are talking face-to-face with a person.

This section provides tips for proper e-mail behavior and etiquette. These tips can help you avoid offending those to whom you send e-mail, and help you avoid getting offended or hurt yourself. The tips are actually a subset of many explicit and implicit social norms that have developed regarding interaction on the Internet. These norms generally go by the clever name of "netiquette." Several collections of netiquette tips are available on the Internet in different forms. Here are some examples:

- Don't write messages using only capital letters. PEOPLE WILL THINK THAT YOU ARE SHOUTING!

- Don't send anything by e-mail that you would not be willing to say to someone's face.

- Before responding to a message in anger, wait for 24 hours. By then, you probably won't want to send it, and you will be glad that you waited.

- Send messages to the fewest recipients necessary. In other words, don't send to a group of people (or to a distribution list) a message that is appropriate for an individual.

- Don't be upset if you don't get an instant reply to a message. Many people check their e-mail messages only sporadically and might not receive your message right away. Other people receive hundreds of messages a day (I generally receive almost 400 messages per day) and might not have time to respond right away. Be patient.

- Do not berate others in public. Publicly criticizing others (often for their violation of these norms of netiquette) is known as *flaming* on the Internet. Flaming occurs with disturbing frequency, with unfortunate consequences for public discourse. Don't be part of this problem.

- Use sarcasm with extreme caution. People often depend on nonverbal cues—such as facial expressions and voice inflections—to detect sarcasm or understand its context. An e-mail message that exhibits sarcasm, but is devoid of these nonverbal cues, might sound either nasty or stupid.

- Reread your messages before you send them. The quickness with which you can send e-mail messages makes it very easy to send ones you haven't proofread. Such messages might contain major errors or even be incomprehensible.

In this chapter, you learned the basics of using electronic mail on the Internet, and particularly how to use the PINE electronic mail program. You should now be able to read, send, reply to, and file messages on PINE. You were also introduced to e-mail etiquette, a necessary component to coexisting with potentially millions of other users on the Internet. In the next chapter, you learn to find the addresses of students and instructors at universities and colleges all over the world.

13

Locating People

Objectives

After reading this chapter, you will be able to

- Find e-mail addresses and other directory information about faculty, staff, and students at academic institutions

- Use the Notre Dame list of directories of academic institutions

Now that you have learned how to send electronic mail by using PINE, it's time to move on to the next logical step: finding the e-mail addresses of people to whom you want to send mail. This chapter explains how to find the e-mail addresses of people on the Internet.

Unfortunately, no single, unified Internet address directory exists, so finding a person's e-mail address on the Internet can often be as much of an art as finding useful documents on a particular subject. However, because you are primarily searching for information to help you conduct research and write papers, this chapter's discussion focuses primarily on finding e-mail addresses of people at universities and colleges—a much easier task.

The Basic Strategy

The basic strategy for finding the e-mail address of someone at a particular academic institution is simple. Consider how you would find the telephone number of someone in Tucson, Arizona, for example. You would probably go to the library, find a telephone directory for Tucson, and look up the person's name in that directory. A strategy for finding a person's e-mail address at a particular institution is similar. Most educational institutions that are on the Internet maintain an e-mail address directory of their own faculty, students, and staff. To find someone at that institution, you just need to search the directory for that institution.

Of course, you may have some complications. First, you have to know where to find the e-mail address directory for a particular institution. Second, you have to use multiple technologies to make those directories available (nothing is ever simple, is it?).

Only two years ago, you had to use the UNIX whois command, for accessing address directories located on whois servers. In addition, you had to use the appropriate tools to search CSO phone directories for institutions that use CSO servers to maintain their directories.

Things are a bit easier today, however. Several institutions have brought together collections of different e-mail address directories from hundreds of academic (and some commercial and research) institutions. These institutions make their collections accessible through a simple set of Gopher menus or World Wide Web links. These collections of e-mail address directories also hide the gory details of whois servers, whois+ servers (yet another technology), CSO servers, and so on. In short, these collections give you a simple way to search for addresses without knowing the technical details. This is the way that searching directories *should* work, and fortunately (unless you want to spend your life learning the technology necessary to doing your work), this is the way that directory searching does work.

The best collection of academic institution directories is probably the one made available through Gopher at Notre Dame. As is often true on the Internet, Notre Dame doesn't actually maintain or control these directories itself. The university simply provides a collected list of links to the appropriate directories so that you can access them from one place and one common interface.

You can get to the Notre Dame list of directories in several ways:

- The URL for the list is

    ```
    gopher://gopher.nd.edu/11
    /Non-Notre%20Dame%20Information%20Sources
    /Phone%20Books--Other%20Institutions
    ```

    You can go to this location directly from your Web client.

- You can simply connect to the main Notre Dame Gopher by using your Web client to connect to `gopher://gopher.nd.edu`. From there, you can choose the menu item Non Notre Dame Information Sources, and from the submenu that appears, you can choose the item Phone Books at Other Institutions.

- You can use your Web browser to connect to the People and Places page, a useful page put up by Netscape Corporation to provide some links to various sources that can help you find addresses. The location of this page is

    ```
    http://home.netscape.com/home/internet-white-pages.html
    ```

    You can reach the Notre Dame list of directories by following the Notre Dame link from this page. Toward the end of this chapter, you'll learn about some other resources available from this page.

Now use the directories available from this list to find two different people at two different institutions. The first is myself, Geoffrey McKim. You can find my e-mail address and directory information from the Indiana University directory. The second is Bill Clinton, for whom you will search in the University of Illinois directory. For this example, you access the Notre Dame list by using the last of the three methods just described. Of course, you can also use one of the other methods, and if you have Gopher access only, you will want to use one of the other methods.

To find these two people, follow these steps:

1. With your Web browser, go to the Netscape Corporation People and Places page, available at location `http://home.netscape.com/home/internet-white-pages.html`. Figure 13.1 shows the Netscape Corporation's People and Places page.

Figure 13.1

The Netscape
Corporation's
People and Places
page.

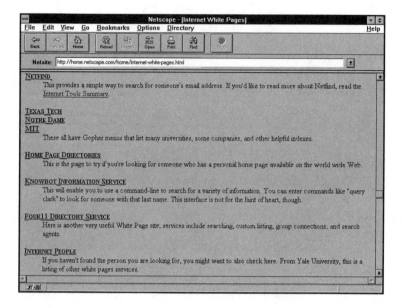

TIP *If you are using the Netscape browser, you can use a shortcut to the People and Places page. Just select the item Internet White Pages from the Directory menu.*

2. You want to access the Notre Dame list of directories, so follow the link NOTRE DAME.

Figure 13.2 shows the Notre Dame list of directories. As you can see, the directories are basically organized by continent or region.

NOTE *At the end of the list are a couple of other groupings: International Organizations and X.500 Gateway (experimental). International Organizations is exactly what it sounds like—a link to directories of major organizations that aren't necessarily connected to any particular continent or region. The other option is a little more complex. X.500 is the name of an international standard created in an attempt to unify these sorts of directories of information that are scattered throughout the Internet.*

X.500 has long held much promise for mmaking this kind of searching easier. Furthermore, the standard is independent of whatever particular technology an institution uses to maintain its own directory. However, X.500 still has many problems and is restricted primarily to experimental use. In general, unless you are very interested in exploring, you should stick with the standard list of directories organized by region.

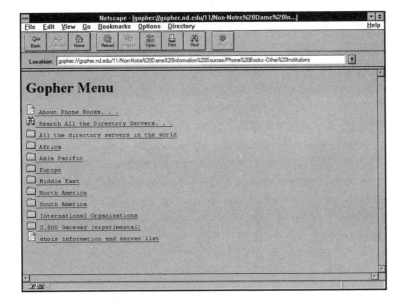

Figure 13.2

The Notre Dame list of directories.

3. Because both of the institutions (Indiana University and University of Illinois) for which you are searching directories are in North America, follow the link North America.

Figure 13.3 shows the beginning of a long list of academic and research institutions in North America. These organizations are listed alphabetically. You can scroll down the list to find the institution you are looking for. For this example, go down to the Indiana University directory.

4. After scrolling to the Indiana University directory, follow that link.

You are prompted to enter your search term, as shown in figure 13.4. At this prompt, you enter the name you want to search for, or at least as much as you know of the name.

Note that the technology used to maintain the directory at Indiana University is whois (the search screen itself says so). However, you don't actually need to know this, because you have the nice Gopher interface to help you search.

Because you want to search for my name in this directory, use *mckim* as a search term.

Figure 13.3
The Notre Dame list of North American academic and research institutions.

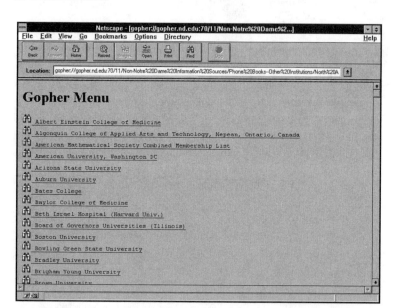

Figure 13.4
The Notre Dame prompt to enter a search term.

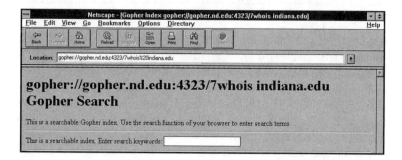

5. Type **mckim** and press Enter to search the Indiana University directory.

Figure 13.5 shows the rather cryptic result of this search: one Gopher text document labeled `Raw search results`. This result is correct, however. You simply need to read this text document to see the results of your search of the directory.

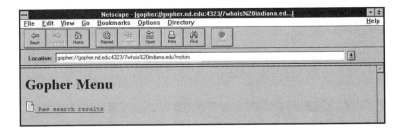

Figure 13.5
The Gopher text document that provides the results of your search.

6. Follow the link `Raw search results`.

Figure 13.6 shows the results of the search. In this example, you see my directory entry in the Indiana University directory. The directory entry shows a bit more than just my e-mail address (although it does indeed show that address—`mckimg@indiana.edu`). The entry shows also the department I work in, my campus address, and the location of my personal home page.

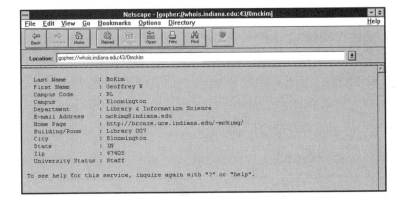

Figure 13.6
The results of your search.

Not all institutional directories present the same types of information, however. To see what another directory entry looks like, continue this exercise by searching for an address at the University of Illinois at Urbana/Champaign.

7. Go back two levels to return to the long list of academic institutions in North America.

8. Scroll down until you find the University of Illinois at Urbana/Champaign directory. Note that these directories are alphabetized strictly by the full name of the university. Thus, the University of Illinois is listed under the letter *U*, not *I*.

9. Follow the link to the University of Illinois at Urbana/Champaign directory.

Figure 13.7 shows the search screen for the University of Illinois directory.

Figure 13.7

Gopher-based interface to the University of Illinois directory.

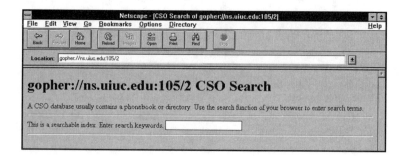

Note that this time the directory uses CSO technology, unlike that used at Indiana University. (In fact, CSO was developed by and named for the University of Illinois Computing Services Organization.) However, you still access the directory in the same way—you enter the search term for which you want to search, or as much of it as you know.

10. Now type the name of someone you would like to search for at the University of Illinois. As an example, you can try searching for Bill Clinton. Just type **bill clinton** and press Enter.

Searching in these directories is not case sensitive; nor does it matter in which order the words in your query appear. The directory will return entries at the University of Illinois that have both the word *bill* and the word *clinton* in them. If you searched for **clinton** only, you would retrieve all records that contained the word *clinton*.

> **NOTE** *A nickname database works behind the scenes with this directory and many others. For example, even though Bill Clinton's real name is William Clinton, a query for* **bill clinton** *would still retrieve his directory entry, if he were at the University of Illinois.*

Directory entries at the University of Illinois provide the name, department, title, campus address, e-mail address (when it exists), and campus phone number.

> **NOTE** *Each institution provides different pieces of information in its phone directory. For example, some directories now provide URLs for personal home pages, or even pictures of the people in the directory. In addition, many institutions now have more sophisticated directories that can be accessed only through the Web. Each directory usually has a unique interface and often provides many more searching options than the simple Gopher-based interface you have looked at. You can find these directories by looking at the home page for the institution. For example, Indiana University has a nice Web-based directory of all students, faculty, and staff available from its home page (located at* `http://www.indiana.edu`*).*

As long as you are looking for people at academic institutions, the searching doesn't get much more difficult than in the preceding examples. Of course, not all academic institutions have electronic directories available on the Internet. For example, Northern Kentucky University, which has recently acquired an Internet connection and even a Web home page, does not yet provide an Internet-accessible directory of its faculty, students, and staff. Thus, looking up the addresses of people at such institutions is nearly impossible. In such cases, you are probably better off actually calling the institution's computing center and asking about the availability of e-mail addresses. In addition, there is always some lag time between the time that an institution puts up an electronic directory and the time the institution adds the directory to the Notre Dame list.

The NetFind Tool

Another tool, NetFind, is available from the Netscape Corporation's People and Places page (refer to figure 13.1). The NetFind tool is often written about, and in theory the idea behind the tool is excellent. However, because your results are modest compared to the effort you must expend, this chapter's coverage of NetFind is brief.

When you searched for people in academic institutions in the preceding examples, you first had to go to the institution's directory and then do a search of that directory. Obviously, it would be easier to enter just the name and the institution—and have the computer automatically find that institution, do the search, and return the results to you. This is the concept behind NetFind.

Instead of going to individual directories, you just enter the name of the person for whom you want to search, along with as many other cues about the person's location that you know (such as his or her institution, department, and type of organization). The NetFind server then uses these cues automatically to narrow your search, search the correct directories, and return the results to you.

NetFind is based on the "knowbot" concept, in which a computer program takes your query, automatically figures out for you what to search for and where to search, and returns the right results to you—while hiding the details of the technology from you. Unfortunately, NetFind isn't yet ready for "prime time." The databases tend to be outdated, you never seem to guess the right cues to search the right databases, and inevitably the key database server is down when you want to search it.

My experience in using and teaching NetFind is that it generates more frustration and error messages than it helps in locating addresses. Your experience may differ, however, and it is probably worth trying this tool at least once. The link to NetFind is available right from the Netscape Corporation's People and Places page.

Finding people on the Internet can be a bewildering experience. There simply isn't a comprehensive directory of people and their e-mail addresses. Each academic institution usually maintains its own unique interface. However, with a little patience, and with the aid of tools such as lists of university address books, you can frequently come up with exactly the name and address you are seeking. Now that you know how to communicate with individuals over the Internet, you learn to find groups of people—discussion lists, electronic conferences, and bulletin boards—on the Internet that share your interests.

14

Electronic Discussion Groups

Objectives

After reading this chapter, you will be able to

- Subscribe to, unsubscribe from, and participate in electronic discussion groups

- Use the Directory of Scholarly Electronic Conferences to find which electronic discussion group is appropriate for your area of study

- Understand the expanded Inter-Link list of all discussion groups, both academic and nonacademic

This chapter discusses an important but often overlooked source of information on the Internet: electronic discussion groups. These groups have many different names, such as electronic conferences, LISTSERVs, lists, and e-conferences. However, the basic principle behind e-mail-based electronic discussion groups is simple: People interested in a common subject or area of discussion form a distribution list of their e-mail addresses.

Members of the distribution list can send a message and have it automatically distributed to the whole list. Usually, although not always, administrative functions such as *subscription* (signing up for the list) and *unsubscription* (removing your name from the list) tend to be automated. Such functions are handled by sending commands through e-mail to the distribution list software.

JARGON ALERT!

When you subscribe to a discussion group, you sign yourself up for an electronic mailing list. If mail is sent to the list, you will receive a copy of the message as e-mail if you are subscribed. Many lists require you to be subscribed before you can post to the list.

When you unsubscribe to a discussion group, you take yourself off an electronic mailing list. In this case, you no longer want to receive mail sent to the list.

E-mail has long been the lowest common denominator as far as network access goes. (Even if a user lacks Web access, the user can still have e-mail access.) For this reason, e-mail-based electronic discussion groups have been among the most popular and successful of all academically oriented Internet tools. Literally hundreds, if not thousands, of different e-mail-based discussion groups exist on almost every academic topic imaginable. (Finding such discussion groups is the topic of the last part of this chapter.) There are even more discussion groups that cover nonacademic topics. Professors, librarians, and students have made good use of such discussion groups for some time.

Introducing LISTSERV and Majordomo

Several systems are used for e-mail-based electronic discussion groups. The two most common are LISTSERV and Majordomo. Until recently, LISTSERV predominated; for this reason, all electronic discussion groups are often referred to generically as LISTSERVs. However, because the LISTSERV software is based on an older and fairly inefficient computer architecture, a new system, Majordomo, was developed to run on more modern equipment (UNIX computers). Majordomo's use has grown quite rapidly over the Internet, and the system is now widely used. Fortunately, both systems are similar, with only minor differences in commands, as this chapter shows.

Several other systems are also used for working with electronic discussion groups, including COMSERVE, LISTPROC, MAILBASE, and MAILSERV. All these systems work almost identically to LISTSERVs. Finally, another type of electronic discussion group, the Usenet newsgroup, works on a different principle and doesn't use e-mail for message distribution. Usenet newsgroups are a major Internet topic of their own and are discussed in more detail in Chapter 15.

Working with LISTSERVs

LISTSERVs are the oldest and most common e-mail-based electronic discussion groups. They are based on a network that predated the Internet, called BITNET, although they have adapted to the Internet quite well.

LISTSERV names have two parts, consisting of the name of the LISTSERV itself and the name of the computer that handles the LISTSERV. For example, URBAN-L is the name of a LISTSERV dealing with issues in urban planning. The full address of the LISTSERV is **URBAN-L@vm3090.ege.edu.tr**. Actually, this is the e-mail address that you use if you want to send a message to all subscribers of the LISTSERV. The address to which you send administrative messages—for subscriptions, unsubscriptions, and configuration changes—is **LISTSERV@vm3090.ege.edu.tr**. This pattern is typical. Postings to the LISTSERV itself are sent to the e-mail address *listservname@hostname*, where *listservname* is the name of the LISTSERV and *hostname* is the name of the computer on which the LISTSERV is located. However, you send commands to the address **LISTSERV@***hostname*, where *hostname* is also the name of the computer on which the LISTSERV is located.

The primary functions that you need to perform with a LISTSERV are to subscribe to a LISTSERV, to unsubscribe from a LISTSERV, and to send a message to the list. In addition, you need to know how to find more information about the LISTSERV software.

Subscribing to a LISTSERV

When you subscribe to a LISTSERV, you sign up for the discussion group's distribution list. To subscribe to a LISTSERV, follow these steps:

1. Compose a mail message to **LISTSERV@***hostname*, where *hostname* is the name of the computer on which the LISTSERV is located. It doesn't matter which mail program you use.

2. Leave the subject field of the mail message blank.

3. In the first line of the message's body, type

subscribe *listname firstname lastname*

where *listname* is the name of the LISTSERV (for example, URBAN-L), and *firstname* and *lastname* are your own first and last names.

4. Send the message.

Usually within a few minutes (but occasionally within a few hours), you receive a message from the LISTSERV software confirming that you are subscribing to the list. This message typically describes the list's purpose, tells you how to unsubscribe, and sometimes lists other commands that you can send to the LISTSERV.

Unsubscribing from a LISTSERV

When you unsubscribe from a LISTSERV, you remove yourself from the discussion group's distribution list. To unsubscribe from a LISTSERV, follow these steps:

1. Compose a mail message to **LISTSERV@*hostname***, where *hostname* is the name of the computer on which the LISTSERV is located.

2. Leave the subject line of the mail message blank.

3. In the first line of the body of the message, type

unsubscribe *listname*

where *listname* is the name of the LISTSERV (URBAN-L, for example).

4. Send the message.

Usually within a few minutes (but sometimes within a few hours), you receive a message from the LISTSERV software confirming that you have unsubscribed from the list.

Sending a Message to the List

To send a message to the list, follow these steps:

1. Compose a mail message to *listservname@hostname*, where *listservname* is the name of the LISTSERV and *hostname* is the name

of the computer on which the LISTSERV is located. The mail message should contain exactly what you want the members of the list to see.

2. Send the message.

Depending on whether the LISTSERV is moderated and how overloaded the computer running the LISTSERV is, your message might be distributed to list members in a few minutes or even in a couple of days (particularly if the LISTSERV is moderated and the moderator is absent for some reason). If you have subscribed to the LISTSERV, you receive a copy of the message that you sent to the list.

Getting Help with LISTSERV Commands

The LISTSERV software actually offers quite a few commands. If you want to find out more about the commands available, you can request a reference page from the LISTSERV. To request this page, follow these steps:

1. Compose a mail message to **LISTSERV@***hostname*, where *hostname* is the name of the computer on which the LISTSERV is located.

2. Leave the subject line of the mail message blank.

3. In the first line of the body of the message, type

    info refcard

4. Send the message.

Usually within a few minutes (but occasionally within a few hours), you receive a message from the LISTSERV with information about the LISTSERV commands available.

> **TIP** *Always send LISTSERV commands to the address LISTSERV@hostname, not to the LISTSERV itself. Otherwise, all subscribers to the list might receive copies of your commands meant for the LISTSERV software and will become annoyed with you.*

Electronic discussion groups based on COMSERVE, LISTPROC, MAILBASE, and MAILSERV software work identically to those based on LISTSERV software, except that the subscription and administrative command address begins with **COMSERVE**, **LISTPROC**, **MAILBASE**, and **MAILSERV**, respectively.

Working with Majordomo Lists

Majordomo lists are quite similar to LISTSERVs; only a few details in the commands vary. Like LISTSERVs, Majordomo lists also have two-part names, consisting of the name of the list and the name of the computer that handles the list. For example, the Indiana University School of Library and Information Science runs a Majordomo list, slis-l, for issues dealing with the school and the profession. The full address of the Majordomo list is **slis-l@indiana.edu**. Again, as with LISTSERVs, this is the e-mail address to which you send messages to all the list's subscribers. You send subscriptions, unsubscriptions, and other administrative messages to **majordomo@indiana.edu**. You send postings to the list to the e-mail address *listname@hostname*, where *listname* is the name of the Majordomo list and *hostname* is the name of the computer on which the Majordomo list is located. However, you send commands to the address **majordomo@*hostname***, where *hostname* is also the name of the computer on which the list is located.

Again, the primary functions that you will probably want to perform are to subscribe, unsubscribe, send a message to the list, and find out more about Majordomo commands.

Subscribing to a Majordomo List

To subscribe to a Majordomo list, follow these steps:

1. Compose a mail message to **majordomo@*hostname***, where *hostname* is the name of the computer on which the list is located. It doesn't matter which mail program you use.

2. Leave the subject line of the mail message blank.

3. In the first line of the body of the message, type

   subscribe *listname*

   where *listname* is the name of the Majordomo list (such as **slis-l**).

4. Send the message.

Usually within a few minutes, you will receive from the Majordomo software a message confirming that you have subscribed to the list. This message typically describes the list's purpose and tells you how to unsubscribe.

Note that the only difference between subscribing to a LISTSERV and subscribing to a Majordomo list (besides the addresses themselves) is that you don't have to send your name to a Majordomo list, as you must with a LISTSERV.

Unsubscribing from a Majordomo List

To unsubscribe from a Majordomo list, follow these steps:

1. Compose a mail message to **majordomo@*hostname***, where ***hostname*** is the name of the computer on which the Majordomo list is located.

2. Leave the subject line of the mail message blank.

3. In the first line of the body of the message, type

    unsubscribe *listname*

    where ***listname*** is the name of the Majordomo list (such as **slis-1**).

4. Send the message.

Usually within a few minutes, you will receive a message from the Majordomo software confirming that you are unsubscribed from the list.

Sending a Message to a Majordomo List

To send a message to a Majordomo list, follow these steps:

1. Compose a mail message to ***listname*@*hostname***, where ***listname*** is the name of the Majordomo list and ***hostname*** is the name of the computer on which the list is located. The mail message should contain exactly what you want the members of the list to see.

2. Send the message.

Depending on whether the list is moderated and how overloaded the computer running the list is, your message may be distributed to list members in a few minutes or even in a couple of days. If you are subscribed to the list, you receive a copy of the message that you sent to the list.

Getting Help with Majordomo Commands

Majordomo software doesn't have nearly as many commands available as the LISTSERV software does. However, to find out more about the commands that are available, follow these steps:

1. Compose a mail message to **majordomo@*hostname***, where ***hostname*** is the name of the computer on which the list is located.

2. Leave the subject line of the mail message blank.

3. In the first line of the body of the message, type

   help

4. Send the message.

Usually within a few minutes, you will receive a message from the list with information about the Majordomo commands available.

The following is a brief list of the most useful Majordomo commands:

subscribe <list>	Subscribes to the specified <list>.
unsubscribe <list>	Unsubscribes from the <list>.
who <list>	Finds out who is subscribed to the specified <list>.
info <list>	Retrieves general introductory information for the specified <list>. This information is provided by the maintainer of the list and may not exist for all lists.
help	Retrieves a list of Majordomo commands available to you.

> **TIP** *Always send Majordomo commands to the address* majordomo@hostname, *not to the list itself. Otherwise, all subscribers to the list might receive copies of your commands meant for the Majordomo software and will become annoyed with you.*

Locating the Right Discussion Group

As with most other Internet resources, the biggest problem in making effective use of discussion groups is knowing of their existence and location. Often you find out about a discussion group (a Majordomo list, a LISTSERV, or a similar discussion group) through word of mouth, through e-mail, or from colleagues, professors, and other students. However, an available tool, the Directory of Scholarly Electronic Conferences, can help you find appropriate discussion groups more systematically. Now in its ninth major revision, the Directory of

Scholarly Electronic Conferences is a old-timer on the Internet and is still one of the most useful directories available.

The following example accesses the Directory as a Gopher resource. It is available at the following location:

```
gopher://gopher.usask.ca/1/Computing/Internet Information
/Directory of Scholarly Electronic Conferences
```

> **NOTE** *You can also access the Directory as a Web resource at the following location:* `http://www.mid.net/KOVACS`. *The inter-face will look different, but the information is the same.*

Figure 14.1 gives you an idea of what the Directory looks like as a Gopher resource. The structure is quite simple, just a series of text lists of discussion groups, arranged by subject category. In addition, the Directory provides a way to search these lists of discussion groups (with the option Search Directory of Scholarly Electronic Conferences).

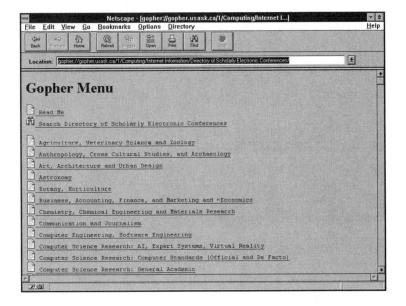

Figure 14.1

The Directory of Scholarly Electronic Conferences from Netscape.

Each of these lists provides certain information about the scholarly discussion groups, including descriptions and subscription information. You can explore the kinds of information the Directory provides by following these steps:

1. With your Web browser retrieve the Directory of Scholarly Electronic Conferences at the following location:

   ```
   gopher://gopher.usask.ca/1/Computing/Internet Information
   /Directory of Scholarly Electronic Conferences
   ```

2. To look at the list of electronic conferences in the areas of Anthropology, Cross Cultural Studies, and Archaeology, follow the link with that name.

   Figure 14.2 shows a small part of the resulting text, which is a list of scholarly conferences in those fields, arranged alphabetically by discussion group name.

Figure 14.2

Beginning of the list of discussion group names generated by the Directory of Scholarly Electronic Conferences.

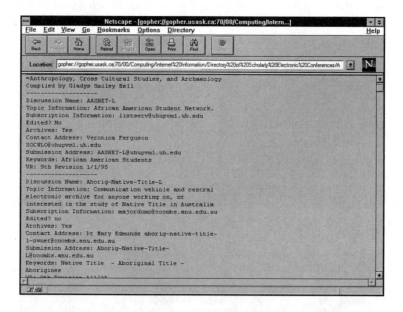

The following are some pieces of information provided about each discussion group:

Discussion Name	The discussion group's name.
Topic Information	A brief description of the group's purpose. The editors of the Directory usually indicate the appropriate audience.

Subscription Information	The address to which you send subscription and other administrative requests. This item usually indicates whether the list is a LISTSERV, a Majordomo discussion list, or another type of list.
Edited?	Whether the discussion group is edited or maintained by an editor.
Archives	Whether archives or back files of past discussions are available.
Contact Address	A contact address for the maintainer of the list.
Submission Address	The address to which you send messages that you want to distribute to the list. Make sure that you don't send any administrative requests (such as requests for subscription or unsubscription) to this address. Instead, you must send such requests to the address provided in the Subscription Information section.
Keywords	A list of keywords describing the purpose of the list. You can search through these keywords to retrieve discussion lists that match your search terms.
VR	In which revision of the Directory of Scholarly Electronic Conferences and on which date the discussion group was added.

3. Go back to the Directory's main screen (the previous screen) by pressing the left-arrow key (in Lynx) or clicking the left-arrow icon (in a graphical browser).

   You should again see the screen shown in figure 14.1.

If you want more information about the Directory, you can retrieve the Read Me document. It contains information about the Directory's scope, as well as additional instructions for subscribing to and unsubscribing from lists, and for obtaining any archived discussions of the available lists.

Now continue by searching for a list on a particular topic.

4. Follow the link `Search Directory of Scholarly Electronic Conferences`.

   Figure 14.3 shows the search page for the Directory of Scholarly Electronic Conferences. You can search for text by typing it in the box and pressing Enter.

Figure 14.3

The search page for Directory of Scholarly Electronic Conferences.

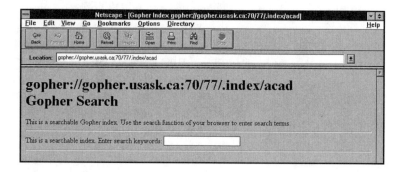

Now search for discussion groups on urban architecture.

5. Type **urban and architecture** (because you want to retrieve discussion groups whose descriptions or keywords contain both *urban* and *architecture*). Then press Enter.

   Gopher then searches through the information about each discussion group and returns only those discussion groups that match your query.

   Figure 14.4 shows the results of your query. The first line contains administrative information about the Directory (copyright, revision date, and so on). Each entry after that is a single discussion list that matches the query. In this case, only one list is displayed: the URBAN-L LISTSERV.

6. Retrieve additional information about the URBAN-L LISTSERV by following the link.

As you can see in figure 14.5, you now have all the information you need to subscribe to URBAN-L. You send subscription, unsubscription, and administrative requests to `listserv@vm3090.ege.edu.tr`. To send messages to the list itself, you use the address **URBAN-L@vm3090.ege.edu.tr**. You also get a couple of contact addresses in case you have any questions about the list.

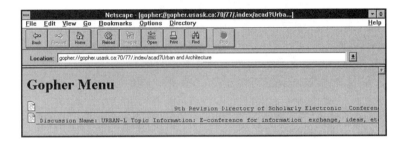

Figure 14.4
Results of the query urban and architecture.

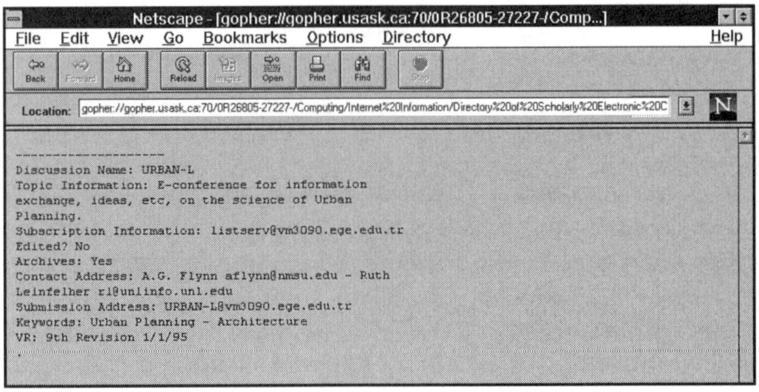

Figure 14.5
A sample discussion group entry from the Directory of Scholarly Electronic Conferences.

Now try another quick example that displays a different type of discussion list. This time, search for discussion groups that deal with classical music.

7. Go back two links to the Directory search page (refer to figure 14.3).

8. Type **classical and music** and press Enter.

   Figure 14.6 shows the results of this search. Now take a look at the last link on the page, `rec.music.classical`.

9. Follow the link `rec.music.classical`.

Figure 14.6

Results of the query classical and music.

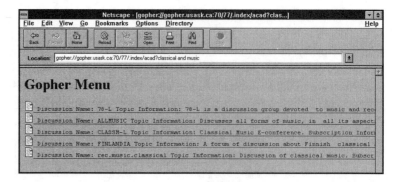

The name of this discussion group, `rec.music.classical`, looks a bit different from others you have seen in this Directory. This group is actually a Usenet newsgroup, a type of discussion group that doesn't use e-mail at all. You can always identify Usenet newsgroups because their names consist of a series of single words or prefixes separated by periods. Other examples are `sci.cryptography`, `comp.sys.apple.announce`, and `soc.culture.bosnia`. Chapter 15 discusses Usenet newsgroups in more detail.

Choosing an Appropriate Discussion Group

Electronic discussion lists vary widely in the quantity, quality, and level of discussion. Some discussion groups generate so many messages each day that it becomes impossible for most people to keep up with them. The excessive traffic of some discussion groups can become annoying, and often leads subscribers to unsubscribe. However, some discussion groups have so few postings that a critical mass of participation never develops to get any discussion off the ground. Finally, the level of discussion may vary widely as well. Some discussion groups are quite open to students and novices. Others offer discussions that are so technical that they are useless to most students.

You must judge for yourself whether a discussion group is appropriate for your needs. If you subscribe to a list and then find that the level of discussion is inappropriate for you or that you are overloaded with information, simply unsubscribe from the group.

Guidelines for Participating in Electronic Discussion Groups

This section offers some guidelines for participating in electronic discussion groups:

- Obey all the guidelines for using e-mail that were provided in Chapter 12.

- When you first subscribe to a new discussion group, you should wait a couple of weeks before posting anything to the group. You can then get a feel for what the group is like—the level of the participants, the topics they tend to discuss, and so on. This reading of a group without posting is called *lurking*.

- Don't ask discussion group members to do your homework for you. Don't post such messages as "I have to write a paper on classical music, and I was wondering if anyone has any ideas." Questions should be much more focused than this. Although experts are usually quite helpful to novices, they also expect novices to spend some time getting to know how the group works first.

- Sometimes a FAQ (frequently asked question) list is available for a discussion group. A discussion list might post the FAQ every couple of weeks; in other cases, you might have to find the FAQ through one of the Web or Gopher search engines. If a FAQ is available, read it before you participate in the group. FAQs address many of the beginner's concerns and are a good way to become oriented to the discussion list quickly. Not all groups have FAQs, though.

- Don't send administrative requests to the group.

- If you send to the group a message asking a question and you receive helpful replies through private e-mail, post to the group a summary of all replies. Then other members who might have the same question can benefit from the responses.

JARGON ALERT! *A FAQ is a list of frequently asked questions and answers to the questions for a particular discussion group or about a particular topic. FAQs are meant to eliminate the need for new members of a discussion group to ask the same questions of the older members.*

(continues)

(continued)

Lurking *in a discussion group means reading messages on the list without posting any of your own or without making your presence known in some other way. It is generally a good idea to lurk in a group for a few weeks before posting, in order to understand the social norms and terminology of the group.*

Another Source for Finding Discussion Groups: The Inter-Links/Dartmouth List

Another resource that can assist you in locating discussion groups is the Inter-Links directory of discussion groups. Actually based on a list of discussion groups maintained at Dartmouth University, the Inter-Links service provides a search engine for searching this list.

This list is much larger than the Directory of Scholarly Electronic Conferences because Inter-Links contains groups that cover nonacademic topics as well as those that cover academic topics. However, the information that the service provides about these lists is usually not as comprehensive or up-to-date as the Directory of Scholarly Electronic Conferences. Therefore, you should search the Directory of Scholarly Electronic Conferences if you want to find a group that covers academic topics, but search the Inter-Links directory if you want to find a nonacademic group.

Figure 14.7 shows the Inter-Links discussion group search page. You can access this page at the following address:

```
http://www.nova.edu/Inter-Links/cgi-bin/lists
```

From this page, you can enter your search terms and search for other discussion groups.

Terms and Abbreviations Used in Discussion Groups

An entire culture (sometimes multiple cultures) has developed around people who participate frequently in electronic discussion groups. This culture has its own social conventions, lexicon, and abbreviations. Many of these terms and abbreviations are bound to confuse new participants, so table 14.1 lists some common abbreviations, symbols, and terms specific to the electronic discussion group culture. These terms also apply to the Usenet newsgroups discussed in Chapter 15.

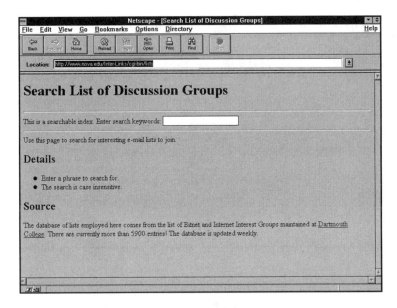

Figure 14.7

The Inter-Links discussion group search page.

Table 14.1 Common Terms and Abbreviations Used in Electronic Discussion Groups

Term or Abbreviation	Meaning
BTW	By the way.
FAQ	Frequently asked question, or a list of frequently asked questions. The term refers to a question whose answer is considered obvious or elementary (and is undoubtedly included in the FAQ list), or to the list of frequently asked questions associated with a particular discussion group.
flame	To denounce or berate someone publicly on the Internet. A *flame war* is a nasty and protracted volley of flames among participants in a discussion group.
IMHO	In my humble opinion. Participants usually use this abbreviation when pontificating on the Internet.
RTFM	Read the manual. This is a common response to a question whose answer is considered obvious to anyone who has read the documentation or FAQ for the discussion group.

(continues)

Table 14.1 Continued	
Term or Abbreviation	**Meaning**
Smiley	A keyboard symbol, also known as an *emoticon*, that Internet users use to indicate certain emotions. There are literally hundreds of potential smilies, but only the following three are used with any regularity and contribute to the meaning of a message:
	:-) A regular smiley, which the sender uses to convey warm feelings for the recipient (although it occasionally can convey gentle sarcasm).
	;-) A winking smiley, which usually indicates sarcasm.
	:-(A frown, which usually indicates unhappiness.

In this chapter, you learned how to make use of what many people consider the most exciting and powerful aspect of the Internet: the ability to bring together groups of people with interests in common from around the world. You learned how to work with these discussion groups and how to find such groups for any interest, academic or nonacademic. Participate in good cheer and always keep an open mind, and you will find many of these discussion groups highly interesting and useful to you. The next chapter introduces another type of Internet technology used to help people communicate about topics of interest: Usenet newsgroups.

15

Usenet Newsgroups: Electronic Bulletin Boards

Objectives

After reading this chapter, you will be able to

- Understand the structure of Usenet and the newsgroups that comprise it

- Use a Web browser to read Usenet newsgroups

- Obtain the list of frequently asked questions (FAQs) associated with a newsgroup

Although Usenet newsgroups can be very informative, extremely addicting, and lots of fun, they offer little that is academically useful, except in the fields of computing and technology. However, this assessment could very well change. As more people outside those fields start to use the Internet, the subjects of discussion are bound to broaden. Already, newsgroups for the social sciences and humanities are beginning to appear. This chapter presents the basics of how to read and use Usenet newsgroups.

The Structure of Usenet

Usenet is essentially an international network of electronic bulletin boards, categorized and organized by topic. Usenet actually predates the Internet, although most of the computers that provide Usenet services are now connected over the Internet. In a sense, Usenet is a giant, very complex, and geographically dispersed electronic bulletin board system.

In Usenet terminology, an individual electronic bulletin board is called a *newsgroup*, which is an electronic discussion group on a single topic. Users post messages to the newsgroup and read messages that other users post to the newsgroup. Literally thousands of newsgroups are available, with such cryptic names as `rec.music.classical`, `soc.culture.bosnia`, and `comp.infosystems.www.browsers.ms-windows`.

All newsgroups are categorized hierarchically by topic, in one giant hierarchical structure. Fortunately, each part of a newsgroup's name reflects the newsgroup's category. The newsgroup name begins with the broadest category, or *level*, on the left and proceeds to the narrowest category on the right.

Consider, for example, the newsgroup name `rec.music.classical`. `rec` indicates that the newsgroup is in a category dealing with recreational activities. This is the newsgroup's broadest category. `music` indicates that the newsgroup is in a subcategory of recreational activities dealing with musical activities, and thus narrows the newsgroup's scope. Finally, `classical` indicates that the newsgroup is in a subcategory of music, classical music.

Of course, a newsgroup's name isn't limited to three levels. For example, a newsgroup called `rec.musical.classical.recordings`, which is a subcategory of `rec.music.classical`, deals exclusively with discussions of classical music recordings. This subcategory does not contain discussions of other classical music subcategories like theory and performances.

There are scores of categories at the top level (the leftmost level reflected in the newsgroup name) and literally hundreds in the lower levels. Some of the categories in the top level include those listed in the following table.

Category	Focus of Topics
rec	Recreation
soc	Social sciences and culture
biz	Business
sci	Science and mathematics
comp	Computing-related issues
alt	Almost anything
humanities	The humanities (but not yet the arts, which are under **rec**)
bionet	Biology

To make things just a bit more complicated, these newsgroups evolve over time. New newsgroups are created almost every day to deal with new topics of interest. The newsgroups then divide to form new ones. In fact, newsgroups multiply and evolve much like life forms.

Some time ago, a newsgroup called **comp.infosystems** dealt with the technology of information systems on the Internet. Eventually, when it became apparent that this topic was too broad for effective discussion, the newsgroup split into many different newsgroups, each dealing with a different aspect of information systems on the Internet. For example, groups like **comp.infosystems.gopher** and **comp.infosystems.www** formed. In time, even these newsgroups became too unwieldy, especially as the Web became more popular. Currently, dozens of subgroups of **comp.infosystems.www** exist, including the following: **comp.infosystems.www.browsers.ms-windows**, **comp.infosystems.www.html-authoring**, and **comp.infosystems.www.browsers.mac**. The exact process by which this splitting occurs is an interesting example of distributed, Internet democracy in action—a topic beyond the scope of this book. Before creating a new newsgroup, the Internet community first undertakes a complicated procedure that involves discussion and voting.

Not all users at all places can access all categories. For example, in addition to the previously mentioned categories, which are all international, there are national categories (such as **us** and **fr**), statewide categories (such as **in** for Indiana and **or** for Oregon), institutional categories (such as **iu** for Indiana University), and even categories for smaller organizations. For example,

Indiana University has a newsgroup called **ucs.security** that covers computing security issues. However, this newsgroup is in the category **ucs** (University Computing Services), which is available only at Indiana University. Therefore, the newsgroups available to you at any given location will vary.

Accessing Usenet Newsgroups

To access and work with Usenet newsgroups, you need two things: a news server and a newsreader. A *news server* actually stores the information in the newsgroups and passes the information on to other news servers throughout the world. This news server is normally provided by your institution, university, or college. If you subscribe to a commercial Internet service, it probably provides a Usenet server. You need to know the Internet address of this server; you should be able to get this information from a computer lab attendant at your college or university, or from someone with your commercial Internet service.

You then need software that enables you to access the news server and the newsgroups themselves. This software is called a *newsreader*. As you might expect, you have choices of newsreaders available for each type of computer. For the Macintosh, newsreaders include Nuntius and NewsWatcher; for Windows, WinVN and Trumpet are available; and for UNIX, the most popular newsreaders are rn, trn, tin, and nn.

Different newsreaders have different sets of features, which can get quite complicated and sophisticated. However, all newsreaders enable you to do the following tasks:

- Connect to a Usenet server
- Subscribe to newsgroups (to *subscribe* to a newsgroup simply means to tell your newsreader that you want to monitor a certain newsgroup)
- Read messages posted by others on newsgroups
- Post messages to newsgroups

Everything else that a newsreader enables you to do is gravy (and many of these newsreaders really have quite a bit of gravy). However, if all you need are these core functions and you want to keep things as simple as possible, you can actually use several Web browsers as newsreaders. In particular, Netscape, Mosaic, and Lynx all function as newsreaders quite nicely. The examples in this chapter use Netscape to read Usenet newsgroups.

Using Netscape to Read Usenet News

Before you use Netscape to read Usenet news, you must set up Netscape so that it can communicate with your news server. To do so, you must know the address of your local news server. You can set up Netscape to read news by going into Preferences and filling in the news field with your news server's Internet address.

After setting up Netscape, you can begin reading news with Usenet. The following exercise takes you through the process of reading a Usenet posting. Remember that your own news server might carry different groups, so you might not see every group mentioned here. To read a Usenet posting, follow these steps:

1. Make sure that Netscape is open.

2. Choose Go to Newsgroups from the <u>D</u>irectory menu.

   Figure 15.1 shows an example of the resulting screen. This screen lists the newsgroups to which you subscribe. If you subscribe to a newsgroup, this just means that you have told Netscape that you would like to follow a particular newsgroup. Your list of subscribed newsgroups is simply a list of all the newsgroups you regularly read, displayed in one list. You can always subscribe and unsubscribe to newsgroups whenever you want.

   > **NOTE** *Your list of subscribed newsgroups may look considerably different from the one in figure 15.1. In fact, if your news server doesn't automatically subscribe you to any newsgroups, you may not even see a list of subscribed newsgroups at the beginning—instead, you will simply see the complete list of newsgroups available to you.*

3. Although you could type in the box (shown in figure 15.1) the name of the newsgroup you want to look at directly, go ahead and browse the complete list of newsgroups. To do this, scroll down to the bottom of the page and click the View all Newsgroups button.

   Figure 15.2 shows an example of the resulting complete list of newsgroups (arranged alphabetically) that are available to you. Again, your list may be quite different from the one displayed.

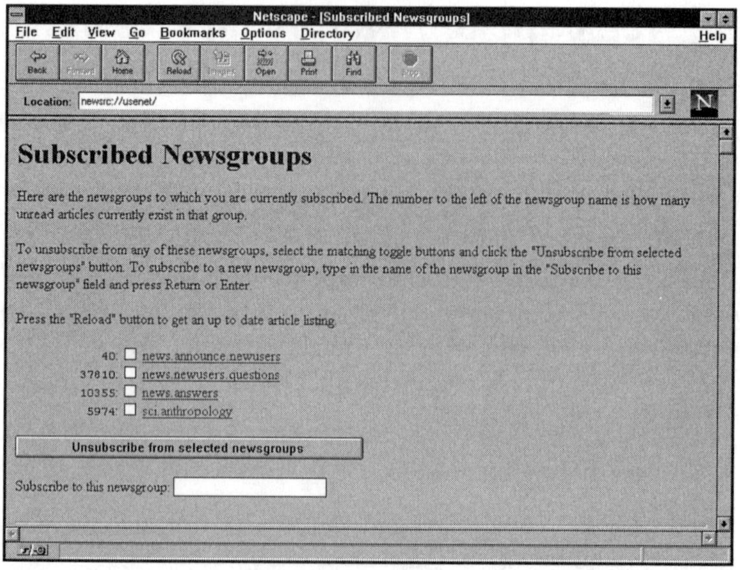

Figure 15.1

A sample list of newsgroups to which you are subscribed, using Netscape.

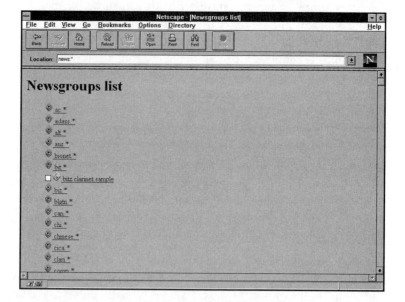

Figure 15.2

A list of broad newsgroup categories available, using Netscape.

From here, you can browse these newsgroup categories. By following the link represented by a category (that is, by clicking the category), you can expand the hierarchy into all the subcategories and newsgroups that make up the category. In this example, you want to look at the sci hierarchy (for newsgroups about topics of a scientific nature) and browse the newsgroups in this category.

> **NOTE** *When you read news with Netscape for the first time, your Netscape browser must transfer the entire list of newsgroups from your news server. If your news server carries many newsgroups, this process of transferring the list of newsgroups from your news server might take a few minutes, especially if you are dialing from home with a modem. It won't take nearly as long the next time you read news!*

4. Scroll down to the icon labeled `sci.*` and click it to go to the science-related newsgroups.

    Figure 15.3 shows the resulting list of newsgroups in the science category, arranged hierarchically. Take a look at the `sci.anthropology` newsgroup.

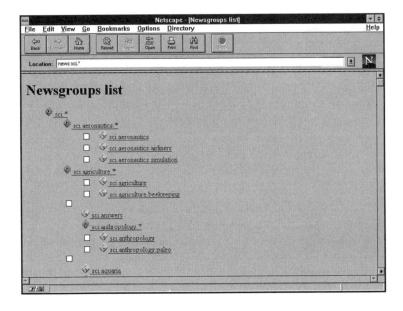

Figure 15.3

The list of newsgroups in the science category, displayed hierarchically.

5. Click `sci.anthropology` to look at the postings to this newsgroup.

    Figure 15.4 shows a screen full of postings to the `sci.anthropology` newsgroup. Notice that the postings themselves are arranged hierarchically. Each hierarchy consists of a series of postings on a single topic of conversation. These hierarchies of postings based on topics are called *threads*. You can think of threads as being like conversations: A user begins a thread by posting a new topic to the newsgroup, another user responds to the posting, someone else responds to the response, and so on.

Figure 15.4

Postings to the
`sci.anthropology`
newsgroup.

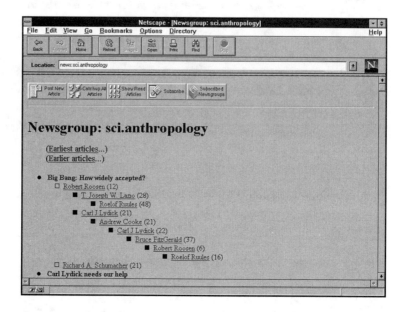

Threads of conversation can continue indefinitely, and many threads can go on simultaneously. You can see several threads on the screen, with such titles as `Big Bang: How widely accepted?` and `Carl Lydick needs our help`. The names of the authors of the postings are listed hierarchically under the title of the thread. For example, in the `Big Bang: How widely accepted?` thread, you can see that Robert Roosen made the first posting. Then T. Joseph W. Lazio made a response to the original posting, and Roelof Ruules made a response to Lazio's response. You can also tell that Carl J. Lydick made a response to the original posting as well.

Responses to a particular posting are indicated by having the author of the response's name indented under the author's name of the original posting. This use of indenting enables you to follow rather easily the overall shape and direction of the conversation. Although most newsreaders do present the postings in the form of threads of conversation, most of them do not display the threads graphically the way Netscape does.

NOTE *When you read a newsgroup with Netscape, it usually plops you right at the end of the news, so you are reading the most current postings. You can use the* Earlier articles... *and* Earliest articles... *links (shown in figure 15.4) to view earlier postings.*

TIP *Entering a newsgroup can be disorienting at first. Most of the threads will have begun before you started reading, so most of the items discussed won't mean much to you. It usually takes a couple of weeks to get involved in a newsgroup and be able to make sense of the threads and personalities involved. Just be patient and keep reading!*

Now read one of these postings. Each of the postings that are available to be read are displayed as a link by Netscape. To read the posting, you can simply follow the link.

NOTE *News servers keep postings for only a certain amount of time (depending on the newsgroup and the policies of the news server). For this reason, you may not be able to retrieve a particular posting because it is no longer available from the news server. Articles that are no longer available will be listed as such in the list of postings. You will probably not be able to retrieve the exact articles used in these examples. Instead, just browse any posting that sounds interesting!*

6. Look at the posting made by Robert Roosen as part of the Big Bang: How widely accepted? thread (not the original posting, but the response toward the bottom of the list).

   Note a couple of elements of the posting (see figure 15.5). At the beginning of the posting are several of pieces of information:

   Subject   The subject of the posting. This subject defines the thread.

   Date   The date the sender made the posting.

From   The e-mail address and name of the person who made the posting. Note that the e-mail address is a link; if you follow it, you can send mail to that person through Netscape.

Organization The organization with which the sender is affiliated (in this case, CTS Network Services).

Newsgroups   The two different newsgroups to which the sender made the posting. Sometimes senders make postings to more than one group at a time, if the topic or posting deals with multiple topics.

References   Other messages in the thread that the posting is following.

Figure 15.5

A sample posting to the `sci.anthropology` newsgroup.

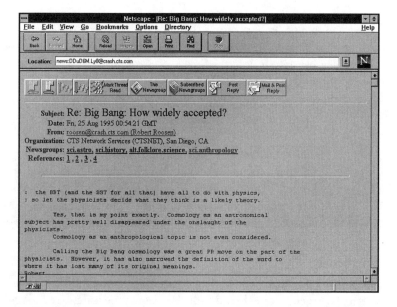

The rest of the text is the posting itself. Some paragraphs may have greater-than symbols (>) at the beginning. This symbol indicates that the text following the symbol was not written as part of this posting; instead, the text was probably part of a previous posting to which this posting is responding. The sender often includes such previous postings to provide context. The principle is similar to including in your papers passages from other texts that you are discussing.

The group of buttons at the top indicates the three actions you can take:

Subscribed Newsgroups	Takes you back to the list of the newsgroups to which you subscribe
Post Reply	Enables you to post to the newsgroup a response to the current message
Mail & Post Reply	Enables you to post your follow-up to the current message and to send the response by e-mail to the sender of the message to which you are replying

Suppose that after reading this posting, you decide that this newsgroup is worth following. In that case, you will want to subscribe to the newsgroup. First, you can return to the list of postings by simply clicking the Back button (the left-arrow icon). You can use this button whenever you use Netscape.

> **TIP** *You can always use the Back button in Netscape to return to where you were before you followed a link, whether you are using Netscape to view Usenet, Web, Gopher, or FTP resources.*

7. Click the left-arrow button to return to the list of postings and threads.

8. Click the Subscribe button to subscribe to this newsgroup.

9. Click the Subscribed Newsgroups button to go to the list of newsgroups to which you subscribe, shown previously in figure 15.1.

Now, whenever you go to your newsgroups with Netscape, you will see the list of newsgroups to which you subscribe. (In this case, the only listed newsgroup is sci.anthropology.) This feature makes it easy to follow a particular list of groups over a period of time.

Proper Conduct on Usenet

The same guidelines for proper conduct in electronic discussion groups pertain to Usenet newsgroups. You should definitely make sure that you follow a newsgroup for a couple of weeks before you post to it. Then you can see what the newsgroup is like and what social conventions apply before you post a message and risk annoying fellow participants.

You have probably already figured out how to post a message to a newsgroup—by clicking the Post New Article button. Be aware, however, that one of the cardinal sins on Usenet is to send test postings to national or international newsgroups. Many local news servers provide local newsgroups explicitly for the purpose of testing newsreaders. (For example, ucs.test is the local test newsgroup at Indiana University.) You might want to look for such a newsgroup at your own site.

TIP *Don't send test postings to national newsgroups (such as the message "Just trying to see if this works…") unless you want to receive scores of nasty e-mail messages berating you.*

Frequently Asked Questions on Usenet

Many Usenet newsgroups maintain a list of frequently asked questions (FAQs) associated with the newsgroup. The purpose of such lists is to save group members from having to wade through the same simple questions repeatedly whenever a new user starts to read the newsgroup. You should read the FAQs before making any postings to the group. After reading the FAQs, you will better understand and enjoy the newsgroup and its dynamics.

The Massachusetts Institute of Technology (MIT) maintains an archive of FAQs for various newsgroups. You can find this archive at the following URL:

```
ftp://rtfm.mit.edu/pub/usenet-by-hierarchy
```

You can access the archive by Web browser, Gopher client, or even FTP client (by using FTP to connect to **rtfm.mit.edu** and moving into the directory **pub /usenet-by-hierarchy**). From here, you can browse the directories of FAQ lists, which are organized in the same categories and hierarchies as the newsgroups themselves. Figure 15.6 shows the first level of the directory of MIT's archive of FAQs.

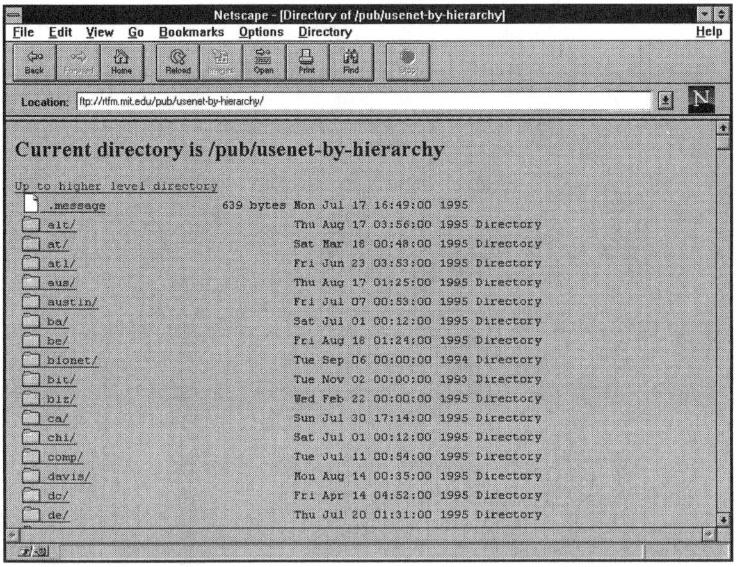

Figure 15.6

The first level of
MIT's archive of
FAQs.

235

Finding Appropriate Usenet Newsgroups

The best source for finding Usenet newsgroups appropriate to your needs is the Directory of Scholarly Electronic Conferences, described in detail in Chapter 14. The Directory contains extensive listings of scholarly discussion groups, both as e-mail distribution lists and Usenet newsgroups.

Using Other Web Browsers to Access Usenet Newsgroups

Although the examples in this chapter use the Netscape browser to access Usenet newsgroups, you can also use Mosaic and Lynx browsers. Because Mosaic is similar to Netscape, you probably won't have any problem using Mosaic to read newsgroups after reading the preceding discussion. Even Lynx works similarly, although getting to the news menu is a bit cumbersome.

To read news with Lynx, follow these steps:

1. Make sure that you are in Lynx.

2. Go to the URL **news:*** (type **g** to go to a URL, type **news:***, and press Enter).

You are telling Lynx to present a menu of all newsgroups. Figure 15.7 shows the results of this command.

Figure 15.7

The list of newsgroups as viewed from Lynx.

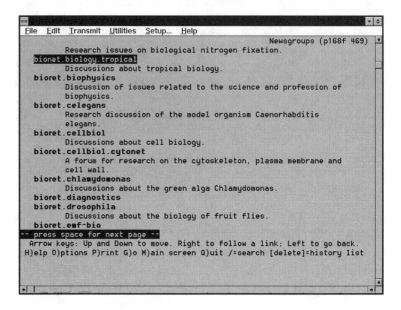

Although Lynx doesn't provide the nice, hierarchical organization of newsgroups that you get with Netscape, you do get an alphabetic listing of newsgroups through which you can scroll and select a newsgroup. After you select a newsgroup, you can look through it or post to it by using the menus.

Of course, if you have only UNIX-based access to the Internet, you are probably better off using a dedicated newsreader rather than Lynx, because you will have many more features available. In any case, Lynx simply isn't very easy to use as a newsreader.

Usenet can be extremely addicting, and it can take up all your available time if you let it. New newsgroups seem to appear every day, covering every topic imaginable. You can probably find a newsgroup for any hobby that you have, from sports to pets to music to literature to cars to beer. Such newsgroups can be quite fun to follow.

Usenet also provides a wealth of information about computing topics. You might expect as much, since until recently Usenet was almost exclusively the domain of computer professionals, who still represent most of the Usenet community. As new users like you move onto the Internet and start using it to support your studies and research, even more newsgroups will appear that are not strictly of interest to computer professionals.

16

Evaluation of Internet Resources

Objectives

After reading this chapter, you will be able to

- Recognize the need for evaluating Internet resources before you use them

- Identify the criteria for evaluating Internet-based resources

- Use library Internet servers to find Internet resources that have already been evaluated

Evaluation is one of the most open-ended and difficult aspects of using Internet information for your research and term papers. Even when you have found a piece of information on the Internet, judging its quality is often difficult.

In the print world, much of the judgment of quality has been done for you by others. The presence of a book in your academic library means that the book has undergone some sort of evaluation: the publisher saw fit to publish the book (and take a financial risk on it), and the librarians who build the book collections thought the book was worth purchasing. Of course, this evaluation process isn't perfect. Sometimes publishers publish bad books, and librarians occasionally acquire bad books for libraries. But at least you know that the book passed some kind of quality control by editors and librarians.

In journal publishing, the standards of quality control are considerably higher than in book publishing. Before being published, a journal article must pass an evaluation by experts in the field. This process, known as *peer refereeing* or *peer review*, is one of the hallmarks of scholarly and academic communication. In the best and most respected academic journals, this evaluation is done without the reviewers knowing who the author is. That way, the reviewers can't be influenced by the professional or academic status of the author—their evaluation is based solely on the quality of the material.

The Importance of Evaluating Internet Resources

On the Internet, many layers of quality control are lost. Almost anyone can be a publisher or an author, especially on the World Wide Web. Even a high school student can create Web resources that look, on the surface, better than the flashiest and most expensive books. The entry barriers to paper publishing are fairly high, but the entry barriers to Web publishing are extremely low. A person with very little of interest to say can say it—and make it look quite impressive.

Furthermore, a person can retrieve Internet-based resources without the intervention or the resources of a library. Although this capability may seem like a good thing (why go through a library when you can get the resources directly?), you should be aware of a pitfall. A library's role, as it builds a collection, has always been one of evaluation and selection, along with purchasing and maintenance. Before librarians purchase materials, they evaluate them, making sure that the limited library budget is spent wisely on books and materials that add to the value of the intellectual resources of the institution. When you bypass the library, you bypass its quality control and evaluative functions.

Everyone a Librarian

Everyone should be a critical reader, especially when choosing resources for use in research and essay writing. When using Internet resources, however, you must be a *more* critical reader. In fact, you must take on the role of the librarian and thus provide your own quality control. Before you decide whether to use the resources you encounter on the Internet, you must evaluate them. The following discussion provides tips for evaluating Internet resources. You should consider four criteria for evaluating these resources: depth and scope, source, degree of quality control, and currency.

Depth and Scope

When you evaluate the *depth* and *scope* of an Internet resource, you are determining whether the coverage of the subject is complete. For example, does the creator of the resource make a comprehensive effort to collect all the information available, or is the resource simply a collection of the creator's favorite resources on the subject? An Internet resource does not need to be exhaustive, any more than a book needs to be exhaustive. However, you should ask yourself whether major areas of the subject are left uncovered or whether any obvious "holes" are evident.

Source

Source is one of the most important criteria for evaluating Internet-based resources. Where does the material in question come from? Are any of the facts, statistics, or quotations attributed to a source that you can verify? If not, you should probably avoid the resource. If the source for facts and statistics is not cited, the information may be unreliable and should not be used in your papers. Does the information come from an organization known to produce quality materials in the field? For example, information placed on the Internet about astronomy that comes from NASA or from an astronomy department at a university should be given greater consideration than information placed on Joe Smith's personal home page (because Joe Smith's hobby happens to be astronomy).

The source of a resource can be very difficult to determine, particularly if you got to the resource by following a link from a different resource. There may be no good indication of the source of the linked-to resource. Sometimes you just have to look at the URL of the linked-to resource and take a guess as to its source.

240

One example of a good Internet resource in which the source of the data is made clear is the National Center for Educational Statistics, located at URL **gopher://gopher.ed.gov:10000**. This resource, shown in figure 16.1, contains several elements that might make you think that the data provided is reliable. First, by following the link Overview about NCES, you will come to another document, About the NCES, which describes exactly how the NCES obtains the data it presents. Second, as the figure shows, NCES provides the data and raw source material used to generate its statistics: NCES Data (surveys & raw data). These are good clues that the information in this resource is reputable and reliable. Incidentally, the fact that the resources available from the National Center for Educational Statistics Gopher are of high quality is part of a general pattern: Internet resources provided by the Federal Government and its agencies tend to be of high quality and are usually excellent places to go for information.

Figure 16.1
The NCES
Gopher menu.

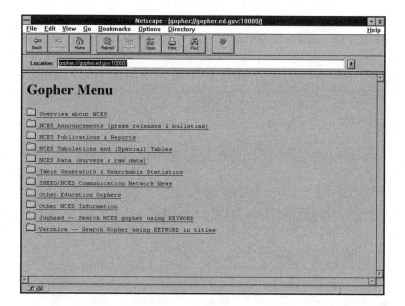

TIP *Internet resources provided by the Federal Government tend to be of uniformly high quality. From the congressional information server called THOMAS to the National Science Foundation Web to the Department of Education resources to the Library of Congress, government resources should be among the first resources you look for, when appropriate. Both Yahoo and the WWW Virtual Library have good directories of government resources.*

Degree of Quality Control

The *degree of quality control* is very difficult to assess, especially if you aren't already an expert on the subject. (If you are a student using the Internet for reference on a subject, you probably aren't an expert.) You can, however, look for some obvious clues to the degree of quality control of a resource. Are the links accurate, or are they perpetually incorrect, leading to error messages? Do you see typos and misspellings, which could suggest more serious factual errors? Is there a credited "editorial board" of experts associated with the resource? (The Directory of Scholarly Electronic Conferences has such a board, for example.) If experts, particularly professionals and faculty members, are willing to put their names on a resource (in essence, putting their reputations on the line), the resource is likely to be trustworthy.

Currency

Whether a resource is *current* is a serious issue with Internet-based resources. At first, the question of currency may seem ironic, because Internet-based resources have the potential to be more up-to-date than printed books or journal articles. However, you should be aware of a couple of problems. Although you can usually tell the publication date of a book or an article, you cannot always tell when an Internet resource was created or updated. An Internet resource often has no date associated with it at all.

Furthermore, many Internet resources are created by people "on the margin" and not as a core part of their jobs. These people create resources just for the novelty of it or for the experience. Building an Internet resource is usually more fun and exciting than maintaining it, so updating it often gets neglected. When you examine an Internet resource for potential use in your research or for a term paper, pay attention to how current its information is. If the resource has lists of events, are they outdated? Is there a "publication" date for the resource, or a date of last update, and if so, when was it?

As an example, the WebElements periodic table database, maintained at the University of Sheffield, is an excellent resource that is well maintained and up-to-date. The resource is located at `http://www.shef.ac.uk/~chem/web-elements`, and part of it is shown in figure 16.2.

As you can see, the author is clear about who is responsible for maintaining the data and for the date of "publication" (1995). In addition, the final paragraph (not shown in the figure), on element nomenclature, mentions that a committee will be meeting in August to make a determination on element nomenclature. One test of how current this resource is, is to see whether this notice disappears or is modified after the committee meets in August. Generally, you need to be cautious about the currency of Internet resources, as they have a tendency to drift toward obsolescence.

Figure 16.2
The WebElements periodic table resource.

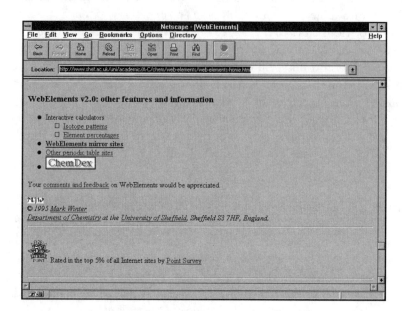

Preevaluated Resources: Library Collections and E-Journals

Another approach to the evaluation of Internet resources is to leave the task of quality control to the libraries and the peer-review process. Libraries have always based their decisions for purchasing books and journals on the quality of materials, and many libraries are now using the same approach with Internet resources—that is, librarians are selecting the best to include as part of the official "collection." This approach may seem a bit silly and bureaucratic, considering that many people think of the entire Internet as a "virtual library." In reality, this service is a great benefit to you, as a user of the Internet, because you are assured that librarians have made some attempt to evaluate a resource in advance and have deemed it worthy enough to be included in the collection.

The peer-review process has also found its way into the Internet in the form of electronic journals, or *e-journals*, as they are often called. (Certainly the nature of the resources on the Internet does not preclude the use of peer review and evaluation.) Although not all electronic journals are peer reviewed, many were created expressly to provide information in a more timely manner over the

Internet, while duplicating the peer-review and quality-control procedures of print journals.

Many different collections of library-evaluated Internet resources are now available. In fact, most major libraries have on the Internet (or will have soon) some kind of collection of resources for their patrons to use. One easy way to find these collections is to look at the Internet servers (usually Gopher or Web servers) of various libraries and examine what they have made available. You can use a particular starting point and then follow the links to other library Web and Gopher servers. A good starting point for locating library Web servers is the libweb Library Information Servers via WWW list, maintained at the University of Washington.

Libweb, located at `http://www.lib.washington.edu/~tdowling/libweb.html`, is shown in figure 16.3. Note the date of last change at the top of the page. This date shows that the page is being maintained and is probably current. From here, you can easily explore the library Web servers of various libraries around the world, where you can find resources of high quality.

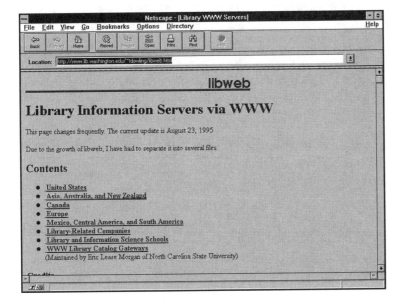

Figure 16.3

The libweb Library Information Servers via WWW list page.

Now try using libweb to go to a couple of other library Web servers and see what is available from there. Follow these steps:

1. With your Web browser, go to `http://www.lib.washington.edu/~tdowling/libweb.html`, the location of libweb.

Figure 16.3 shows the libweb page, with Library Web servers categorized by region.

2. Follow the United States link to go to a list of library Web servers in the United States.

3. Scroll down the list and follow the link to the Library of Congress Web server.

You can see some of the resources that are available from the Library of Congress home page, shown in figure 16.4. For example, you can get to THOMAS, a server that provides legislative information and contains up-to-the-minute information about congressional action, laws, and pending bills. You can also get to other government information resources at the national and state level. The link Indexes to Other World Wide Web Services provides more links to resources that the Library of Congress has deemed of value. Now take a look at another library Web server.

Figure 16.4

The Library of Congress World Wide Web home page.

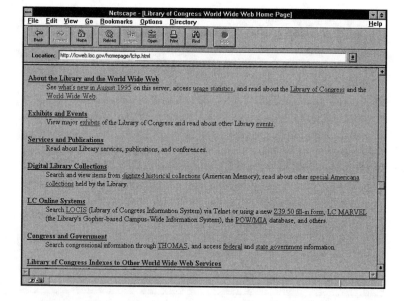

4. Go back one link to the libweb list of library Web servers in the United States.

5. Scroll down to the link to the libraries of North Carolina State University.

6. Follow the North Carolina State University link to the home page for the North Carolina State University Libraries, shown in figure 16.5.

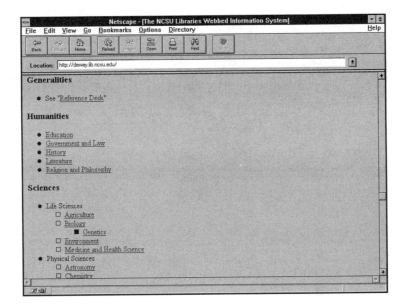

Figure 16.5

The North Carolina State University Libraries home page.

This page is definitely one of the better library home pages. It is maintained by Eric Lease Morgan, one of the best-known organizers of Internet information, as well as a developer of many Internet tools. This home page contains, among other links, a whole series of selected Internet references organized by subject and available directly from the home page. The page points to numerous resources in the sciences, social sciences, and humanities.

7. Follow the History link to go to the History page at NCSU.

This page, shown in figure 16.6, is an excellent example of the broad scope of resources provided by this Web server. Organized by type of resource, this page provides access to everything from journal catalogs in history to scholarly journals to collected works in history.

Figure 16.6

The History page from the North Carolina State University Libraries.

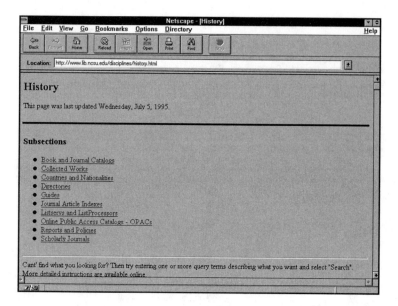

Ultimately, you are responsible for deciding whether an Internet-based resource will be useful in your research. As you make your resource selections, keep in mind what you should evaluate: the depth and scope of the resource, its source, the degree of quality control, and the currency of the information. You should also be aware of the collections, mostly available through libraries, that have already been evaluated for you.

17

Giving Credit: Citing Internet Resources in Your Projects

Objectives

After reading this chapter, you will be able to

- Recognize the need to cite Internet resources when you use them as sources in your papers

- Recognize the pieces of information that you should include in any citation of an Internet resource

- Refer to some examples of citations of Internet resources available to you

This chapter covers one of the less glamorous facets of doing research on the Internet: the citing or footnoting of Internet resources. Although citations and bibliographies may be unglamorous, they are an essential part of writing papers at every level. There is no accepted way to cite Internet resources, particularly those available through the Web and Gopher. This chapter presents one way of citing resources—one way of fulfilling the purpose of a citation.

What Is a Citation and Why Give It?

Citations are a fundamental aspect of scholarly communication and research. In fact, in many papers and publications, the citations and bibliographies are as important as the text itself. Note the following reasons for providing citations:

1. *Citations are a way of acknowledging credit and academic debt.* Members of the academic community don't tend to get paid directly for publication, at least not for journal publication. Instead, payment is made in the form of public recognition for having been the first person to come up with an idea, a phrase, or a concept. Such recognition comes as a citation or reference in a bibliography. If, for example, I use your idea in a paper, I am expected to give you credit for having come up with that idea by citing your work in my paper. Conversely, if you use my idea in a paper, you are expected to give me credit in your paper. Thus, citation is the currency of academic life, and stealing ideas without giving credit is like stealing money or goods.

2. *Citations provide a way for your readers to trace the source material that you used to build your paper.* The citations enable readers to verify your sources and trace your arguments back to the sources.

3. *Citations give your readers a means of getting further information on the topic.*

A citation must do two things: (1) credit the person or institution responsible for a certain idea, phrase, or concept; and (2) enable the reader to locate, retrieve, and read the source being cited. Everything else—where you put the periods, whether you follow the date with a comma or period, whether you underline or italicize—is simply a matter of convention. Convention, mind you, is usually taken seriously by journals that publish scholarly works, and, quite frequently, by the professors who grade your papers.

Although no well-established standards exist for the citation of Internet resources, you must make sure that you include the following pieces of information in any citation of an Internet resource:

- *The author of a particular work.* The author may not be an individual but may be an institution, an organization, or a department. (Technically, when the author is an organization, the author is called a "corporate author.")

- *The date of publication of a particular work.* Of course, the publication date may be difficult to determine. If you can find a date of copyright or publication somewhere on a resource, use that date. If the resource is an e-mail message or a Usenet newsgroup posting, use the date of the posting.

- *The title of the resource.* In a Web- or Gopher-based document, the document's title may be the title of the home page. In an e-mail message or a posting to a Usenet newsgroup, the title may be the subject of the message or posting.

- *The location of the resource on the Internet.* Although the URL is not yet a standard, consider giving the resource's location in the form of a URL. The URL gives all the information necessary to retrieve the document from anywhere on the Internet, including the type of Internet resource it is (such as a Gopher or Web resource). If the resource is an e-mail message (from either an individual or a LISTSERV), include an e-mail address that the reader can use to obtain the document.

Internet Citation Styles

You can use two types of citation in your text: (1) a citation that appears at the place where you make the reference, and (2) a citation that appears at the end of the paper. Although the first type (generally called a citation or footnote) used to be quite common, the trend in academic publishing is to dispense with footnotes and to insert a brief citation, in parentheses, right where the reference is made in the text. This brief reference in the text must correspond to a full citation at the end of the paper. This type of brief citation is generally called an *in-line citation* because it occurs in the same line as the text to which it refers. (I use this type of citation myself, and the examples in this chapter are of references at the end of the paper, meant to be used with in-line citations.) The in-line citation is usually brief, consisting of the author and date, or just the author if you have only one reference for the author in your paper. The most popular manuals of style, including those of the Modern Language Association and the American Psychological Association, recommend in-line citations.

At the end of a paper comes the complete bibliographic information for all references cited in the text, usually in alphabetic order by author. This list is still called the *bibliography* (or sometimes *references*), even though the bibliography may contain works in electronic form. I sometimes refer (facetiously) to such bibliographies as "webliographies."

The examples that follow are for use in a bibliography. As noted, the in-line citations are simple: Just use the last name of the author and place it in parentheses within the sentence that cites the resource. If you have more than one author with the same last name, use the last name and first initial. If you have more than one source by the same author, include the year as well. Then make sure that you include the full bibliographic information for that source in your bibliography.

> **NOTE** *No matter what you learn in this chapter about citing resources, if your instructor tells you to use a specific style for citation, footnoting, or bibliography, use it. You would hate to get marked down for anything as silly as that.*

Citing an E-Mail Message

The most important thing to remember when you cite an e-mail message is to keep a copy of it, in case you need to document your use of the message. In fact, if you cite an e-mail message in a paper, you should probably print out the message and keep a copy for your files.

Use the following form for such a reference:

> Message sender. (Year, Month Day). *Subject of the Message* [e-mail to the name of the recipient]. Available e-mail: e-mail address of the message recipient.

Note an example:

> McKim, Geoffrey. (1995, August 8). *Should I Upgrade to Windows 95?* [e-mail to W. Gates]. Available e-mail: mckimg@indiana.edu.

If you were to cite this e-mail message in your paper, you would place the preceding reference at the end of the paper. At the point at which you would like to cite the message, you would insert an in-line citation like (McKim, 1995).

Citing a Usenet Newsgroup Posting

Use the following form for citing a Usenet newsgroup posting:

> Name of poster. (Year, Month Day). *Subject of the Thread* [Usenet discussion]. Available: news:name of newsgroup.

Note the use of the URL in specifying the availability of the posting.

Here is an example:

> McKim, Geoffrey. (1995, January 1). *Ethnography of Computing Systems* [Usenet discussion]. Available: news:soc.anthropology.

Once again, you might use an in-line citation like (McKim, 1995) along with this reference.

Citing a Web or Gopher Document

Use the following form for citing a Web or Gopher document:

> Name of author. (Year, Month Day). *Title of the Document* [World Wide Web or Gopher]. Available: URL of resource.

Watch out for the following specific cases:

- The author may not be an individual but may be an organization, a corporation, or a department.

- A date of publication may not be available for the resource. If no date is available, use the date that you checked the resource.

Here are a few short examples of citation of Internet information:

> Winter, Mark. (1995). *WebElements* [World Wide Web]. Available: http://www.shef.ac.uk/uni/academic/A-C/chem/web-elements/web-elements-home.html.

> Indiana University School of Library and Information Science. (1995). *IU SLIS (IUB) WWW Home Page* [World Wide Web]. Available: http://www-slis.lib.indiana.edu.

> National Association of Press Photographers. (1995, August 12). *National Press Photographers Association* [World Wide Web]. Available: http://sunsite.unc.edu/nppa.

Indiana University. (1994). *About our Main Menu* [Gopher]. Available: gopher://gopher.ucs.indiana.edu:1067/00/ucspubs/gopher/.IUGOPHERinfo/main_menu.

If you would like more information, along with a more comprehensive style manual, you may want to obtain Xia Li and Nancy Crane's *Electronic Style, A Guide to Citing Electronic Information* (1993, Meckler). This is an excellent and well-documented guide to citation of electronic information, containing hundreds of examples covering almost every contingency. The only problem is that this reference predates the World Wide Web and is therefore badly in need of an update. Thus, the preceding suggestions for citing Web and Gopher documents are simply suggestions. However, they do fulfill the necessary criteria of acknowledgment and location for citations. These suggestions should be helpful until a better, more comprehensive standard for citing electronic documents emerges.

You have come a long way in 17 chapters, covering all phases of your search for useful Internet information. You started with the tools used to access Internet resources: FTP, Telnet, Gopher, and the World Wide Web. You then moved on through the information search process itself, including search techniques and concepts, search engines, library catalogs, and a demonstration of how some commercial services might be of use to you. Next, you learned how to use people as resources, focusing on electronic mail, electronic discussion groups, and Usenet newsgroups. Finally, you learned how to evaluate Internet resources and cite them in your research.

This book should provide a good start as you begin to make the Internet useful in your studies. The book will not be an end, however. As more high-quality, well-designed, and well-maintained resources are brought up on the Internet, it will become even more important for you to learn to find information. The tools will get easier, of course; dramatic progress has already been made on that front. Using the Internet will never be as easy as watching television—and we don't want it to be. The beauty of the Internet is the quantity and diversity of information that is available to you from a single place. Sorting and searching through that information will always require some thought, thought that you as a student are now in a prime position to give.

Appendix

Where to Find It

This appendix gives summary information about the different Internet sites and tools accessed in this book. All locations are given in the form of Uniform Resource Locators (URLs). In most cases, the URLs of the resources refer to Web pages (and thus begin with `http://...`). Ohers refer to files that must be retrieved by FTP. These files can still be retrieved using a Web browser, of course, since Web browsers provide FTP capability as well.

Browser/Client Software

This section gives information about where to find the various pieces of client software mentioned in this book. Many other browsers are available, but these have the best combination of features and are easy to use.

Telnet Clients

NCSA Telnet for Macintosh

    ftp://ftp.ncsa.uiuc.edu/Mac/Telnet

WinQVT/Net for Windows

    ftp://ftp.cica.indiana.edu/pub/pc/win3/winsock

World Wide Web Browsers

Netscape for Windows and Macintosh

> `ftp://ftp.netscape.com/netscape`

> `http://www.netscape.com`

Mosaic for Windows and Macintosh

> `ftp://ftp.ncsa.uiuc.edu/Mosaic`

Lynx for UNIX

> `ftp://ftp2.cc.ukans.edu/pub/lynx`

Miscellaneous

Fetch FTP Client for Macintosh

> `ftp://sumex-aim.stanford.edu/info-mac/Communications/TCP`

Data Viewers and Helper Applications

This section contains a short list of data viewers and helper applications that can be used to work with various media formats available on the Internet. Several good lists of helper applications are also available from the Internet. These are especially useful since they are continually updated and contain links to the helper applications themselves. URLs for these lists are given in the next section.

Image Viewers

WinGIF for Windows (GIF graphic viewer)

> `ftp://ftp.cica.indiana.edu/pub/pc/win3/desktop`

LView for Windows (GIF and JPEG graphic viewer)

> `ftp://ftp.cica.indiana.edu/pub/pc/win3/desktop`

JPEGView 3.31

> `ftp://sumex-aim.stanford.edu/info-mac/Graphics`

Sound Players

Mplayer for Windows

```
ftp://gatekeeper.dec.com/pub/micro/msdos/win3/desktop
```

WHAM Sound Player

```
ftp://gatekeeper.dec.com/pub/micro/msdos/win3/sounds
/wham133.zip
```

SoundMachine for Macintosh

```
http://wwwhost.ots.utexas.edu/mac/pub-mac-sound.html
```

Video Players

MPEGPLAY for Windows

```
ftp://gatekeeper.dec.com/pub/micro/msdos/win3/desktop
```

AVI Video for Windows

```
ftp://gatekeeper.dec.com/pub/micro/msdos/win3/desktop
/avipro2.exe
```

Sparkle (Video) for Macintosh

```
http://wwwhost.ots.utexas.edu/mac/pub-mac-graphics.html
```

Compression and Uncompression

StuffItExpander

```
ftp://sumex-aim.stanford.edu/info-mac/cmp
```

PKUNZIP for DOS/Windows

```
ftp://ftp.cica.indiana.edu/pub/pc/starters
```

Page Description Languages

Adobe Acrobat for Macintosh

```
http://www.adobe.com/Acrobat/Acrobat0.html
```

Adobe Acrobat for Windows

> `http://www.adobe.com/Acrobat/Acrobat0.html`

GhostScript PostScript viewer

> `ftp://ftp.cica.indiana.edu/pub/pc/win3/desktop/gsview.zip`

Lists of Helper Applications

These lists of helper applications are probably more useful than any of the preceding URLs. The lists provide common helper applications for Macintosh and Windows and are generally kept up-to-date.

> `http://www.voicenet.com/~mmax/help/App.html`

> `http://www.netscape.com/assist/helper_apps/index.html`

Search Tools

This section gives information about where to find the Internet searching and directory tools mentioned in this book.

Web-Based Search Tools

Yahoo

> `http://www.yahoo.com`

WebCrawler

> `http://www.webcrawler.com`

TradeWave Galaxy

> `http://www.einet.net`

Lycos

> `http://www.lycos.com`

WWW Virtual Library

> `http://www.w3.org/hypertext/DataSources/bySubject`

InfoSeek

    `http://www.infoseek.com`

Magellan

    `http://www.mckinley.com`

Gopher-Based Search Tool

VERONICA

    `gopher://gopher.unr.edu`

Other Resources and Reference Materials

This section provides the locations of the supplementary resources and guides that can help you as you seek information on the Internet.

HYTELNET

    `http://www.lights.com/hytelnet`

    `http://library.usask.ca/hytelnet`

Clearinghouse of Subject-Oriented Internet Resource Guides

    `http://www.lib.umich.edu/chhome.html`

Directory of Scholarly Electronic Conferences

    `http://www.mid.net/KOVACS`

Inter-Links/Dartmouth List of LISTSERVs

    `http://www.nova.edu/Inter-Links/cgi-bin/lists`

CARL/UnCover Document Delivery

    `http://www.carl.org`

Usenet Frequently Asked Questions Lists

    `ftp://rtfm.mit.edu/pub/usenet-by-hierarchy`

PINE E-mail home page

`http://www.cac.washington.edu/pine`

Netscape People and Places

`http://home.netscape.com/home/internet-white-pages.html`

Notre Dame List of Phone Directories

`gopher://gopher.nd.edu/11`
`/Non-Notre%20Dame%20Information%20Sources`
`/Phone%20Books--Other%20Institutions`

Index

X–Y–Z